# LEGAL EASE
## AND
# LIFE HACKS

# LEGAL EASE
## AND
# LIFE HACKS

## Essays on Pursuits
## of Excellence

Angelia M. Nystrom – JD LLM

Knoxville, Tennessee, USA
crippledbeaglepublishing.com

Cover design by Lauren Harris

Hardcover ISBN 978-1-970037-84-5, 978-1-970037-85-2
Paperback ISBN 978-1-958533-63-5, 978-1-958533-64-2

Library of Congress Control Number: 2021923076

Articles originally appeared in DICTA, an official publication of the Knoxville Bar Association. Reprinted with permission.

Published and printed in the United States of America.

# What if you wrote a book but did not know it?

All of you who know Angelia (or get to know her through her writings) do or will appreciate that she is a remarkable woman. You will be hard pressed to find someone who can match her work ethic, sense of humor, intellect, or ability to plan a party. Over the last twenty years, I have seen first-hand how she makes things better than they were before. This applies to legal teams, nonprofit organizations, and husbands!

Over the years, Angelia's writings have brought great joy to members of the legal community. She has profiled the life and leadership stories of many remarkable attorneys. Some of her writings are actually about the practice of law; however, the ones that seem to resonate with everyone are her stories and advice on cooking, life hacks, and the occasional tale of my poor judgement in basic household tasks. Last year one of her columns went viral when a local sportswriter Tweeted about a column in which Angelia provided play-by-play coverage of taking a cooking class hosted by Vols basketball star Yves Pons. This viral moment had me thinking that her writings should be shared with a wider audience than the legal community.

So behind her back, as a surprise Christmas present, I compiled Angelia's writings from over twenty years and put them into the book you now have in your hands. Thank you for reading it and allowing me to share with you the wise words of my in-house counsel and perfect wife.

With deep gratitude,
Hugh Nystrom

P.S. Special thanks to Marsha Watson, Executive Director of the Knoxville Bar Association, and Jody Dyer of Crippled Beagle Publishing for your help in pulling this project together.

A percentage of each book sold will be donated to three organizations Angelia holds dear: the Knoxville Bar Foundation, the Tennessee Bar Foundation, and the Herbert College of Agriculture at the University of Tennessee (for the Emily Bruner Scholarship Endowment, which was started by the Knoxville Garden Club). I will use any remaining profits to take Angelia out to dinner or on a well-deserved vacation.

# Foreword
## The Honorable Cynthia Richardson Wyrick

FEW AUTHORS CAN WRITE IN A KNOWLEDGEABLE AND ENGAGING WAY about topics as diverse as Tennessee politicians, lawyers, and community leaders such as Lamar Alexander and Bill Haslam; important Supreme Court decisions; foodie favorites like Benton's Bacon, banana pudding, wine pairings and coffee selection; parenting tips and making holidays special from the perspective of a working "swim mom"; shoes from high heels to Chuck Taylors; sports of all sorts, many from a Big Orange perspective; health pointers; TV, movie, book and music reviews and recommendations; cars; pets; and countless others. In this book, award-winning author Angelia Nystrom has done just that with easy-to-read, down-to-earth, humor. While the book is so captivating that you will want to read straight through, because it is comprised of a series of articles that read like short stories, you can also take it along to read when you have a few minutes of unexpected downtime. If you know Angelia, you already understand why this book is such a page-turner, but for those of you who don't, let me introduce you.

ANGELIA NYSTROM AND I HAVE BEEN FRIENDS FOR ABOUT TWENTY-FIVE YEARS NOW. When we started our careers, Angelia and I were practicing law in neighboring small East Tennessee towns, but it took a trip to the Tennessee Bar Association (TBA) headquarters in the "big city" of Nashville for us to meet. There, we discovered our shared small-town roots and mutual desire to give back to the profession and our communities through involvement in the TBA. We became fast friends, and our volunteer work gave us the opportunity to share adventures across the country. It even earned us an important title in the TBA Young Lawyers Division (TBA YLD) before we had reached the ripe old age of thirty. Then TBA YLD President Jim Wheeler bestowed upon us the title of "Grand Old Ladies" of the YLD, and while he assured us that he did so because of our years of service to the division, it might have taken us a while to forgive him for the "honor."

ANGELIA IS AN ACCOMPLISHED ATTORNEY WITH SIGNIFICANT EXPERTISE in estate planning. While she began her career in private practice, for the last several years she has served as Executive Director of Specialty Programs for the University of Tennessee

Institute of Agriculture. Angelia is also a leader in the legal profession and in her community. Additionally, she is a well-respected author and speaker. Outside of work, she is a loving wife and swim mom extraordinaire who has a flair for whipping things up in the kitchen and being the consummate hostess. Angelia is one of those rare people who can tromp around the cow pasture or present a legal argument in the courtroom with equal authority and ease.

NO INTRODUCTION OF ANGELIA IS COMPLETE WITHOUT EXPANDING ON HER LEADERSHIP AND SERVICE to her profession and community. Angelia has held countless leadership roles in the American, Tennessee, and Knoxville Bar Associations, Tennessee Bar Foundation, Knoxville Estate Planning Council, the Smoky Mountain Planned Giving Council, and many others. These organizations have frequently called upon her to put her legal knowledge and writing and speaking skills to use for their benefit. In her community, Angelia has served as President of the Carson-Newman University Alumni Association and is active in the United Way of Greater Knoxville, the Junior League Community Circle, Leadership Knoxville's Curriculum Committee, the American Heart Association, and Go Red for Women, to name a few. Angelia has also managed to mesh her roles as community servant and swim mom by serving for many years in leadership roles with the Greater Knoxville Area Interclub Swimming Association and the University Swim Club, ultimately serving as president of both.

ANGELA'S RURAL ROOTS AND DIVERSE PROFESSIONAL AND PERSONAL EXPERIENCES HAVE EDUCATED HER about a unique cross-section of people, places, events, and topics of importance. Angelia has used her keen ability to see these experiences through the lens of humor, allowing her to forward lessons learned in a light-hearted yet meaningful way. Don't pass up the opportunity to learn from and laugh with Angelia through the experiences she shares in the pages ahead!

*Cynthia "Cindy" Richardson Wyrick is a United States Magistrate Judge serving the Eastern District of Tennessee at Greeneville and a Past President of the Tennessee Bar Association. She is also a BIG Angelia Nystrom fan.*

# CONTENTS

# TELEVISION AT IT'S MOST IMAGINATIVE

## A Review of Ally McBeal

I have always been a television nut. Suffice it to say that several friends and I scheduled our law school classes around the television shows that we liked. Oh, and I don't think I ever turned mine off during Bar Review. I work in front of the television, read in front of the television, and run on the treadmill in front of the television. I like the light and the sound. Yes, I am a television nut.

However, I rarely find a show that captures my full attention. *Ally McBeal*, which is on Monday night on Fox, is such a show. Ally is producer David E. Kelley's vibrant, imaginative creation that takes us inside the head of young lawyer Ally McBeal, played by newcomer Calista Flockhart. After

17

only eight episodes, the series has won a Golden Globe for Best Comedy series, and Flockhart has won an individual award for Best Actress.

The series, which has become a favorite of twenty-somethings (of which I am still a member, at least for the next nine months), opened with Ally, a twenty-seven-year-old Harvard law grad, working in a large Boston law firm. She is sexually harassed by an older partner in the firm who has an affinity from grabbing young women's backsides. After Ally reports him to the other partners, he determines that his problem is obsessive-compulsive, a defense which he bolsters by grabbing the behind of every woman he sees. Rather than fire the partner, the firm determines that it would rather be sued by Ally, who resigns her position. As she is leaving the firm, she runs into former classmate, Richard Fish, who invites her to join his firm, Fish & Cage & Associates.

Fish, played by Greg Germann, is hilarious as he doles out advise with his "Fish-isms." Other than carrying on an affair with the much-older Judge Whipper Cone (Dyan Cannon), Fish's primary goal in life is "to make money—piles of money. It's all about the piles."

The other partner in the firm is John Cage, affectionately known as "The Biscuit." "The Biscuit," played by veteran character actor Peter MacNichol, is the moral fiber of the firm (although he is arrested for soliciting a prostitute in the second episode). The classic eccentric nerd, "The Biscuit" has an odd approach to the practice of law, often pausing to "take a moment" at oddly inappropriate times and playing bagpipes to alleviate nerves.

After joining the firm, Ally learns that Billy Thomas (Gil Bellows), her former childhood/high school/law school sweetheart, is also an associate with the firm. Ally is at her best with Billy, as that is when the viewer is allowed to "get inside her head" to see what she is thinking. Upon meeting Billy, who had left her at Harvard so he could go to Michigan where he had a better chance of making law review, Ally imagines frolicking with Billy in a giant coffee cup. When she learns that he is married to Georgia, a fellow lawyer played by Courtney Thorne-Smith (formerly of Melrose Place), Ally smiles the "how nice" smile while arrows are going through her heart.

The supporting cast includes Jane Krakowski (last seen as Cousin Eddie's marijuana-growing daughter in the original *National Lampoon's Vacation*) as Ally's legal assistant, Elaine. Elaine is pushy and always has to have her nose in everyone's business. As Elaine's overinflated sense of self-importance grows, we see her through Ally's eyes, with her head inflating like a giant balloon. When she feels that Ally is not paying her due respect, she retorts that Ally is "snappish" (a term which has, on occasion, been used to describe me early in the morning).

Renee, played by Lisa Nicole Carson, is Ally's roommate. Outgoing an unafraid, Renee, the assistant DA, is what Ally would like to be. In one episode, Renee remarks that Ally is Julie Andrews-esque, a claim which Ally denies although she knows the description is accurate.

Another of *Ally's* endearing qualities is the music, which is performed by Vonda Shepard. Shepard performs at the local bar where Ally and friends congregate at the end of the day. If you listen closely, the music being performed mirrors what is happening on the show. (A CD of the music from the show is set for release later this year).

I'm hooked on Ally McBeal because she, like me, is a young professional trying to balance her career and private life, often feeling like one is or both are out of control. I've felt like Ally when she was dumped by Ronnie Chaney—like garbage in a dumpster pouring into a garbage truck. I've had my foot in my mouth on more than one occasion. And I've felt like my head is in a guillotine. When things have gotten to be almost too much to handle, I have felt like I could be a street person if it were not for having to give up my outfits. In short, although the situations Ally finds herself in are much unlike mine, the feelings she has about those situations and about life in general are very much like my feelings. Ally, like me, is trying to make her own way in the world. For me (and for most of my friends who watch the show), that is what makes *Ally McBeal* so entertaining.

If you like lighthearted humor and haven't made a date with Ally McBeal on Monday night at nine o' clock, I suggest that you do that. And if you don't watch *Ally*, please don't call my house while the show is on— I tend to get "snappish" when the phone rings during that hour.

*January 1998*

# PRACTICE TIPS PRACTICE TIPS PRACTICE TIPS

## LITIGATING AGAINST THE KINGS OF THE ROAD
### – A Plaintiff's Perspective

by: Angelia Maria
Nicholson, Garner & Duggan

While there has been much publicity in recent months regarding the dangers that sport utility vehicles pose to occupants of regular motor vehicles in collisions, little mention is ever made concerning the dangers posed by tractor-trailers and other motor carriers to members of the passenger vehicle driving public. According to the latest statistics from the Insurance Institute for Highway Safety, Large Truck Fatalities, large trucks represent only 3% of all registered motor vehicles yet they account for 22% of all deaths in multiple vehicle collisions.

8                                                                February 1998

# PRACTICE TIPS

## Litigating Against the Kings of the Road – A Plaintiff's Perspective

While there has been much publicity in recent months regarding the dangers that sport utility vehicles pose to occupants of regular motor vehicles in collisions, little mention is ever made concerning the dangers posed by tractor-trailers and other motor carriers to members of the passenger vehicle driving public. According to the latest statistics from the Insurance Institute for Highway Safety, Large Truck Fatalities, large trucks represent only three percent of all registered motor vehicles, yet they account for twenty-two percent of all deaths in multiple vehicle collisions.

As a result, many plaintiff's attorneys will have the opportunity at some point in their careers to litigate against a motor carrier. In order to do so effectively, plaintiff's attorneys should be aware of the laws regulating the motor carriers and their drivers and should plan the litigation process accordingly.

An understanding of applicable law will assist in evaluating the case prior to initiating the litigation process. The Federal Motor Carrier Safety Regulations (FMCSR) are the sole safety standards professional truck drivers and motor carriers must follow in operating commercial motor vehicles. The purpose of the FMCSR is to "help reduce or prevent truck and bus accidents, fatalities, and injuries by requiring drivers to have a single commercial motor vehicle driver's license and by disqualifying drivers who operate commercial motor vehicles in an unsafe manner." 49 C.F.R. 383.1(a).

The commercial driver's license (CDL) is required by the federal government but issued by the driver's home state. (A driver can have only one CDL). The written exam for the CDL tests the driver's knowledge of driving rules and safety regulations, as well as an understanding of air brakes, hazardous materials, and pre-trip inspection procedures.

The FMCSR establishes minimum safety standards for both drivers and the trucking companies for which they work. Because a company and a driver satisfy the minimum standard, however, does not obviate their responsibility to meet a higher standard of care that is reasonable under the circumstances.

According to 49 C.F. R. 391.11, trucking companies have a nondelegable duty to hire only qualified drivers. The regs clearly establish what constitutes a "qualified driver." Defendant drivers who fail to satisfy one or more of the listed criteria subject themselves and the motor carrier to a viable punitive damages claim in many jurisdictions.

Within thirty days after the driver's initial hire, the regs pose a duty on the carrier to inquire of every state agency that has issued a CDL to the driver during the past three years and also to investigate the driver's employment record for the three previous years. All materials gathered must remain in the driver's employment file.

After the initial hire and investigation, the carrier must continue to supervise the driver to ensure that the driver does not operate the vehicle for more than the maximum hours of operation. Additionally, the carriers are required to inspect, repair, and maintain their vehicles. Violation of any of these regs can subject the carrier to liability under the theories of negligent entrustment, negligent hiring and retention, and negligent vehicle maintenance.

If a situation arises where one or more of these regulations may have been violated, there are a number of tips to make the pursuit of litigation more successful and easier:

1. Immediately—as soon as the client walks out your door, if not before—send a letter by certified mail, return receipt requested, informing the carrier, the carrier's insurance carrier, and the driver of your representation. The letter should clearly state that all physical evidence pertaining to the accident, including the vehicle itself, will be necessary to investigate and prosecute your claim and that they should be retained and not disturbed.

2. Locate and secure the vehicles to prevent destruction of the evidence. If necessary, file a motion for temporary restraining order to prevent destruction or tampering of the evidence until a thorough inspection is completed.

3. Hire an investigator to photograph and videotape the crash site and the vehicles involved.

4. Get recorded statements from all witnesses, police officers, emergency workers, the tow truck operators, the defendant driver, and the representatives of the motor carrier. Additionally, review written reports of investigating police officers, MS workers, and emergency room physicians.

5. Hire an expert check the truck for mechanical difficulties.

6. Obtain a driver's license record and traffic offense report on the defendant driver in the state where the driver's CDL was issued, as well as in all states where the driver may have been employed.

7. Consider whether you need to hire an accident reconstructionist and whether you need to produce a computer animation of the crash. This can be quite expensive ($10-20,000 or more) but can be a powerful tool for use at trial or in settlement negotiations.

8. File a lawsuit naming the motor carrier and the driver involved in the accident. Along with your complaint, file extensive discovery requesting all logs of the trip the driver was making at the time of the accident, the driver's employment file, all maintenance records on the vehicle involved, all documents evidencing the carrier's compliance with

the regs, the driver's driving record, and copies of all road tests the driver was asked to perform.

9. Finally, it may be useful to file a non-party subpoena to the defendant driver's previous employers to obtain a complete copy of the driver's employment file, including the application, violation history, and employment status and termination.

Cases involving motor carriers are difficult and require a tremendous amount of time and effort to pursue. However, they can be litigated successfully with a good working knowledge of the applicable regs and with careful planning and preparation. For a more extensive discussion of motor carrier litigation, see Daniel S. Chamberlain's article in the February 1998 issue of *Trial Magazine*.

*February 1998*

# Movie Review
# The Truman Show
### by Angelia Morie / Nicholson, Garner & Duggan

I'll start off by saying that I have never been a big fan of Jim Carrey. I've said before and I'll say again that I thought "Dumb and Dumber" should have been "Dumb and Dumber and Dumbest", with me being the "Dumbest " for paying $6.50 (or whatever movies cost back then) to see it. I won't even tell you what I thought about "Ace Ventura: Pet Detective."

I started to change my mind about Jim Carrey when I saw "Liar, Liar" last summer. While it was no "Forrest Gump", it was cute without being totally silly. "The Truman Show", however, has made me rethink my feelings about Jim Carrey and his talent (or, as I previously thought, lack thereof.)

Prior to seeing "The Truman Show", I had heard the hype about how spectacular it was to see Jim Carrey completely out of his element. Just this once, believe the hype. Refreshingly, "The Truman Show" lacks the characteristic "Silly Putty" limb antics of Jim Carrey. Instead, it is a provocative and daring drama that chronicles the life of Truman Burbank.

"The Truman Show"'s basic premise is that Carrey's character, insurance salesman Truman Burbank, is the star of a live television show that airs globally 24 hours a day, seven days a week. The whole world is watching, only Truman doesn't know it. Unlike MTV's REAL WORLD, where the characters know that their lives are being taped, poor Truman thinks he is just living his life like an ordinary person, completely unaware that the scenic Florida island that he calls "home" is really a giant movie set or that his hopelessly chipper wife, played by Laura Linney, is really an actress playing a part, as are all his friends, neighbors, and coworkers.

Truman is smart enough to realize that something is not quite right. He begins to wonder why he sees the exact same people at the exact same time every morning. He also wonders why his wife extols the virtue of various kitchen products and foods at inappropriate times and then always holds them up so the labels show. As the truth begins to dawn on him, he begins to object to leading an examined life.

The most fascinating aspect of "The Truman Show" is the mechanics of the television show itself. I found it fascinating how many cameras were needed to record Truman's every move. Also quite funny was the fact that troublesome actors were routinely written out. (Wouldn't it be nice if real life were so simple?)

If you are looking for a moral theme in "The Truman Show", Carrey does aptly make the point that one should live one's own life and not just watch other people's lives on TV. (And I'm sure this applies to movies as well). "The Truman Show" is captivating. It provides laughs; it provides drama; and it makes a point.

And it is well worth the admission price.

# MOVIE REVIEW

## *The Truman Show*

I'll start off by saying that I have never been a big fan of Jim Carrey. I've said before and I'll say again that I thought *Dumb and Dumber* should have been *Dumber and Dumber and Dumbest*, with me being the "Dumbest" for paying $6.50 (or whatever movies cost back then) to see it. I won't even tell you what I thought about *Ace Ventura: Pet Detective*.

I started to change my mind about Jim Carrey when I saw *Liar, Liar* last summer. While it was no *Forrest Gump*, it was cute without being totally silly. *The Truman Show*, however, has made me rethink my feelings about Jim Carrey and his talent (or, as I previously thought, lack thereof).

Prior to seeing *The Truman Show*, I had heard the hype about how spectacular it was to see Jim Carrey completely out of his element. Just this once, believe the hype. Refreshingly, *The Truman Show* lacks the characteristic "Silly Putty" limb antics of Jim Carrey. Instead, it is a provocative and daring drama that chronicles the life of Truman Burbank.

*The Truman Show*'s basic premise is that Carrey's character, insurance salesman Truman Burbank, is the star of a live television show that airs globally 24 hours a day, seven days a week. The whole world is watching, only Truman doesn't know it. Unlike MTV's *The Real World*, where the characters know that their lives are being taped, poor Truman thinks he is just living his life like an ordinary person, completely unaware that the scenic Florida island that he calls "home" is really a giant movie set or that his hopelessly chipper wife, played by Laura Linney, is really an actress playing a part, as are all his friends, neighbors, and coworkers.

Truman is smart enough to realize that something is not quite right. He begins to wonder why he sees the exact same people at the exact same time every morning. He also wonders why his wife extols the virtue of various kitchen products and foods at inappropriate times and then always holds them up so the labels show. As the truth begins to dawn on him, he begins to object to leading an examined life.

The most fascinating aspect of *The Truman Show* is the mechanics of the television show itself. I found it fascinating how many cameras were needed to record Truman's every move. Also quite funny was the fact that troublesome actors were routinely written out. (Wouldn't it be nice if real life were that simple?)

If you are looking for a moral theme in *The Truman Show*, Carrey does aptly make the point that one should live one's own life and not just watch other people's lives on TV. (And I'm sure this applies to movies as well.) *The Truman Show* is captivating. It provides laughs, it provides drama, and it makes a point. And it is well worth the admission price.

*June 1998*

# PRACTICE TIPS

## "Best" and "Super" Lawyers Can Advertise Inclusion on List

The Board of Professional Responsibility has issued an Advisory Ethics Opinion, stating that lawyers may advertise if they were named to the "Best Lawyers in America" or "Super Lawyers" listings. It is permissible, as long as the lawyer does not "go further and refer to themselves subjectively as 'super' or 'the best,'" the BPR warns.

Advisory Ethics Opinion 2006-A-841, issued on September 21, 2006, interprets Formal Ethics Opinion 2004-F-149. There was some doubt as to the interpretation of the Formal Ethics Opinion in light of a recent New Jersey ethics opinion, which prohibited New Jersey lawyers from touting such designations as "Best Lawyers" or "Super Lawyers" or participating in their surveys. (The opinion now has been put on hold by the New Jersey Supreme Court).

Formal Ethics Opinion 2004-F-149 provides guidance regarding what general types of claims or representations included in attorney advertising are false or misleading advertising as contained in Tennessee Rule of Professional Conduct (RPC) 7.1. RPC 7.1, Communication Concerning a Lawyer's Services, provides as follows:

*A lawyer shall not make false or misleading communication about the lawyer, the lawyer's services, the lawyer's charges for fees or costs, or the law as relates to the services the lawyer will provide. A communication is false or misleading if it:*

*a) contains a material misrepresentation of fact or law or omits a fact necessary to make the statement considered as a whole not materially misleading; or*

*b) is likely to create an unjustified expectation about results the lawyer can achieve or states or implies that the lawyer can achieve results by means that violate the Rules of Professional Conduct or other law; or*

*c) compares the lawyer's services or fees with other lawyers' services or fees, unless the comparison can be factually substantiated.*

Comment to RPC 7.1 provides, in pertinent part, as follows:

*... The prohibition in paragraph (b) of statements that may create an "unjustified expectation" would ordinarily preclude advertising a bout results obtained on behalf of a client, such as the amount of a damage award or a lawyer's record in obtaining favorable verdicts and advertisements containing client endorsements.*

In addressing what constitutes permissible language in advertising, the BPR first addressed whether commercial speech such as lawyer advertising is afforded First Amendment protection. The BPR cited Central Hudson Gas and Electric Gas and Elec. Corp. v. Public Serv. Comm'n of N.Y., 447 U.S. 557, 100 S.Ct. 2343, 65 L.Ed.2d 341 (1980). In Central Hudson, the U.S. Supreme Court held that a four-part test of intermediate scrutiny must be employed to determine whether commercial speech is protected by the First Amendment. Commercial speech is afforded qualified First Amendment protection only if it is not false or misleading. If the commercial speech is not actually or inherently false or misleading, a state may reasonably regulate speech that it deems potentially misleading if the harms which the state seeks to alleviate are real, and where the proposed regulation "directly and materially advances the state's interest in preventing the specific type of deception at hand." Douglas v. State, 921 S.W.2d 180, 184 (Tenn. 1996), quoting Edenfield v. Fane, 507 U.S. 761, 770-771, 113 S.Ct. 1792, 1800, 123 L.Ed. 2d 543 (1993).

Accordingly, the BPR concluded that claims or representations contained in lawyer advertising are afforded only qualified First Amendment protection. Communications violative of RPC 7.1(a), (b), and (c)-those communications which contain material misrepresentations of law or fact, those which are likely to create an unjustified expectation about a particular result the lawyer can achieve, or those which compare a lawyer's services or fees with another lawyers' services or fees in a fashion which cannot be factually substantiated-are potentially false or misleading and, accordingly, are prohibited where additional disclosures are not included. Further, the BPR concluded that lawyer advertisements cannot contain subjective-- particularly self-imposed-- characterizations of descriptions of the lawyer, the quality of legal services offered by the lawyer, the level of fees charged, or any comparison of one lawyer's law firm to another law firm unless such comparison can be factually substantiated. Thus, in the absence of factual substantiation, a lawyer shall not advertise that he or she (or his or her law firm) is "No. 1," the "best," "one of the best," "better," "top," "excellent," "qualified," "highly qualified," "experienced," "most experienced," "reputable," "efficient," "preferred," or that the lawyer's or law firm's fees are the lowest. Such terms may be likely to create unjustified expectations about the results to be obtained by the lawyer. These characterizations (and many others too numerous to list) are necessarily relative and ambiguous terms comparing lawyer services and are inherently misleading in the absence of factual substantiation.

Accordingly, Tennessee lawyers may permissibly advertise that they have been included in "Best Lawyers in America," "Super Lawyers" publications, or other listings as long as the lawyer does not go further to tout that he or she is the "best" or is a "super lawyer."

*4 November 2006*

# WORTH YOUR TIME

## Barnsley Gardens: A Spirited and Magical Resort

Legend has it that the ghost of Julia Scarborough Barnsley roams the grounds of Barnsley Gardens in Adairsville, Georgia, which is about an hour south of Chattanooga. In 1842, as the Italian manor house was constructed under the watchful eye of her husband, Godfrey Barnsley, Julia succumbed to tuberculosis. Distraught, Godfrey left his six children in the care of a governess and abandoned the estate that he named Woodlands. A year later when he returned to visit his children, Julia's ghost appeared to Godfrey at the fountain in the front garden and appealed to him to complete construction on the villa and surrounding gardens. Inspired, he completed the grand estate that would be home to his family for nearly one-hundred years. But the years were not kind to the Barnsley family or their beloved estate. Godfrey lost his fortune during the Civil War, and his estate was ransacked by Union soldiers. In 1906, a tornado ripped the roof off of the manor house, and it fell into ruins. The family lived in a kitchen wing until the estate was sold in 1942. In 1988, the estate was rescued by a German prince named Hubertus Fugger, who restored the estate to its previous grandeur.

Today, Barnsley is a new type of resort destination, with luxurious cottages and first-class service. Remnants of the Italian villa still stand in the midst of the gardens which were inspired by the designs of the famed landscape designer, Andrew Jackson Downing.

I first learned of Barnsley Gardens by accident. One night during a rare bout of insomnia, I decided to play on the Internet. I ran a Google search on resorts with sporting clays, fly-fishing, and golf (my husband's three favorite things), and Barnsley popped up. After a bit of research, I purchased a "weekend getaway" for my husband as a Christmas gift. In what he now terms "redneck gift of the Magi," he gave me a shotgun (which is better than the vacuum cleaner I got for my birthday, but I digress).

We decided to spend New Year's Eve and New Year's Day at Barnsley. On the afternoon of our arrival, we first went to the ruins of the old manor. Candles greeted us as we toured the ruins at dusk. The old kitchen wing, which is adjacent to the ruins, is now a museum that contains artifacts and information about Barnsley Gardens' rich history.

Ideal for couples, families, or corporate getaways, the accommodations at Barnsley Gardens are modeled after an English village, with cottages designed with one, two, or four bedrooms and each containing at least one wood-burning fireplace. The rooms feature heart pine floors, high ceilings, and four-poster beds with Egyptian cotton bedding. The amenities and service are first-class, and room service is available twenty-four hours a day.

In addition to great accommodations, Barnsley has activities for everyone in the family. The Fazio-designed golf course nicknamed "The General," is both beautiful and challenging. For the outdoorsman, Barnsley Gardens offers the Orvis center for fly fishing, a challenging sporting clay course (let's just say it is a good thing I don't have to hunt for my own food), guided horseback riding, hiking, and paintball. For someone seeking a more relaxing trip, The Spa at Barnsley offers a wide array of massages and skin treatments.

As a corporate retreat, Barnsley is the perfect place to "get away from it all." There are some 5,000 square feet of space to accommodate conferences. The Pavilion is available for smaller gatherings, and the Town Hall, historic ruins, and gardens are available for more casual get-togethers. Being a self-confessed "foodie," I particularly enjoyed the dining options. The Rice House, which is an old Adairsville home that was dismantled and reassembled on the Barnsley property, puts an epicurean spin on southern cuisine. The main dining room surrounds the original 1854 stone fireplace, while a glass-enclosed sun porch overlooks the historic ruins and gardens. The food was unique (my favorite was the mango succotash), and the wine list is excellent. The Woodlands Grill is a carnivore's delight, serving fine prime beef and fresh fish. The dining area overlooks the golf course, including the ponds which are home to the property's swans. The Woodlands Grill has the feel of an English hunting lodge, with an inviting bar that doubled as a disco on New Year's Eve. On a seasonal basis, the Beer Garden serves German beers, sausages, pretzels, and other fare in a casual atmosphere. An open fire pit keeps diners warm at night and makes a great place for toasting marshmallows.

One of the highlights of our recent trip was the visit from Barnsley's own "fairy godmother." When we entered our cottage, the fairy godmother had left a gift and special treats for our two-year-old son. Much to his disappointment, the babysitter who came later in the evening was not the "fairy godmother" from Cinderella. However, by the end of day two, he asked if the babysitter could go home with us, which is pretty heady praise from a two-year-old.

In addition to being family-friendly, Barnsley Gardens is pet-friendly. Barnsley offers a pet turndown service, pet beds and pet bowls. Guests and pets are welcome to roam the twelve and a half miles of hiking trails, and pets are welcome to have a swim in the ponds and lakes or run with other animals on the 1300 acres.

I did not see the ghost of Julia Scarborough Barnsley on our recent visit to Barnsley Gardens. I guess that gives me one more reason to visit again soon…

*February 2008*

# WORTH YOUR TIME

## The Homestead: A Place Where Time Stands Still

When my husband and I were discussing how to celebrate my … gulp … fortieth birthday, there was almost no discussion. While The Greenbrier in West Virginia bills itself as "America's Resort," I call The Homestead "Angelia's Resort." We first visited there when Trace was six months old, and I have been wanting to make a return trip ever since. The latest trip was pure bliss; and, when my wallet recovers, I will be going back.

Nestled amidst the splendor of the Allegheny Mountains, The Homestead has been a favorite of presidents and princes. History abounds at The Homestead, and it is truly amazing to say that you have walked where George Washington, Thomas Jefferson, James Madison, and Thomas Edison once walked.

From the moment we arrived for our most recent stay, we knew that we were in for a magical weekend. Our room was a junior suite in a portion of the hotel known as "The Tower" and boasted ten-foot windows with an unparalleled view of the mountains, which were starting to burst with color. The furnishings were old-world elegant, and the staff was extremely kind in making sure our stay was first class.

While we love the hotel itself, which is a National Historic Landmark, we chose to return to the Homestead for the activities. Our first venture into the great outdoors was a round of golf on The Old Course, which is a Donald Ross-designed course that was completed in 1892 and has the oldest first tee in continuous use. I particularly enjoyed the Old Course (as long as I was not in the sand … the sand traps are brutal) because each hole had a placard with a bit of historical trivia about the course and the U.S. Presidents who played it. The resort also has two other courses: The Cascades, where Sam Snead launched his career (it was his home course), and the Lower Cascades, which uses its varied terrain to influence play and not dictate it. Our next adventure began at The Homestead Shooting Club. When I asked for a birthday gift, I felt like Ralphie from *A Christmas Story*, when I asked for a Beretta 686 Silver Pigeon with a 28" barrel. With new gun in hand, we met Jimmy, our trapper, who has been with the Shooting Club since 1950. Although my friends think I am crazy, I find clay shooting strangely relaxing, and this trip was no different. While it is still a good thing I don't have to shoot my own food, I will tell you that, with Jimmy's help, my shooting percentage on the sporting clay course improved from twenty-five percent to forty percent, and my husband's improved from seventy percent to eighty-five percent (hence, as long as I am married to him, we will not go hungry).

For the serious outdoorsman, The Homestead offers an Orvis center for fly fishing, which my husband particularly enjoyed. On our first trip, he attended the three-day fly-fishing clinic and now cannot seem to get enough. While I did not fish on our trip, I did venture out to the streams, which are truly beautiful. The Homestead also offers falconry, guided horseback riding, carriage rides, hiking, and paintball.

My favorite part of our trip was my visit to The Spa. I have been to spas at a number of resorts, but the spa at the Homestead is my favorite. I particularly enjoyed the European facial and the hot stone massage. After all of the shooting and golf, it was worth every penny. My son particularly enjoyed the indoor pool. The Spa also boasts the spa gardens, which is a popular place for weddings (we saw two on our most recent visit). For those seeking something a little less serene, the Homestead has a gym, outdoor swimming pool and tennis courts. For those wanting indoor activities, The Homestead has a full-service bowling alley ("which serves beer, just like the real thing," to quote a friend I met) and a movie theater, which has a family-friendly movie at seven o' clock nightly, and a PG-13 or R-rated movie at nine o' clock.

As a corporate retreat, The Homestead is the perfect place to relax and focus. I took a tour of the meeting space, which I understand is often used for conventions (although with all of the great activities, I cannot imagine sitting in a meeting).

Being a self-confessed "foodie," I particularly enjoyed the dining options. For over a century, guests have enjoyed the traditions of the renowned Dining Room. Musicians play nightly, and my son enjoyed his first ballroom dance. The dinner cuisine is southern-American, and the entrees are complemented by fine wines from around the globe. While I enjoyed scallops and mussels as a first course and swordfish as a main course (both were excellent), my husband out ordered me with the "Duck Two Ways," which was one of the best things I have ever tasted. (The wine room, which is located next to the Dining Room, is particularly impressive.) The Casino Club restaurant is located at the Old Course and is housed in a building built in 1895 for ladies' indoor badminton. The food is southern traditional, and is every bit as good as the dinners served in the Dining Room. Sam Snead's Tavern is located in the village in a turn-of-the century bank building, and features Virginia mountain cuisine such as Virginia mountain trout and Black Angus beef. The food is delightful, and the dress is casual.

My favorite meal was my "birthday dinner" at the 1766 Grille, which is celebrated as one of Virginia's finest restaurants. Known for its spectacular views and even more spectacular cuisine, the art of tableside preparation is celebrated at the 1766 Grille. My son particularly enjoyed the fact that all of the desserts on the menu are "flaming desserts" and are prepared at your table. It was truly a magical evening.

The highlight of the trip was our visit to the Jefferson Pools, which are so named because Thomas Jefferson frequently "took the waters" there. The magnificent warm mineral springs are located about five miles from the resort and are housed in octagonal wooden buildings that are on the National Register of Historic Places. The pool inside is about 120 feet in circumference and contains about 40,000 gallons of constantly flowing, clear, mineral spring water. It is considered the oldest spa facility in the United States. The Jefferson Pools have family hours from 10 a.m. until noon daily and are "adults only" after noon. During "adults only" hours, clothing is optional (my option was "on"). Facilities are co-ed during family hours, but men and women have separate facilities at all other times.

Time truly does stand still at The Homestead. Stress seemed to disappear, and I did not feel one day over thirty-nine while I was there. I guess that gives me one more reason to visit again soon…

*October 2008*

# ATTORNEY PROFILE

## Tom Ramsey

I was both delighted and honored to be asked to write this month's Attorney Profile on Tom Ramsey, who is our incoming KBA President. After all, I have known Tom for a decade and a half, and we do pretty much the same thing...just in different locations. Tom and I sat down one afternoon so that I could get material for this article. When I asked Tom what he wanted me to write, he told me that he was ordinary and that there wasn't "...anything that interesting...." Although I thought I knew Tom pretty well, I will tell you that I learned things about him that I did not know when we sat down to talk about this article. His journey as an attorney and now to the presidency of the KBA is anything but ordinary.

Tom Ramsey's journey to service in the Knoxville Bar actually began in 1953. That year, a gentleman named William Caldwell Wilson, a founding member of Ambrose, Wilson, Grimm, and Durand, became the sixth president of the Knoxville Bar Association. In 1962, Mr. Wilson's grandson, Tom Ramsey III, was born. Raised in Kingsport (along with two sisters, a brother, and an identical twin brother...yes, there are two of them), Tom attended Jackson Elementary, John Sevier Middle School, and Dobyns-Bennett High School. After graduation from Dobyns-Bennett where he was an outstanding soccer player in 1980, Tom headed to Knoxville to the University of Tennessee, from which he graduated in 1984 with a degree in political science. More importantly, though, in 1982 while at UT, Tom met his future wife, Kim, an engineering student. If you have not met her, Kim Ramsey is as nice as she is smart. Kim formerly served as the Town Engineer for the Town of Farragut and is currently with a private engineering firm. Tom had the good sense to marry her in 1986...on her birthday! I will tell you that it is a sign of supreme intelligence and perfect planning to have a spouse whose birthday is on the same day as your wedding anniversary...one day to remember, one gift to purchase.

Also, in 1986, Tom followed the path of his twin brother and entered law school at the University of Memphis. Following graduation in 1989, Tom came to Knoxville to work in the firm that his grandfather had founded many years before. After a couple of years, Tom took a job with Robertson & Overbey and then formed the Isaacs, Rayson & Ramsey Law firm in 1994. In September of this year, Tom and Scott Elmore formed Ramsey Elmore, PLLC, a firm focusing on estate planning, probate, corporate planning, and real estate.

Tom's practice today focuses on sophisticated estate planning, probate administration, corporate planning, and real estate. I believe that there is a defining moment when an attorney decides in what area he or she wants to practice. Tom will tell you that his defining moment came with the death of his paternal grandfather. That same year, he was asked to administer his grandfather's estate. Based on the experience of handling his grandfather's estate, Tom stated that it became clear that estate work and all it entails should be the focus of his practice. Since that time, Tom has built one of the most successful and respected estate and probate practices in Knoxville. He has been recognized in various publications as one of the best of the Bar in estate planning and probate administration. When he is not in the office, Tom can often be found speaking to lawyers and community groups for the KBA on matters involving estate planning and probate.

During the hours when he is not practicing law, you can most often find Tom coaching on a soccer field. Tom has been coaching soccer almost continuously since I first got to know him some fifteen years ago. Tom is currently the coach of the West Valley Middle School Soccer Team, where son Reid, age twelve, is a standout player. Ryan, Tom and Kim's oldest, is fifteen and a sophomore at Bearden High School, where he is... you guessed it... a big contributor to the school's soccer team. Tom and Kim are also the proud parents of a daughter, Abby Ann, who is six and in the first grade at Bluegrass Elementary School. When I asked Tom whether Abby Ann had been bitten by the soccer bug, Tom laughed and informed me that Abby Ann is "...into all things 'girl'." Based on Tom's description of Abby Ann, I am certain that, although she is considerably younger than her brothers, she is in charge at the Ramsey household.

If you don't know Tom personally, I hope you will take a few minutes to get to know him. Tom is caring, intelligent, hard-working, and devoted to his family, to his clients, and to service in the Bar. His clients are fortunate to have such a man as their advocate, and the KBA is fortunate that such a man is our next President.

*December 2008*

# COVER STORY

## Tennessee Introduces Long-Term Care Partnership

Without proper planning, the cost of long-term care can be the greatest threat to financial security.[1] Although long-term care insurance has been available for a number of years to help defray the costs of long-term care, few people have purchased such policies, instead opting to "spend-down" in order to qualify for Medicaid benefits to cover long-term care in the event such care is needed. While many estate planning and elder law attorneys have encouraged the purchase of such insurance, the majority of clients have failed to protect themselves with the purchase of long-term care insurance, with many feeling that there was little incentive for the expenditure of funds on an insurance that they may never use. This may soon change. Tennessee's new Long-Term Care Partnership will likely provide incentive for purchase of long-term care insurance.

### The Long-Term Care Partnership

Tennessee has now joined twenty-four other states in giving its citizens an incentive to purchase long-term care insurance. Effective October 1, 2008, the Tennessee Long-Term Care Partnership (the "Partnership") is a public-private venture designed to encourage and reward Tennesseans who take an active role in planning ahead for future long-term care needs instead of relying on the state's Medicaid program, administered through the Bureau of TennCare, to finance their long-term care.[2] The Partnership allows Tennesseans to have an additional level of asset protection because, for every dollar that a Partnership-qualified policy pays out in benefits, a dollar of personal assets can be protected when applying for long-term care coverage under TennCare.[3] With the purchase of a long-term care policy, Medicaid becomes the payor of last resort, which means that individuals can be private-pay patients with regard to long-term care, giving them more choices as to facilities and types of services and, further, that the state Medicaid budget saves money since the individual has proceeds from the insurance policy to pay for care prior to qualification for long-term care benefits.

The Long-Term Care Partnership is truly a partnership in that it involves private insurers, long-term care agents and brokers, the Bureau of TennCare, the Department of Human Services, and the Tennessee Department of Commerce and Insurance all working together to administer the program.[4] Although the Partnership is overseen by the federal centers for Medicare and Medicaid services, each state that participates has a great deal of autonomy in its administration.[5]

## The Partnership-qualified Policy

As noted above, the Partnership rewards Tennesseans who purchase long-term care insurance policies to help cover the costs of their long-term care. It is important to note, though, that not all long-term care insurance policies allow their insureds to be Partnership participants. In order to take advantage of the Partnership benefits, a Partnership participant's policy must be "Partnership-qualified", meaning that it must meet three basic requirements. First, the policy must contain the provisions set forth in the National Association of Insurance Commission's ("NAIC") model law.[6] Further, all plans sold in Tennessee must be approved by the Tennessee Department of Commerce and Insurance prior to use.[7] Second, the policy must be tax-qualified, meaning that the Internal Revenue Service does not tax the policy's benefits.[8] Finally, the policy must contain certain inflation protection provisions at the time it is sold. If a person purchasing a policy is under the age of sixty-one at the time of the purchase of the policy, then the policy must compound annual inflation protection at some level. If the person is between the ages of sixty-one and seventy-five at the time of the purchase of the policy, then some level of inflation protection must apply; however, no minimum level is established. Finally, if a person is over the age of seventy-five at the time of purchase of a long-term care policy, the policy may provide inflation protection; however, no inflation protection is required.[9]

For Tennesseans who have previously purchased policies, the Partnership contains a special "grandfathering" provision. An individual who currently owns a long-term care policy that would otherwise meet the requirements of a Partnership-qualified policy is entitled to exchange his or her policy for a Partnership-qualified policy as long as the purchase of the initial policy occurred on or after February 8, 2006.[10] In order for an insurance company to offer or exchange a Partnership-qualified policy, the insurance company must have the policy or policy rider approved by the Tennessee Department of Commerce and Insurance.[11] All policy forms and riders filed for approval must be accompanied by an Issuer Certification Form.[12]

The Bureau of TennCare will recognize the Partnership-qualified status of policies purchased in other states as long as the policies meet all requirements of Partnership-qualified policies in Tennessee.[13] Thus, benefits paid under a Partnership-qualified policy purchased in another state will be recognized for purposes of determining eligibility in Tennessee.

At the time the Partnership-qualified policy is offered by an insurance agent to a customer, a Long-Term Care Partnership Program Notice must be given to the customer.[14] In addition, the purchaser must be given a Long-term Care Insurance Partnership Disclosure Notice that explains the rules concerning TennCare eligibility.[15]

## Requirements to be a Partnership Participant

A Long-term Care Partnership participant in Tennessee is someone who either: (1) requests TennCare payment for long-term care services after exhausting all benefits of a Partnership-qualified policy; or (2) exhausts all benefits of a Partnership-qualified policy while receiving payment of long-term care services under TennCare; or (3) receives TennCare payment of long-term care services and dies before the Partnership-qualified policy benefits are exhausted.[16] Importantly, this means that holders of Partnership-qualified policies will not be required to completely exhaust all of their benefits under the policy before being able to qualify for Medicaid long-term care benefits under TennCare. Thus, once a person meets the eligibility requirements, he or she may obtain

TennCare long-term care benefits even if he or she has unused benefits under a Partnership-qualified commercial policy.

## Benefits Derived by Partnership Participants During Life

The Partnership is set up so that participants receive benefits during their lifetimes. First, and as previously set forth above, assets may be designated as "disregarded" in an amount equal to the benefits paid out by the Partnership-qualified long-term care policy as of the date of application for Medicaid eligibility.[17] This means that assets are "disregarded" on a dollar-for-dollar basis so that property equal to the amount paid under a long-term care policy is not counted when determining TennCare long-term care eligibility. Secondly, designated assets are not counted toward the TennCare asset limit for eligibility purposes.[18] This means that a person receiving TennCare does not have to spend-down the "disregarded" assets, and, thus, can retain a greater amount each month. Additionally, the designated assets may be transferred to another person without penalty, meaning that there is no "look back" on asset transfer when the transfer includes "disregarded" assets or amounts.[19] Finally, additional benefits paid by the Partnership-qualified policy after the application for Medicaid shall not be disregarded in future review and/or determination for Medicaid eligibility.[20]

## Benefits Derived by Estates of Partnership Participants

After the Partnership participant is deceased, assets which were disregarded for purposes of Medicaid eligibility determination are protected from estate recovery.[21] Additionally, when the amount of assets disregarded during the person's lifetime was less than the total benefits paid by the Partnership-qualified policy, additional assets may be protected in the estate recovery process up to the amount of payments made by the individual's Partnership-qualified policy for services covered under the policy.[22] If no assets were disregarded during the person's lifetime, the personal representative of the decedent's Estate may designate assets to protect from estate recovery up to the lesser of the two previous options— even if the Partnership-qualified policy benefits were not completely exhausted.[23]

## Final Thoughts

Tennessee is now in the forefront of encouraging people to plan for their own long-term care. With the Tennessee Long-Term Care Partnership, Tennessee has joined twenty-four other states in being part of the solution in helping baby boomers solve their long-term care financing needs. By allowing policyholders to protect one dollar of assets for every one dollar of benefits received under a qualified long-term care insurance policy, Tennesseans now have greater incentive to take affirmative steps to finance their own long-term care while protecting more of their assets from estate recovery in the event they ultimately receive long-term care benefits under TennCare. Additionally, when people have insurance to cover at least part of their long-term care, then the state Medicaid budget is spared. Accordingly, clients should be counseled to take advantage of the benefits offered by the Long-Term Care Partnership.

*January 2009*

1Miller, Jessica, "The Changing Face of Long-Term Care," CARING Magazine, August, 1998.
2"Consumer Handout: Introduction to the Long Term Care Partnership Program," Tenn. Dept. of Commerce and Ins., 2008.
3Bulletin RE Requirements and Responsibilities Brought About by the Adoption of the Long-Term Care Partnership in Tennessee," Tenn. Dept. of Commerce and Ins., Sept. 22, 2008.
4"Consumer Handout: Introduction to the Long Term Care Partnership Program," Tenn. Dept. of Commerce and Ins., 2008.
5Id.
6Bulletin RE Requirements and Responsibilities Brought About by the Adoption of the Long-Term Care Partnership in Tennessee," Tenn. Dept. of Commerce and Ins., Sept. 22, 2008.
7Id.
8Id.
9Id.
10Id.
11Id.
12Id.
13Id.
14Id.
15Id.
16"Consumer Handout: Introduction to the Long Term Care Partnership Program," Tenn. Dept. of Commerce and Ins., 2008.
17Id.
18Id.
19Id.
20Id.
21Id.
22Id.
23Id.

# AROUND THE BAR

## Supreme Court Dinner Preview: James F. Neal

Respected. Competitive. Accomplished. Competitive. Down-to-Earth. Competitive. These words aptly describe Nashville attorney James F. Neal, who is the featured speaker at this year's KBA Supreme Court Dinner.

In nearly five decades of trying cases, Jim Neal, founding member of Neal & Harwell, PLC, can count on one hand the number of cases he has lost in front of jury ... pretty heady stuff considering some of the cases he has handled. For his accomplishments, Mr. Neal was recently named one of the ABA's "Top 70 Over 70: Lions of the Trial Bar." When asked about his impressive record, Neal replied, "Yeah, I love winning. But I hate losing even more. Just the thought of losing makes my body shrink from five foot eight to five foot six."

Born in Oak Grove, Tennessee, Neal's competitive spirit was apparent from an early age. After graduating from high school, he traveled to the University of Wyoming to play football under another Tennessee legend, Bowden Wyatt. As a student at UW studying physical education, Neal didn't start out intending to be a great trial lawyer. Aubrey Harwell, his law partner since 1971, says that Neal was a mediocre student at best. Says Mr. Harwell, "Jim is famous for saying, 'I scheduled all of my classes before noon so I would be finished when I got up.'"

After graduation from UW in 1951 and serving in the Marine Corps from 1952-1954, Neal came back to Tennessee to attend law school at Vanderbilt. While he was an average student in college, Neal was a stellar student at Vanderbilt, graduating number one in the class of 1957. Following graduation, he took a job in Washington, D.C. and attended classes at Georgetown University at night, earning a Master's in Tax in 1960, with the intention of being a tax lawyer.

When John F. Kennedy was elected President in 1960, Neal, who had become an acquaintance of the Kennedy family during his time in Washington, campaigned to be the head of the Tax Department at the Department of Justice. Instead, he was appointed and served as the U.S. Attorney for the Middle District of Tennessee from 1964 through 1966. He served as Special Assistant to the U.S. Attorney under Bobby Kennedy and prosecuted famed Teamster boss Jimmy Hoffa in 1964. Later, he served as Associate Special Prosecutor on the Watergate Special Prosecution Force from 1973-1974, where he prosecuted H.R. Haldeman and John Erlichman.

States Aubrey Harwell, "No one in Nashville has been involved in as many high-profile cases. He was involved in the Ford Pinto cases, the Twilight Zone helicopter crash case with director John Landis, the Ray Blanton matter, and defense of Al Gore during the latter days of the Clinton Administration." Other notable cases include the defense of Exxon in its trial related to the Valdez oil spill in 1994 and the University of Alabama booster case.

Neal has credited his success in the courtroom to lessons learned under Coach Wyatt on the football field. Neal has recalled that Coach Wyatt was famous for saying, "The team with the fewest mistakes during the game will win." Says Neal, "It was true in football, and it is true in the courtroom." Jim Neal's professional success extends beyond the courtroom. In 1978, Neal declined the nomination for FBI Chief. Although the Tennessee Democratic Party urged him to run for governor in 1982, he considered but ultimately rejected the offer. Instead, he was appointed Chief Counsel on the U.S. Senate Select Committee on Undercover Operations in the Department of Justice. He was given the

UW Distinguished Alumnus Award in 1994 and was inducted into the UW Athletics Hall of Fame in 1994. He received the Distinguished American Award from the National Football Foundation and Hall of Fame, the Johnny Cash Americanism Award from the Anti-Defamation League of B' Nai B' Rith, and the Distinguished Alumnus Award from Vanderbilt University. In 2003, he was awarded an honorary doctorate from the University of Wyoming.

Trey Harwell, Nashville Bar Association President and member of Neal & Harwell, credits Neal's success as a trial lawyer to his ability to relate to people. "He is the most down-to-earth person you will ever meet. He is a great trial attorney, and if you spend any time with him, you will know why." He stated that Neal has a way about him which makes people feel at ease. Trey relayed a famous story from the firm. "Mr. Neal had people in from out of town for a meeting. Prior to the meeting, he ripped his pants. Not wanting to conduct a meeting in ripped pants, he took them off and gave them to his assistant to sew up. Not wanting to delay or cancel the meeting, he conducted it in his boxer shorts." Trey also recounts that Jim Neal is known for his love of cigars. But he doesn't smoke them—he eats them. Says Trey, "He will come in in the morning what we call his 'Class A' clothes. But by the end of the day, they are covered in tobacco stains. It doesn't bother him at all."

Aubrey Harwell is quick to point out that Neal's success is also due to his competitive nature. "If you go to lunch with him, he will say, 'Let's flip for the bill.' If he loses, he will say, 'Let's flip again. Two out of three.' He just cannot stand to lose."

Although they founded Neal & Harwell together in 1971, Aubrey Harwell still refers to Jim Neal as his mentor and role model. In nearly forty years of practicing together, Mr. Harwell states that they have never had an argument. He says, "Jim Neal is one of my heroes—even after forty years."

*August 2009*

# COVER STORY

## U.S. Supreme Court Ruling a Game-Changer for Campaign Spending

The long-awaited decision in Citizens United v. Federal Election Commission[1] was issued on January 21. In a 5-4 ruling, the U.S. Supreme Court rolled back campaign finance restrictions meant to limit corporate and union influence on elections and determined that corporations and unions may now directly and expressly advocate for the election or defeat of candidates for federal office as long as they do not coordinate their efforts with specific campaigns or political parties. Many predict that the impact of the decision will be immense and far-reaching and will drastically impact U.S. politics, the 2010 mid-term elections, and future legislation.

## I. Legislative and Procedural History

As amended by § 203 of the Bipartisan Campaign Reform Act of 2002 (BCRA), which is also known as McCain-Feingold, federal law prohibited corporations and unions from using their general treasury funds to make independent expenditures for speech that is an "electioneering communication" or for speech that expressly advocates the election of defeat of a candidate.[2] An "electioneering communication" is "any broadcast, cable, or satellite communication" that "refers to a clearly identifiable candidate for Federal office," is made within thirty days of a primary election,[3] and is publicly distributed.

In McConnell v. Federal Election Commission,[5] the U.S. Supreme Court upheld limits on electioneering communications in a facial challenge, relying on the holding in Austin v. Michigan Chamber of Commerce[6] that political speech may be banned based on the speaker's corporate identity.

The Citizens United decision stems from a controversy caused by a clash between Citizens United, a 501(c)(4) organization, and regulations crafted by the Federal Election Commission (FEC). In January 2008, Citizens United released a documentary, *Hillary: The Movie ("Hillary")*, which was critical of Sen. Hillary Clinton, who was then a candidate for the Democratic presidential nomination. Anticipating that it would make *Hillary* available through cable television on-demand services, Citizens United produced television ads to run on broadcast and cable television. Concerned about possible civil and criminal penalties for violating election laws, Citizens United sought declaratory and injunctive relief. The U.S. District Court for the District of Columbia denied Citizens United a preliminary injunction and granted the FEC summary judgment. An appeal followed.

The Supreme Court heard oral arguments on March 24, 2009, and a decision was expected in the summer of 2009. However, on June 29, 2009, the Supreme Court issued an order directing the parties to reargue the case on September 9 after submitting briefs that included broader First Amendment concerns.

## II. The Decision

In a historic 5-4 decision, the U.S. Supreme Court overruled the District Court, specifying that the First Amendment protects corporations and unions the same as individuals with regard to the ability to spend money to influence elections. Speaking for the majority, Justice Kennedy found that § 441b's restrictions on expenditures were invalid and could not be applied to spending like that in the film in question. Kennedy wrote, "The restrictions … function as the equivalent of a prior restraint, giving the FEC power analogous to the type of government practices that the First Amendment was drawn to prohibit."[7]

The Court also overruled the Austin case, which had previously held that a Michigan campaign finance act that prohibited corporations from using treasury money to support or oppose candidates in elections did not violate the First and Fourteenth Amendments. The Court concluded that §441b's restrictions were invalid and that there was no basis for allowing the Government to limit corporate independent expenditures. In reaching their conclusion, the Court also overruled that part of McConnell that upheld BCRA § 203's extension of § 441b's restrictions on independent corporate expenditures. Justice Kennedy stated, "§ 441b's prohibition on corporate independent expenditures is an outright ban on speech, backed by criminal sanctions. ... Because speech is an essential mechanism of democracy—it is the means to hold officials accountable to the people— political speech must prevail against laws that would suppress it by design or inadvertence." In determining that corporate entities are entitled to the same First Amendment protection as individuals, Justice Kennedy stated, "Differential treatment of media corporations and other corporations cannot be squared with the First Amendment, and there is no support for the view that the Amendment's original meaning would permit suppressing media corporations' political speech."

The Court did determine that BCRA §§ 201 and 311 are valid as applied to the ads for *Hillary* and to the movie itself. Thus, the disclosure and disclaimer requirements will be kept in place. These requirements involve reports that have to be filed with the FEC on electioneering communications, and the ads themselves must carry a disclaimer stating who is responsible for the content.

## III. Reaction to the Decision

Reaction to the decision has been swift and passionate. In general, conservatives and libertarians have praised the ruling as preservation of the First Amendment and freedom of speech, while liberals and advocates for campaign finance reform have criticized it as greatly expanding the role of corporate money in politics.

In support of the decision, campaign finance expert Jan Baran, a member of the Commission on Federal Ethics Law Reform, has written, "The history of campaign finance reform is the history of incumbent politicians seeking to muzzle speakers, any speakers, particularly those who might publicly criticize them and their legislation. It is a lot easier to legislate against unions, gun owners, 'fat cat' bankers, health insurance companies, and any other industry or 'special interest' group when they can't talk back."[8]

Campaign finance attorney Cleta Mitchell, who had filed an amicus brief on behalf of two advocacy groups, wrote that "The Supreme Court has correctly eliminated a constitutionally flawed system that allowed media corporations (e.g., The Washington Post Co.) to freely disseminate their opinions about candidates using corporate treasury funds, while denying that constitutional privilege to Susie's Flower Shop Inc. ... The real victims of the corporate expenditure ban have been nonprofit advocacy organizations across the political spectrum."[9]

In responding to a question as to how he believed corporate money would reshape politics as a result of the Court's decision, University of Miami School of Business assistant professor Christopher Cotton expressed his belief that the effect would be minimal.[10] He stated that there may be very little difference in seeing eight or nine ads as opposed to one or two.[11] Further, he expressed confidence in the voters, believing that they recognize that the richer candidates are not always the better candidates.[12] University of California law professor Eugene Volokh also believed that corporate money would have little effect on politics, believing that corporations would fear alienating consumers by supporting candidates.[13]

In response to the notion that the ruling would allow foreign entities to gain political influence in situations where domestic corporations are under foreign control, Bradley A. Smith, Capital University Law professor and former chair of the Federal Election Commissions, pointed out that the decision did not overturn the ban on political donations by foreign corporations.[14]

On the other hand, President Barack Obama has been one of the harshest critics of the decision, calling it a green light for special interest money in politics. He stated that the decision "gives the special interests and their lobbyists even more power in Washington—while undermining the influence of the average Americans who make small contributions to support their preferred candidates."[15] In his 2010 State of the Union address, he further condemned the decision, saying that it opens the floodgates for special interests, including foreign corporations, to spend without limit in U.S. elections.[16]

Senator John McCain, co-crafter of BCRA, said, "There's going to be, over time, a backlash...when you see the amounts of union and corporate money that's going into political campaigns."[17] Republican Senator Olympia Snowe agreed, stating, "Today's decision was a serious disservice to our country."[18]

Former Supreme Court Justice Sandra Day O'Connor has also criticized the decision. She warned, "In invalidating some of the existing checks on campaign spending, the majority in Citizens United has signaled that the problem of campaign contributions in judicial elections might get considerably worse quite soon."[19] She cautioned that the ruling may impact state judicial elections, allowing corporations to increasingly influence those who are supposed to be unbiased arbiters of the law.[20]

## IV. Going Forward

The Citizens United case has erased the subtle distinction between corporate donors, which are subject to regulation, and individual donors, who largely are not. Corporations now have the same free speech rights as individuals. The case lifts the ban on the use of corporate treasury funds in federal elections and the requirement that corporations use PAC's to advocate for a candidate. The FEC will now be tasked with taking the opinion and crafting new rules to ease the limits on corporate spending. What solution that they craft is anyone's guess. While the full effect of the ruling remains to be seen, it is certain that the ruling will alter corporate spending on future elections.

*March 2010*

1 558 U.S. _____ (2010).
2 2 U.S.C. § 441b.
3 2 U.S.C. § 434(f)(3)(a).
4 11 CFR § 100.29(a)(2).
5 540 U.S. 93, 203-209.
6 494 U.S. 652.
7 558 U.S. _____ (2010).
8 Baran, Jan Witold (2010-01-25). "Stampede Toward Democracy." *New York Times*. http://nytimes.com/2010/01/26/opinion/26baran.html.
9 Who is helped, or hurt, by the Citizens United decision'? *Washington Post*. 2010-01-24. http://www.washingtonpost.com/wp-dyn/content/article/2010/01/22/AR2010012203874.html?hpid=opinionbox1.
10 "How Corporate Money Will Reshape Politics: Restoring Free Speech in Elections." *New York Times* blog. 2010-01-21. http://roomfordebate.blogs.nytimes.com/2010/01/21/how-corporate-money-will-reshape-politics.
11 Id.
12 Id.
13 Id.
14 Smith, Bradley (2010-01-27). "President Wrong on Citizens United Case." National Review. http://corner.nationalreview.com/post/.
15 "Obama Criticizes Campaign Finance Ruling." CNN *Political Ticker*. Turner Broadcasting System, Inc. 2010-01-20.

http://politicalticker.blogs.cnn.com/2010/01/21/obama-criticizes-campaign-finance-ruling/.
16 Obama, Barack. State of the Union Address (2010-01-27).
17 Amick, John (2010-01-24). "McCain skeptical Supreme Court decision can be countered." Washington Post. http://voices.washingtonpost.com/44/2010/01/mccain-skeptical-supreme-court.html.
18 United States Senate (2010-01-21). Snowe troubled by U.S. Supreme Court ruling to remove limits on corporate and union spending in political campaigns." Press Release. http://snowe.senate.gov/public/index.cfm.
19 Liptak, Adam (2010-01-26). "O'Connor Mildly Criticizes Court's Campaign Finance Decision." *The Caucus Blog*. New York Times Company. http://thecaucus.blogs.nytimes.com/2010/01/26-oconnormildly-criticizes-courts-campaign-finance-decision/.
20 Id.

## ATTORNEY PROFILE

## Supreme Court Dinner Preview Sen. Lamar Alexander: Deep Roots and a Long Shadow

In a March 2008 article, Alison McSherry of Roll Call wrote that when you cross the threshold of Sen. Lamar Alexander's office in Washington, it feels as though you have left Washington and entered the backwoods of Tennessee. Instead of the traditional white paint and diplomas, Sen. Alexander's office has a graying barn wall decorated with relics from Appalachia. The hallways are decorated with memorabilia from musicians like Elvis, Johnny Cash, and Hank Williams, Jr. When asked about the relics that adorn his office, Sen. Alexander stated, "My thought was that Tennessee and Tennesseans were more interesting than I am." Truth be told, however, Sen. Alexander has Tennessee roots that run deep, and he is one of the most interesting and colorful people you will meet.

Born in Maryville in 1940 to a kindergarten teacher and elementary school principal, Andrew Lamar Alexander is a seventh generation Tennessean and a member of Sons of the Revolution. As a harbinger of things to come, Sen. Alexander was elected as Governor of Tennessee Boys State during his senior year at Maryville High School. Following graduation, he attended Vanderbilt University, where he was a member of the track team and Sigma Chi fraternity. He graduated from Vanderbilt in 1962, Phi Beta Kappa (and school record holder in the 440 relay), and then graduated from New York University School of Law in 1965. Following a clerkship for the Honorable John Minor Wisdom of the U.S. Court of

Appeals for the Fifth Circuit, Alexander embarked on a career in politics, which has now spanned over forty years.

After working in Sen. Howard Baker's office from 1967 to 1969, he moved to Washington to work for Bryce Harlow, who was executive assistant to Richard Nixon. In 1970, he moved back to Tennessee to serve as campaign manager for Winfield Dunn's successful gubernatorial bid. Although his own gubernatorial bid in 1974 was unsuccessful, Alexander gained national notoriety in 1974 when he was named one of Time magazine's 200 Faces of the Future.

In 1978, Alexander decided again to run for governor. He made a name for himself, walking over 1,000 miles across the state, wearing his signature red and black shirt, often staying in constituents' homes and eating home-cooked meals. At the age of thirty-seven, Lamar Alexander became the forty-fifth governor of the state of Tennessee. He made history four years later when he became the first Tennessee governor elected to a second four-year term. As governor, he helped Tennessee become the third largest auto producer in the U.S. and the first state to pay teachers for teaching well. He also started the Tennessee Governor's Schools for outstanding students. During his second term, he gained national prominence when he was elected Chairman of the National Governors Association.

Following his governorship, Alexander was named President of the University of Tennessee, where he served from 1988 until 1991, when he was appointed U.S. Secretary of Education by President George H. W. Bush, serving until 1993. When Sen. Fred Thompson decided against seeking re-election, Lamar Alexander was persuaded to run for the open Senate seat being vacated by Thompson. In 2002, Sen. Lamar Alexander became the first Tennessean to be popularly elected both governor and senator. He was re-elected in a landslide in 2008.

As the Senior U.S. Senator from Tennessee, Alexander is recognized as a relatively moderate voice in the Republican party who is willing to work across the aisle. He has been at the forefront of the energy debate and has worked tirelessly as a champion for education. He has worked his way through the ranks, becoming the Chairman of the Senate Republican Conference at the beginning of 2008. He also serves on committees overseeing education, clean air, highways, science, appropriations, and the Tennessee Valley Authority.

Sen. Alexander has received numerous awards, including the Guardian of Seniors' Rights Award, the Defender of Children Award, the U.S.

Chamber of Commerce Spirit of Enterprise Award, the Defender of the Mountains Award, the National Association of Manufacturers Award for Manufacturing Legislative Excellence, and the National Federation of Independent Business "Guardian of Small Business Award." He has also been named American Action Network's Legislator of the Year. In 2006, the NCAA named him to the list of "100 Most Influential Student Athletes" in the last one-hundred years.

As interesting and distinguished a career as Sen. Alexander has had, there is so much more. Lamar Alexander's life and interests have been as varied as the state of Tennessee. The author of seven books, Alexander has taught American character at Harvard University's Kennedy School of Government. He also helped found the nation's largest provider of worksite daycare.

Alexander is also a classical and country pianist. In April 2007, he played piano on Patti Page's re-recording of *The Tennessee Waltz* and has performed at Nashville's Schermerhorn Symphony Center. To celebrate a recent birthday, he and his family climbed Mt. Kilimanjaro. An avid walker and outdoorsman, he is also a collector of walking sticks. His office houses his collection of walking sticks, including one that belonged to one of his heroes, Sam Houston, and another that belonged to Pres. Franklin D. Roosevelt.

During the Reagan Administration, Sen. Alexander served on the Commission on American Outdoors. Recently, scientists in the Great Smoky Mountains National Park found a new species of insect, which looks as though it is wearing a red and black plaid shirt. Appropriately, it has been named the Cosberella lamaralexanderi, making Sen. Alexander the only U.S. legislator to have an insect bear his name.

Recently, I was honored to share the podium with Sen. Alexander at an event. In his speech, he paid homage to his good friend, the late Alex Haley. He quoted Haley, telling the audience to "find the good and praise it." With a long and accomplished political career and a personal life and interests as varied as the state of Tennessee itself, Sen. Alexander is a mirror of the good that is Tennessee and worthy of all of the praise that comes his way. The KBA is honored to have him as speaker at the Supreme Court Dinner on August 31. It is an event not to be missed.

*August 2011*

# GUILTY PLEASURES

## For True Guilty Pleasures, Regret Not Required

It's not the first cupcake, it's the second. And the third. On the same day. It's the purchase of the pair of high heels that you affectionately call "sit-down shoes" because no woman in her right mind would try to walk in them. It's listening to Selena Gomez or Justin Bieber in the car on the way to work. It's our secret behavior that we hide from our friends and colleagues.

Guilty pleasures are those low brow, high-calorie things we know we shouldn't enjoy. But we do. A lot. They are those things that we do that harm no one, but which can be a source of embarrassment when we are caught. As Cathy Lynn Grossman of USA Today once wrote, "This is guilt with a wink, not the 'Big G' kind of guilt for which we ask forgiveness, confess to a priest or regret on Yom Kippur."

"Big G" guilt makes us seek forgiveness, but guilty pleasures are innocent indulgences. The twinge of guilt they give us is part of their charm. We are rewarded with distraction from the stresses of everyday life or a vicarious thrill. They make life a little more fun.

Recently, I was outed with my own guilty pleasure. I was sitting in the break room at the office, having lunch by myself later in the afternoon. I turned on the television to my favorite afternoon show, *The Young and the Restless*. I've been a fan of Mrs. Chancellor, Jill Foster Abbott Whateverhernameisnow, and Victor Newman for almost as long as I can remember. I scheduled my law school classes around it. I recorded it on a daily basis for a number of years. But it has always been my little secret. Until now.

I was late into the program when one of my colleagues walked in. I was caught. "Are you watching soap operas?" he asked. "How can you watch that trash?" In a moment of panic, I wondered whether I should turn the TV off and feign ignorance. Or acknowledge my own guilty pleasure. I did what any quick-thinking lawyer would do. I came up with a witty, yet appropriate, response.

My response: "Give me a break. I deal with death, dying, and taxes all day. I *need* this." Soaps are mindless, and I love them. So, I will confess. I love trash. I love soap operas, celebrity gossip magazines, and reality television. I'll also admit that I was almost giddy on our recent beach trip when my dear husband came out of the house with a *National Enquirer* and *Star* magazine that he had picked up at the grocery store. It was pure bliss. I've also been known to change the clocks and put my child to bed early so that I could watch *Teen Mom 2* on MTV. Yep, I indulge in guilty pleasures more that I care to admit.

They say that confession is good for the soul. After confessing my own guilty pleasures to some of my friends, some of them confessed their own.

My dear friend Jessica Shafer (who, coincidentally, introduced me to www.people.com) confessed that her guilty pleasures are celebrity gossip and shoes. Says Jessica, "Celebrity magazines and websites are some of my favorite mini-escapes. And shoes are fabulous because they can really spice up an outfit, and they always fit ... except when you are eight months pregnant with twins."

Tasha Blakney agrees. "I'll have to agree with Jessica on the shoes. You can never have too many of them. Also, I have a ridiculous obsession with cookbooks. I buy them constantly, even the little ones by the grocery store checkout. If I started now, I could never make a recipe from every book I own, but I do love reading them."

Darsi Sirknen likewise loves shoes. And hats. And music. "Music is definitely a pleasure of mine. I don't really consider it a guilty pleasure because I am not ashamed of my choices in music (which run the gamut from bluegrass to gangsta rap), but sometimes my co-workers are embarrassed when we go to lunch together and pull back into the parking garage blasting Ice Cube or, worse, Britney Spears."

We love guilty pleasures most when we can justify them. *Health Magazine* once listed ten guilty pleasures that are actually healthy for us, like dark chocolate and sleeping in. They even backed up their claims with supporting research. Perhaps guilty pleasures are lightweights on the regret scale because their damage is neither deep nor lasting. Neither, alas, are the delights. As Euripides wrote, "Short is the joy that the guilty pleasure brings."

I think I need a little joy tonight, so I am concluding this month's "guilty pleasures" column. Besides, *Toddlers and Tiaras* just came on.

*September 2011*

# GUILTY PLEASURES

## Gluttony and Culinary Guilty Pleasures: Just Call Me "Sinner"

A "guilty pleasure" is defined as something one enjoys and considers pleasurable despite feeling guilt for enjoying it. The "guilt" involved is sometimes simply the fear of others discovering our low-brow or embarrassing tastes.

A couple of months ago, I wrote about my guilty pleasures with regard to television watching and reading material. I'm not (totally) ashamed to admit that I love a good *Lifetime* movie, a *Real Housewife*, or a grocery check-out magazine (hey, it helps with pop-culture trivial pursuit). Of course, that article did not even begin to scratch the surface because I read and watch a lot of crap. Some secrets are better kept private. However, I am secretly proud of my *other* guilty pleasure. I do not like pork. Ham, pork chops, salami, bologna. Yuck. But I LOVE bacon.

I once had a cat that wiggled her nose and salivated when she smelled Kentucky Fried Chicken. I am that way when I smell bacon. I am like the dog on the bacon-flavored Beggin' Strips commercial. "I want bacon! Give me bacon!" I just cannot get enough of that smoky, salty, crispy goodness. Gluttony is the over-indulgence and over-consumption of anything to the point of waste. It is one of the Seven Deadly Sins, and I am a sinner.

I don't remember how it happened. It just did. Hugh brought home a pack of Benton's bacon, and I was hooked. If you have never tried it, Benton's bacon has to be what God eats for breakfast. I love it baked in the oven, sprinkled with brown sugar. At our house, we call that "candy bacon." And it is good.

Last year, I read an article about Sean Brock, who was the chef at Capitol Grille when I lived in Nashville. He had moved to South Carolina and was executive chef at McCrady's in Charleston and had invented bacon-infused cotton candy for his dessert menu. He was opening a new restaurant—Husk—in Charleston, which would feature southern food, including Benton's bacon. I immediately began plotting a trip there.

My husband competes in triathlons, and he found one in Charleston that coincided with our beach vacation. And I found my "in." We headed to Charleston on a Friday, with an eight o' clock dinner reservation. By noon on Sunday, Hugh had completed his triathlon. I had completed my own triathlon – three meals at Husk. I won't go into details about all of the food (the Friday night dinner was the best meal I have ever had. Husk was recently – and appropriately – named "Best Restaurant in America" by *Bon Appetite* magazine), but I will tell you that bacon is featured prominently on the menu. The butter for the bread is mixed with bacon fat, and the cornbread is baked in bacon grease and has bacon pieces in the batter.

The pièce de résistance is the Husk burger, which is a blend of ground beef tenderloin and Benton's bacon. I am not a burger-eater, but I can attest that the Husk burger is the best burger I have ever tried. My son agrees. When I asked what he wanted for dinner on his sixth birthday, his response, "A Husk burger." The apple doesn't fall far from the tree.

For my birthday, I asked my husband for one thing: dinner at Baconfest. He forgot to make a reservation, and it sold out. I almost cried.

Last weekend, Childhelp had their annual fundraiser, Les Trois Chefs. Sean Brock was the celebrity chef, and he designed the menu. The menu featured ... you guessed it ... Benton's bacon and country ham. It was amazing. The silent auction had an item called "The Bacon Lover's Package." It contained two Lodge cast iron skillets, a country ham, and a tour of Benton's Country Hams and Bacon in Madisonville with Allan Benton. While we were looking at the items, a very nice lady made the comment that her friend makes Benton's bacon in a skillet on her grill outside so her house does not smell like bacon.

My question was, "Why would anyone want to do that?" I love that smell.

We love guilty pleasures most when we can justify them. Unfortunately, bacon didn't make the list of ten healthy guilty pleasures in *Health Magazine*. I don't eat bacon every day (or even every week). Sometimes, I cook bacon for my family just so I can smell it. As my fitness trainer once told me, "Everything is fine in moderation." I think I will take him at his word on that.

*November 2011*

# GUILTY PLEASURES

## Guilty Pleasures Equal Holiday Treasures

By the time you read this article, the holidays will have given way to New Year's resolutions (and, if you are anything like me, those will have already been broken). While most of us have little "guilty pleasures" that we enjoy all year, for some of us, those "guilty pleasures" give way to "guilty pleasures on steroids" at holiday time.

I collect cocktail napkins, and my favorite to bring out during the holidays says, "Thank goodness it's that time of year when being fat and jolly is a good thing!" I am not ashamed to admit that I love chocolate-covered cherries. Queen Anne brand. The kind with the gooey centers that ooze down your chin when you bite into them. And I love holiday movies. I cannot wait until December 1 when ABC Family and Lifetime start their '25 Days of Christmas' movie marathons. While my favorite is *Love Actually,* I am not ashamed to admit (well, maybe a little) that I also love *Holiday in Handcuffs* and others of that ilk. These things make me fat and jolly.

But I was convinced that I was not alone, so I asked a number of my friends and colleagues to share their own "holiday guilty pleasures." Leslie

Beale shares in my delight of holiday treats. Says Leslie, "I love anything baked or chocolate. I mean, if it's consumed between Thanksgiving and New Year's the calories don't count, do they? Eating all those things with reckless abandon makes me feel like a kid again, even in between all the holiday stress."

Kristi Davis has two "holiday guilty pleasures." Says Kristi, "The first is driving around looking at Christmas lights. My husband will plan for two to three nights' worth and map out routes for it. The second is Cracker Candy from the *Junior League* cookbook. It's the perfect combination of salty and sweet, and I always make it the week of Christmas. One time, I made some in July because I got a craving, but it just wasn't the same."

LeAnn Mynatt's favorite "holiday guilty pleasure" is spending time with her nephews. "I'll respond this way. When I leave work early to go get my haircut, I feel guilty. When I leave work early to take my visiting nephews to Dollywood, the toy store, to ring the bell for the Salvation Army, or ride the Three Rivers Rambler Santa Express, I don't feel guilty. Turning off the billable clock is hard, except to spend time with loved ones. So, my guilty pleasure is that I don't feel guilty playing with them—I feel guilty when they're in town and I'm at work. Also, I don't feel guilty eating fudge or reading *People Magazine*."

Donald Farinato also enjoys family time as his favorite "holiday guilty pleasure." He loves sitting on the sectional sofa snuggled under a blanket with the kids watching Christmas specials. Donald relays, "I am sorry to say that I do not get to spend as much time with them as I would like, so it is a fun way for us to enjoy some time together. Plus, it will not be too long before it is no longer 'cool' to watch Christmas specials with dad, so I am enjoying it while I can!"

My treasure trove of "holiday guilty pleasures" came from Adrienne Anderson. We have been friends for nearly twenty years, and I can honestly say that I learned some things about Adrienne I didn't know. I learned that Adrienne loves eggnog. "It should be absolutely disgusting—drinking eggs, milk, sugar, nutmeg—but I absolutely love it, all 800 calories and thirty grams of fat per serving! If you see some woman outside Weigel's in her car chugging the eggnog straight from the plastic jug, it is not me!"

Adrienne also loves Little Debbie Christmas tree cakes—the white ones, not the chocolate ones. "I don't know why I am so infatuated with these things. With a great cook like my husband, Jeff, I am usually kind of a food snob. There is no real food ingredient or positive nutritional value in these little cakes, but there is that red piping and sparkly green sugar." She also likes fruitcake, which only makes her "guilty" because ninety-eight percent of the population thinks she is crazy to like fruitcake.

Like me, Adrienne loves Christmas movies, particularly *It's a Wonderful Life* and *A Christmas Story*. Says Adrienne, "I don't feel too guilty about being a Jimmy Stewart fan, but should a forty-eight-year-old woman and her sister be able to recite all the lines from *A Christmas Story?* – 'You'll shoot your eye out!' – My sister actually bought a replica of the Leg Lamp. Hey, 'It's a major award.'"

Adrienne also enjoys her eclectic holiday music collection. In addition to the Mormon Tabernacle Choir, Boston Pops, and Bing Crosby/Burl Ives/Johnny Mathis/Mahalia Jackson versions of traditional Christmas and holiday music, she has these gems: "You're A Mean One, Mr. Grinch," "Rocking Around the Christmas Tree" by Cyndi Lauper, "Up On the Housetop" by The Jackson 5, "The Twelve Days of Christmas" by the Beastie Boys, "The First Noel" by Smokey Robinson, "Santa Baby" (both the Eartha Kitts version and the one by the Pussycat Dolls), "Blue Christmas" by Johnny Cash—not Elvis, and "Christmas Don't Be Late" by Alvin and the Chipmunks. Says Adrienne, "I listen to these songs nonstop on Christmas baking days, and it drives everyone in my family crazy. And even I will admit that Alvin and the Chipmunks are annoying."

But Adrienne's real pleasure is the one with no guilt. "The end of the Christmas Eve Service at my church, when everyone in the congregation holds a candle, and we pass the flame down the row until all the candles are lit, then turn off all the electric lights and sing "Silent Night" *a cappella* by candlelight. It is one of the best moments of the year, every year."

When it comes to the holidays, I am learning that our guilty pleasures are really our holiday treasures. If they make us smile and fill our hearts and lives with joy, we shouldn't feel guilty at all. Those are the things that make memories that last a lifetime.

*January 2012*

# GUILTY PLEASURES

## Guilty Pleasures v. New Year's Resolutions

If you have read this column over the past few months, you know that I have more than a few "guilty pleasures"—those low brow, high-calorie things I know I shouldn't enjoy. But I do. A lot.

You know that I love soap operas, trash TV, and the *National Enquirer.* I'm not ashamed to admit that I have 224 episodes of *Beverly Hills, 90210* on the DVR. And I was delighted when my six-year-old brought me a present home from the grocery store . . . *CBS Soaps Magazine* "because I knew you would love it, Mommy." I must be doing something right with that one.

You also know that I love bacon, especially Benton's bacon. My husband's family has a Christmas tradition of seeing who can find the most unique and humorous gifts. Hugh's brother bought us a board game this year: *Mr. Bacon's Big Adventure.* I kid you not. The object of the game is to join Mr. Bacon on a mouth-watering mosey through Meatland. On the journey, you have to navigate your way through the Mustard Marsh, cross the eerie expanse of the Wiener Wasteland, and sail on the Sausage Sea. If you make it past the deceptive detour of Vegan Alley and avoid getting grounded in Gristle Grotto, you may just make it to the Great Frying Pan at the end of the trail. Most definitely a high-cholesterol, high fat journey. It's like *Candyland* for bacon lovers. Everyone else in the family thought the autographed photo of Telly Savalas holding a kitty that Hugh had shipped from Germany for his brother was the winner, but I thought the bacon game was pretty cool.

You also know that I love chocolate-covered cherries. Queen Anne brand—the kind with the gooey centers. At last count, we devoured twelve boxes of those at our house during the holidays. (And, for reference, the Queen Anne's chocolate-covered blueberries are just not the same.) I should also tell you that I love Reddi-Whip. Straight out of the can. I will squirt it on a spoon prior to eating it, but that is about as mannerly as I get.

As I predicted last month, though, the holidays have given way to New Year's resolutions. A 2007 study by Richard Wiseman from the University of Bristol involving 3,000 people showed that eighty-eight percent of those who set New Year's resolutions fail, despite the fact that fifty-two percent of the study's participants were confident of success at the beginning.

In spite of the overwhelming odds against me, I made three resolutions this year. According to author Frank Ra, "Resolutions are more sustainable when shared, both in terms of with whom you share the benefits of your resolution, and with whom you share the path of maintaining your resolution. Peer-support makes a difference in success rate with New Year's resolutions."

So, here goes. I am going to share my three resolutions. Unfortunately, to my chagrin, two of them are diabolically opposed to my guilty pleasures.

First, my goal is to read more quality books and magazines that will actually teach me about something more substantial than pop culture. In that vein, I have also resolved to watch less trash television and more quality programming. So far, I am not doing so well. I have read nothing and spent the weekend watching a *Harry Potter* movie marathon. There is still hope, though. We have eleven and a half months left in the year.

Second, my goal is to exercise more, eat healthy, and lose the forty pounds of baby weight I am still carrying (my husband says it is not baby weight if your "baby" has started school . . . but I will beg to differ). I am this year's chair of the American Heart Association Go Red for Women luncheon in Knoxville, and I really think I need to set a good example for other women and for young girls as we work to promote heart-healthy living. Thankfully, I do have my husband's complete support on this one.

He is a health-nut who goes to Operation Boot Camp nearly every day and competes in triathlons.

Hugh did suggest that I should take up running to lose weight and suggested I run a half marathon. I'm not sure if he really thinks I can do it or if he just wants my life insurance, but I am going to give it a go. I plan to be in Nashville on April 28 and also plan to cross the finish line in under 4 hours so that I can get a medal. Like a child, I am motivated by rewards. I love a good trophy.

I will confess: given my love of all things bacon and corn syrup, this one is going to be tough. Amazingly, though, I am doing pretty well so far. I have exercised nearly every day and have even bought a rowing machine after I discovered you could burn one hundred calories in five minutes. I can't tell you that I have not eaten any candy or even that I have lost any weight, but there is still time, and I will continue to work at it. When you see me, ask me how it is going. Keep me accountable. Cheer me on at the finish line in Nashville. And, if you have been frying bacon, please stand down-wind so I can savor the aroma.

Finally, I have resolved to take down my Christmas decorations prior to February 1. For someone who once took down the tree on St. Patrick's Day, this is a big deal. So far, most of the exterior decorations have been removed from my house, but the inside still looks like we are waiting for Old St. Nick. With a couple of weeks until the end of January, I am still hopeful on this one.

I will apologize for regaling you with my own guilty pleasures and New Year's resolutions. If you have read this column in the past, you know that I do not hesitate to throw my friends under the bus and expose their guilty pleasures. They have caught on to me. When I put out the call for New Year's resolutions, I did not have a single taker. Not even one.

I may have to resort to trickery for the next column …

*February 2012*

# My Toughest Adversary Wears Stride-Rite Shoes

In 2005, I felt like a "moderately seasoned" lawyer, having been in practice for well over ten years. I thought I was pretty tough. Very tough, actually. Until I learned a valuable lesson. While some adversaries can be scary, a kid can bring you to your knees.

When Hugh and I found out we were going to be first-time parents, we were both fast approaching forty. I recall my dear mother-in-law (who was thirty-five when her first child was born, and there were two more after that) telling us that people always thought that her children were her grandchildren. We laughed and said to ourselves, "That will never happen to us." Fast forward a couple of months when we were buying baby clothes. The salesclerk at the Baby Superstore looked at us (me, being very pregnant), and said, "Some child is going to be very lucky to have such nice grandparents." Thankfully, we were both too stunned to make any sort of remark at all.

Trace was born on October 6, 2005. We are blessed to have a sweet, funny child who never ceases to "tell it like it is." When Trace was nearly two, he saw Hugh drop a gallon of milk onto the kitchen floor and heard him rattle of a string of expletives that would make a sailor blush. Imagine my horror when Trace dropped his Cheerios a couple of weeks later and, verbatim, rattled off that same string of expletives. For weeks, I lived in fear that our dear cherub would rattle off that same string of expletives at church. In the meantime, Hugh lived in the doghouse. Hugh then found a new expletive, "Dadgummit," which took the place of the aforementioned, cringe-inducing tirade. Not long after, Trace dropped some candy on the carpet and yelled, "Tracegummit." Hugh and I were a bit perplexed until the psychologist in his office explained that Dad had said "Dadgummit," so Trace thought he was supposed to say "Tracegummit." Yes, a child can bring you to your knees (and make you feel really stupid at the same time).

More recently, Trace and I were driving home from yet another kid birthday party. From the backseat, he inquired, "Mom, you are past forty. Right?" Yes, dear. Why? "Well, Mom. You are old." Yes, dear, I guess compared to you, I am. "But don't worry, Mom. You are not wrinkled-old. You are just plain old." And then I asked Trace, "Honey, who is wrinkled-old?" With that, my dear child started naming names. I had to laugh a little (and immediately get on the cell phone) when the first person he named was my much younger sister. Yes, a kid can bring you to your knees (and make you laugh while he does it).

Before Christmas, Hugh and I took Trace to the Fantasy of Trees, where he was more excited about the carnival rides than the hundreds of trees, the gingerbread houses, and even Santa. When we made it to the Spinning Strawberries, Trace told me, "Mom, no offense, but I don't want you to ride the Strawberries with me. Only Dad." My feelings were a little hurt until he said, "Because I want him to throw up—not you."

A couple of weeks ago, Trace and I passed the new Barre3 on Bearden Hill. He suggested that I try Hot Yoga. When I asked him "why," he responded, "Because I have heard it is good for old people who need to lose weight." I am still perplexed as to (1) how a six-year-old knows about Hot Yoga (college-aged babysitter is my guess), (2) why he thinks Mom is old, and (3) why he thinks I need to lose weight (I do, but that is beside the point). Yes, a kid can bring you to your knees.

Last week, I was asked to speak at our Sunday morning church service. I was a bit surprised when Trace decided to forgo the children's activities to come to the service to hear me speak. After I had finished, Trace remarked, "That was really good, Mom. You didn't embarrass me at all." I asked if he had expected that I would. Matter-of-factly, he said, "Yes. That's why I picked the service over the kid's stuff. But you did okay."

Kids really do have a way of bringing you to your knees. In late 2010, I had been in practice for over seventeen years. I loved my firm, and I loved my job. Many times, however, it was to the exclusion of my family. I was working at home one night on some sort of project I can no longer recall. Trace was a typical, noisy four-year-old. After about fifteen minutes of non-stop interruption, I told Trace, "You have got to go upstairs. You are too loud, and Mommy needs to concentrate. This is for a client, and it is very important. I have to finish it so it is ready tomorrow." Trace looked at me with sweet little eyes, and said, "Okay, Mom. But can I be your client tomorrow night?" Trace didn't know what he said, but I certainly did. It was a wake-up call that struck me like no loss in a courtroom ever could. At that moment, I vowed to get my priorities in order, even if it meant saying "no" to clients and other obligations so that I could take care of my family. I still panic if I can't find my cell phone or my Blackberry, and I can come undone when the internet goes down; but I work a little harder every day to be sure that I take time for my family, even if it just means playing a mean game of *Mr. Bacon's Big Adventure*.

I faced a number of worthy adversaries in my years since I started practicing law, but I never dreamed that the one that could bring me to my knees was the one who calls me "Mom."

*March 2012*

# GUILTY PLEASURES:

## What Is Calling You?

As a kid, I knew spring had arrived when I heard that sound and those five little words that were music to my ears. "The porpoises are calling you." I recall practically begging my mom to get me out of school at the first forecast of good weather to take off to Pigeon Forge to see the porpoises and dolphins and whatever other marine life they had performing at Porpoise Island. I would also ask for a trip to Magic World or Mountain Ocean or Tommy Bartlett's Water Circus "...while we were at it." It is amazing that I ever became a lawyer because I can never recall a single time she agreed with my position that I deserved an afternoon off. My power of persuasion obviously was lacking, and it is amazing that I chose a career in the law where the power to persuade is paramount.

My power of persuasion has improved, and I no longer have to convince anyone other than myself that I need a break in the afternoon "just because." Porpoise Island, Magic World, Mountain Ocean, and Tommy Bartlett's Water Circus have long since been replaced by outlet malls, chain restaurants, go-cart tracks, and various other attractions, but I still feel the call to break free when the weather is warm. I no longer have the desire to escape to Pigeon Forge on a weekday or a Friday afternoon. In my mid-forties, my afternoon guilty pleasures are a bit more practical.

My favorite guilty pleasure is an afternoon trip to the hair salon. To get my hair dyed. My husband often laughs about this one. He really has no understanding of the fact that it takes four hours and a lot of ammonia to turn my brown hair blonde. But I love it. In the four hours at the salon, I have to turn off the cell phone, and I don't have to engage in any difficult or meaningful conversation. It is the one afternoon every month that I can read *Vogue*, *People*, and *US Weekly* with no guilt whatsoever. I have never seen *Forbes*, *Time*, or *U.S. News* and *World Report* at the hair salon, and I, for one, am glad. It is my time to be free of the world, to clear my mind, and to be the blonde that I was meant to be.

On days when I am feeling more adventurous, nothing is better than a round of golf or a round of sporting clays. Every time I play golf, I am reminded of how much I actually enjoy it. Whether I play really well or whether it is one of those days where I lose two sleeves of balls, I always seem to have a good time. And nothing beats a good round of sporting clays. After my first trip to the gun club with Hugh several years ago, I was hooked. I think he was a little scared when I remarked, "I love the smell of gun powder." I am certain that I saw fear in his eyes when I stated, "There is something strangely relaxing about watching that little clay disintegrate."

I was certain that I am not the only lawyer in this town who gets the desire to play hooky for an afternoon, so I asked a number of my friends what they do if they are fortunate to steal a few hours away from the office on a Friday afternoon. A few were willing to share their own guilty pleasures.

Susan Fendley shares my love of the salon. "I love uninterrupted reading time and mani's and pedi's or a leisurely trip to a specialty grocery store like Fresh Market when I can select what I want—not what I have to buy."

I learned that a number of my friends enjoy the tranquility of the water. Adrienne Anderson says, "I am just hoping to break away some spring/summer afternoon in the middle of the week to go out in my kayak." Another friend, who shall remain nameless, says, "I love drinking massive quantities of margaritas while lounging at the lake."

Darsi Sirknen also likes to escape the office and hit the water. "Assuming its summertime, I love nothing more than going home, getting on the boat, and heading to dinner on the water. The lake is relatively empty on weekday afternoons/evenings, and cruising on the calm water is a perfect stress reliever. In the winter, all I want to do is go home and hibernate."

Ashley Lowe also enjoys escaping to the lake. "There is nothing better than heading to the lake on a Friday afternoon. I love to go out on the boat and wake surf before all of the craziness of the weekend. It is my way to relax and escape the pressures of everyday life."

While the porpoises no longer call me, I am convinced that I knew at a young age that there was something to that longing to escape from the pressure of everyday life, even for a few hours. Even as a seasoned "forty-something," I find that I need to get away—recharge my batteries—if only for a few hours on a Friday (or a Wednesday). While those little "escapes" are probably classified as guilty pleasures, I'm not sure they should be called "guilty" at all. Necessary. But not guilty. It seems that if we are rejuvenated and less tired, we are better to each other and, ultimately, better at what we do. So, what is calling you?

*April 2012*

# GUILTY PLEASURES

## For Love and Basketball

March Madness has officially given way to April Sadness at my house. NCAA basketball has ended, and Trace and I are already counting the days to the beginning of next year's season. To say that we are a "basketball-crazed household" is an understatement. My love-affair with basketball began around 1976 when my dad took me to Stokely Athletics Center to see the *Bernie and Ernie Show*. When he told me he was taking me to a basketball game, I was more interested in the popcorn, souvenirs, and seeing the cheerleaders than I was in the actual game. But something magical happened that night . . . I fell in love with basketball.

My love for basketball grew stronger later that year when Santa brought me a red, white, and blue basketball just like the Harlem Globetrotters used. (It was 1976—the Bicentennial year—so everything was red, white, and blue, and *The Harlem Globetrotters* was the hottest cartoon on Saturday morning television). Needless to say, I was in Heaven. I remember bouncing that ball on the patio every day after school and trying out the skills that I learned from *The Globetrotters* cartoons and from books on basketball that I purchased from the *Weekly Reader* magazine that they sent home from school every week. I begged for a backyard basketball goal, and, although my dad purchased one, he never quite got around to putting it up. In spite of my lack of a goal, I practiced every day. I even began wearing my mother's old basketball necklace (she played in high school) in hopes that some of the magic (and some of her height) would rub off on me. Unfortunately, neither did, and my parents were delighted when, in fifth grade, their four-foot-two daughter made the cheerleading squad. After that, I spent a number of years cheering for basketball instead of actually playing it.

I don't think I ever quit loving basketball . . . It just became temporarily displaced. I discovered cheerleading, and then swimming, and then the law. Basketball took a backseat to lots of other things. I occasionally challenged my husband to pick-up games when we would be vacationing in places with a court (and, yes, I can out-shoot him), but that was the extent of my interest in basketball. At least until Chris Lofton came to UT.

For four years, I watched Chris Lofton play every chance I got. I'll swear, when he would shoot the ball, the angels would sing. To me, it was like watching ballet—poetry in motion. I would venture to guess that I was noticeably "basketball crazy" when my then two-year-old remarked, "My Mommy loves my Daddy, but she really, really loves Chris Lofton." I thought it was funny; Hugh was not amused.

Unfortunately, my family did not share my love of basketball. I recall asking my son if he wanted to see the Lady Vols play in the NCAA tournament a couple of years ago. He remarked, "I'm not so sure I want to watch girls, and I don't even think I want to see basketball." This year, though, he came around. When we renewed our basketball tickets, I convinced Hugh that we needed four—not three. After all, it is much easier to convince Trace to go when he can take a friend—and taking a friend is cheaper than hiring a babysitter.

This past season, Trace enjoyed lots of popcorn, pretzels, and $5 sno-cones with a few of his friends. Miraculously, he started to enjoy basketball. I recall a day when Trace had a friend over for a playdate. Instead of playing with toys, Trace convinced his friend that they needed to watch the Vols play on television with me. I knew we were a basketball-crazed family when Trace's friend remarked, "Man, Mrs. Nystrom. You all sure watch a lot of basketball around here."

Trace recently informed me that he wanted to be Jarnell Stokes when he grows up for three reasons: he is smart; he is a chess master; and he is six feet and eight inches tall. (Unfortunately, Trace will learn soon enough that he will have to settle for two out of three. At six years old, he has yet to hit four feet. I will be happy if he gets tall enough to ride all of the rides at Disney World.) Trace's singular goal is now to play basketball for Coach Cuonzo Martin and the Vols. For weeks, Trace informed Hugh that he was the only boy in our neighborhood without his own basketball goal. His pleas fell on deaf ears with Hugh. Secretly, I kept advising Trace that persistence would pay off. After all, I think I wanted a goal as much as he did.

Trace saw his opening when Hugh held a fundraising breakfast where Coach Martin was the guest speaker. Trace convinced me that he needed to skip school in order to attend the breakfast. As we were walking in, Trace advised that he needed to speak to Coach Martin if he could. "It's really important," he told me.

When we walked in, Coach Martin was in the hallway, and Trace seized the opportunity. He sounded like Ralphie in *A Christmas Story*, asking Santa for the Red Ryder BB gun, when he said, "Coach Martin, I need you to talk to my dad. I am the only boy in my neighborhood without a basketball goal, and I really need one. I am going to play basketball for you someday, but I can't practice. You need to tell him I am missing valuable practice time." Two days later, Trace got his basketball goal.

The arrival of the basketball goal coincided with the end of the NCAA basketball season. Since we cannot watch basketball, we have decided to play. Trace and I have played nearly every day. The goal sits at the end of our driveway in the middle of my day lilies. Our "court" is bordered on the sides by small evergreen trees and roses. I would normally fuss about children running into my plants, but for some reason, I don't. The foliage (and my car) has been hit by the basketball more times than I care to count. I've spent a lot of time with Trace over the past several weeks—most of it on our make-shift court. The mom in me feels really bad when I steal the ball and dunk on him (the goal will lower to 6' so a dunk isn't much of a stretch for me), but the competitor in me secretly does the dance of joy. We play in the early morning before school, and we play at night even after Trace should be in bed. My neighbors are mildly amused. I had to laugh the other day, when my neighbor remarked, "Thank goodness day lilies are hardy plants."

*May 2012*

# AROUND THE BAR

## Governor Bill Haslam: Profile of a Leader

Webb School's motto is "Princeps, Non Homines," which is Latin for "Leaders, Not Ordinary Men." Students are taught from early on that they are to live selflessly and heed the call to serve the greater good. Described by colleagues as "genuine," "unpretentious," and "grounded," Governor Bill Haslam, Webb Class of 1976, continues to live this motto every day.

Born and raised in Knoxville to parents Jim and Cynthia Haslam, Gov. Haslam learned early on that the keys to success included working hard and treating others as he would want to be treated. He credits his parents for instilling their strong faith and work ethic in him and his siblings, Jimmy and Ann. At the age of thirteen, Bill got a job pumping gas at a family-owned service station and quickly learned that running a business took diligence and hard work. He also learned that treating others with kindness and respect was key to gaining customer loyalty.

Bill applied those same lessons to the classroom. In addition to being a stellar student at Webb, Bill was a great athlete. He ran track and played basketball and baseball. In a hint of things to come, Haslam also served in student government. Former schoolmates recall that he always remembered everyone and called them by name. He was known for being genuinely kind.

When Bill was sixteen years old, tragedy struck his family. The sudden unexpected death of his mother changed Bill's perspective. Bill's dad pulled the family together, and they leaned on each other and on their faith to get them through the rough days, with Mr. Haslam advising them that people were not going to feel sorry for them and that they had to continue living. The death of his mother marked a turning point in Bill's life. "It was a total surprise," he has said. "Obviously, if you lose your mom when you are sixteen, it causes you to step back and think, OK, it's not just about the football game this Friday night or who I am going to prom with. You start thinking about harder and tougher issues, and realize really quickly that life is hard and doesn't work for a whole lot of people." It was this understanding and empathy that carried him through high school and into college.

Bill entered Emory University in 1976, and on the first day of class, met Crissy Garrett, a young woman from Memphis, who would later become his wife. While attending Emory, Bill was a volunteer leader for Young Life, a Christian ministry that reaches out to adolescents. During the summers, Bill volunteered for the grassroots political campaigns of Howard Baker and Lamar Alexander and gained a deep understanding of the type of principled leadership needed to govern.

After graduating with a degree in history, Bill and Crissy married and moved to Knoxville, where Bill planned to teach high school history and coach basketball for a few years and then head to a Presbyterian seminary to be a minister. Wanting his son to have an understanding of business, Jim Haslam encouraged his son to enter the business world for a couple of years. Bill had agreed, at his father's urging, to work "for a couple of years" managing his family's small chain of gas stations. In the early years, Bill recalls that he spent long days driving all over the country, identifying, negotiating, and purchasing good locations for new truck stops. Throughout his time at Pilot, Bill learned to allocate resources wisely and satisfy customers. It was there that Bill gained the essential hands-on knowledge that makes the chief executive officer of a complicated enterprise successful. In 1999, Haslam joined Saks Fifth Avenue as the chief executive officer of the emerging e-commerce and catalog division.

In 2003, at the urging of many of his friends, Bill ran for and was elected mayor of the City of Knoxville. The skills he learned in the private sector helped make his administration extremely effective. Re-elected in 2007 with eighty-seven percent of the vote, Bill balanced seven consecutive city budgets, tripled the Rainy Day Fund, insisted that city government focus on providing services in an efficient manner, helped found key education initiatives, and recruited and retained thousands of jobs to the city through development and revitalization.

On November 2, 2010, Bill was elected Governor of the state of Tennessee with sixty-five percent of the vote—winning ninety of ninety-five counties and securing the largest victory of any non-incumbent gubernatorial candidate in our state's history. Samantha Edwards, who worked as an intern in his campaign, says, "It was an amazing experience. Bill was always on the go, but he made sure that he knew everyone who was working on his campaign. He knew everyone's name and something about them and would call you by name every time he saw you. I was impressed with the fact that he treated everyone the same. From the lowest intern to the highest staffer, he treated everyone with respect. He made sure to tell us often how much he appreciated the work we were doing for him. When he said it, you knew he meant it."

For all that he has accomplished in business and in the political arena, Bill Haslam will tell you that his greatest accomplishment is his family, and he is sustained by his faith. He and Crissy just celebrated their thirty-first wedding anniversary. They have also been blessed with three children, a daughter-in-law, son-in-law, and a new grandson. For twenty-eight years, Bill and Crissy have been members of Cedar Springs Presbyterian Church (EPC) in Knoxville, and for twenty-two of those years, Bill has served as an elder. Governor Bill Haslam has been and continues to be a respected leader in business, with his family, in his church and in the political arena. He has succeeded on every level. Those early lessons instilled in him as a child continue to resonate today. He has nothing to prove, yet he continues to serve. That is precisely what makes him a leader and not an ordinary man.

*August 2012*

# GUILTY PLEASURES

## Confessions of a Swim Mom

I've routinely shared with you my own guilty pleasures. You know that I love *Toddlers and Tiaras*. And if you think I have seen *Honey Boo*, you are probably right. But I never thought I would be anything remotely close to a "Stage Mom."

I learned quickly that I would never be a "Soccer Mom." Trace pretty much assured that when, at age four, he stated, "Mom, why do you want me to run down that field when they are just going to turn around and run right back?" I knew "Baseball Mom" was not in my future when he couldn't hit a ball off a tee. And I certainly never thought I would be a "Swim Mom."

Trace's swimming career had an auspicious beginning. The "Mommy and Me" instructor called him "The Tick" because he held onto me with a death-grip. We then tried Mr. Ed's Adventure Swim. Trace took one look at Mr. Ed and got so scared that he pooped his pants.

Undaunted, I told Hugh that learning to swim for Trace was non-negotiable. After much searching, we found a great instructor. After a few lessons, I told her that I wanted him to be able to swim on the summer swim team. She looked at me like I was crazy. Then, it happened. Trace started to learn to swim.

We did join the swim team last year, and with his first race, I was praying that he would make it across the pool. He did. When he touched the wall, he looked at me and asked, "Did I win?" He did. And then he asked, "How many people did I beat?" I knew he was in love, and so was I.

Trace's swimming has become my own guilty pleasure. I love nothing more than to watch him swim laps. I have tried many times to take work with me to the pool or to talk to the other moms during practice, but I just can't do it. I cannot take my eyes off of my child.

It is fulfilling as a parent to see him enjoying something so much and to see him have reasonable success at it. I knew that I could not be the only parent whose child's pursuits have become their own guilty pleasure. I asked several of our colleagues what it is that their children do that, from the outside, could be seen as a chore, but has become their own guilty pleasure because of the joy it brings to their child.

Victoria Tillman's "guilty pleasure" comes from her daughter's participation in two very special sporting events. Ellen is a special needs child and, as a result, doesn't qualify for "regular" sports teams. This past year, though, Ellen was able to participate in the Special Olympics, where she came in second in the fifty-meter race and first in the long jump. Per Victoria, Ellen still talks about receiving her trophies in front of the entire school. Additionally, Ellen's school had a special Pom Squad consisting of six children in the CDC program, and Ellen was selected to be on the team. She was able to practice with the Powell Middle School cheerleaders and cheer at the girls' home basketball games. Ellen had her own uniform, a cheer bag with her name on it, and, before every game, the cheerleaders place ribbons in her hair like all of the other cheerleaders. Victoria was at every game, even though it meant leaving work early one day every week. "When you have a special needs child, there is nothing like seeing them participate in something so normal. I cried the first time she went out on the floor and did cheers with the other girls. It was very special," says Victoria.

Mary Miller's guilty pleasure is helping her son, Will, pursue his artistic talents. Will, a sixth grader, has shown quite a talent for painting and drawing, despite having parents who cannot even draw a good stick figure (Mary's words . . . not mine). He has been juried as a member of Fine Arts Blount, and he often gets to show and sell his work in the Last Friday Art Walks in Maryville. In addition to being a great lawyer, Mary has become a master framer. Says Mary, "His work is very good, but what is really neat is that he has taught us so much about art. He has taught us about the different media and has showed me so many things I would have never noticed about paintings. The irony of this is that he has taught us so much about a world which we knew nothing about."

For Rick Carl, seeing his child experience and work through adversity without giving up is the trait of which he is most proud. His son, Rick, experienced unthinkable adversity watching his mother battle cancer when he was just ten and losing her battle when he was twelve. Through it all, he has maintained and continues to be a good student, with lots of activities and friends.

Rick is now fifteen and a musician. Last May, his band got a gig on Market Square. The show was on a Thursday (a school night), so Dad Rick suggested they load the van on Wednesday night so that they were ready to set up as soon as school was out. Through a perfect storm of events, the van was broken into, and all of the equipment was stolen. Gone. Discovered five hours before sound check.

Dad Rick was able to replace everything by two o'clock, but he knew that the real sound of the band came from the settings and sounds that his son had spent the previous five months inventing, programming, and recording into the keyboards. When he broke the news to Rick, shock turned to panic. As the band set up, Rick sat in a corner with his keys and headphones and calmly re-produced and re-recorded what he had spent the last five months producing. Two hours later, he played perfectly and looked like he was having the time of his life. Dad Rick was amazed.

"When you see your kid, a child who before he was even a teenager, suffered a lifetime of disappointment and heartbreak and the sheer terror of uncertainty, exhibit that kind of focus and determination, you realize that the cliché is true—your kid really can accomplish anything he sets his mind to, and he can already do it better than his old man. This is what makes me proud."

Dwight Tarwater recently saw his son, Davis, accomplish his ultimate goal—an Olympic gold medal. I think Dwight summed it up best when he said, "The desires of a child's heart may be either grand or modest, but their achievement is always pure joy."

*September 2012*

# GUILTY PLEASURES

## And the Penguin Who Hated the Cold

When I was a kid, one of my favorite books was a book by Brenda Brenner called *The Penguin that Hated the Cold*. It was about a little penguin named Pablo who lived in the South Pole but who hated cold weather. In the book, Pablo quickly realizes his dislike for the cold sets him apart from the other penguins. Rather than moping over his inability to fit in or settling for a life of discomfort, he heads north in search of a warmer climate. Through a series of misadventures, Pablo follows his dream to find his niche in the world (and a warm place to call home). The story ends with a smiling Pablo on a hammock on a beach, drinking a fruity drink.

Pablo was a penguin who, by virtue of the fact that he *was* a penguin, should have loved the cold. But he didn't. What should have been the thing he loved the most became the thing he hated. Pablo always struck a chord with me. I always thought it was because of the heartwarming story and the cute illustrations, but I was wrong. Pablo resonated with me because I am a lot like Pablo.

I am a lawyer who hates to read.

Given that my livelihood is dependent on my ability to read and analyze massive amounts of material, I should love to read. But I don't. When we were at the beach this summer, seven of the nine adults in our house were reading the *Fifty Shades of Grey* trilogy. Although it was the topic of nearly every morning news show that month, I resisted. Instead, I read *People, Star Magazine, Garden and Gun,* and *Soap Opera Digest,* among others. A few weeks later, a dear friend and fellow lawyer suggested that I at least read the first one to see what the hype was about. That weekend, Hugh was on a guy's trip, and Trace was with the grandparents. So, I downloaded it . . . just to read a little. After all, there was laundry to be done and there were closets to clean. Seventy-two hours later, the clothes were still dirty. The closets were a mess. But I had read the entire trilogy. For the record, I thought they were horrible. Worst writing ever. Thin plot.... But I couldn't stop reading until I was finished.

Fast forward three weeks. Hugh had rented *The Hunger Games* movie. I reluctantly watched it and begrudgingly loved it. I was heading to Florida on business the following day, and Hugh suggested that I take the first book of the trilogy because "the books are so much better than the movie." On the flight from Atlanta to Orlando, I read half of the first book. Because I was certain I would finish it before the week was over, I ran into the bookstore in the Orlando airport as they were shutting the doors to purchase *Catching Fire* (even though I had it at home). During that week, I read every chance I got . . . during breaks in the conference sessions, at night after the conference ended, and into the wee hours of the morning.

On the last day of the conference, I finished the book. I checked out of the hotel and headed to the airport three hours early . . . to purchase *Mockingjay*. I gladly sat in the airport for three hours so that I could read. When my plane landed in Knoxville at midnight, I drove home . . . And then continued to read. Until I finished the book the following morning. For the record, the trilogy was awesome.

Reading is a guilty pleasure for me. It is also the source of great anguish. A book—good or bad—is like a bag of Lay's potato chips. Once I start, I cannot stop. I become so engrossed in the stories and the characters that I tune everyone and everything else out. For that reason, I hate to read.

I wondered if I was the only person who is this way. My husband informed me that he can stop with a chapter or two and can even read two or three books at a time. I figured he was an oddity, so I took an informal poll.

Kacie Flinn McRee agreed with me. "I like to read suspense thrillers at night. They can become a 'guilty pleasure' at times. Sometimes, I know I should be doing something else, but I just have to read because the book is so good."

Another friend also agreed that reading is a "guilty pleasure." "I dream of vacations where I can sit on the beach under an umbrella and read for hours on end. But of course, that never happens because I have a wonderful wife and children who demand and deserve my time. So, to keep the peace in my home, I have to be judicious about when and for how long I read. For example, if I am at a soccer practice, my son expects me to see everything he does. Although I usually take a book, I have to spend more time watching soccer than reading. Or, if the family is watching a movie, I have learned that reading a book while they watch a movie is frowned upon. I have even tried reading a few pages while helping my younger children get ready for bed, but even that can cause disappointed looks." He went on to state, "What frequently happens is that I read a quick two pages here and there with an occasional late-night binge."

Kelli Thompson disagreed that reading is a "guilty pleasure." Instead, it is a pleasure without guilt. Kelli prefers non-fiction, history, and religion. For fiction, she likes the Michael Vey series. Says Kelli, "The second book just came out a month or so ago, and I read it in a weekend. I can't believe I have to wait a year to learn what happens next."

Right there with you, Kelli.

*December 2012*

# GUILTY PLEASURES

## Guilty Pleasures v. New Year's Resolutions: Round Two

I've admitted that I love soap operas, trash TV and *The National Enquirer*. You know I love bacon and chocolate-covered cherries. Consumed separately or together—it really doesn't matter. You also know that I have tried to do better.

Last year at this time, I did a little research. I found a 3,000-person, 2007 study by Richard Wiseman from the University of Bristol. The study (referenced in a previous passage) showed that eighty-eight percent of those who set New Year's resolutions fail, despite the fact that fifty-two percent of the study's participants were confident of success at the beginning.

Again, in spite of overwhelming odds, I shared my three resolutions. I relied once more on Frank Ra's profession that "Resolutions are more sustainable when shared, both in terms of with whom you share the benefits of your resolution, and with whom you share the path of maintaining your resolution. Peer-support makes a difference in success rate with New Year's resolutions."

First, I vowed to read more quality books and magazines that would be more intellectually stimulating than the pop culture fluff I normally read. I also resolved to watch less trash television and more academic programming. While these things make me a ringer for *Trivial Pursuit* or *Who Wants to Be a Millionaire?*, they don't actually do anything to increase my intelligence. I wanted to be able to pass through the grocery store check-out line without purchasing the *Soap Opera Digest,* which would most certainly end up hidden in my house until I could read it without fear of being caught.

While I cannot say I was entirely successful, I also cannot say this one was a total bust. Although I did continue to read to pop culture fluff, I did read six books that would fall under what my son calls "chapter books." I wouldn't exactly call the *Fifty Shades* trilogy and the *Hunger Games* trilogy "intellectual," but I was proud that they each actually made at least one best-seller list. I think that is at least a step in the right direction.

Last year, my second resolution was to exercise more, eat healthy and lose the forty pounds of baby weight I was still carrying (although the "baby" was born in 2005). I even vowed to run a half-marathon. Although a number of you tried to keep me accountable, I will admit that I was a miserable failure on this one. My exercise regime was inconsistent at best, and I weighed exactly the same thing on January 1, 2013, that I did on January 1, 2012. I did try to eat more healthfully, but bacon and chocolate called my name more times than I cared to admit. And I answered that call. Every time.

Finally, my third resolution was to take down my Christmas decorations prior to February 1. Drum roll, please. The last box was put away and the trees took their place in the garage on January 31. Of 2012. At our house, this is big. I usually never get the trees down by Valentine's Day, and I have been known to leave them up until St. Patrick's Day in the past.

Since I was batting .500 at best for last year (which, in light of the University of Bristol study, was pretty good), I'm trying again this year. Again, I am going to share my resolutions. And, again, they contradict my guilty pleasures.

First, and again, my goal is to read enriching books and magazines that actually expand my mind rather than rotting my brain. Second, I want to exercise more, eat healthy and lose the forty pounds of baby weight. To get a head start on both, I bought a book called *Made to Crave,* which is a book by Christian author Lysa TerKeurst. The premise of the book is that we were made to crave, but that we often substitute craving for God with food. So far, the book is really good. It is thought-provoking, and I am taking a lot away from it. But it still hasn't squelched my desire for a chocolate chip cookie. Or bacon. Or anything else for that matter. The mind is willing, but the flesh is weak.

I have also downloaded some books that my husband (who reads practically everything that is published) has recommended. So far, I haven't opened the first one. But I have eleven and a half months left in the year, so there is still time.

I am not doing so well with the resolution to eat healthy, lose weight and exercise more. Last weekend, Hugh and I attended the Southern Foodways Alliance dinner at Blackberry Farm. The dinner was a seven-course meal, and I think I ate every bit of every course (except for an egg yolk). I even asked if it would be rude to lick the dessert plate. Following dinner, we were escorted to the barn, where we dined on Rice Krispies treats and the absolute best fried bologna sandwiches I have ever had. Needless to say, I have work to do.

I'm also having a rough time with the whole exercise thing. We are a few days into the new year, and I have not darkened the door of a gym. Nor have I hopped on my treadmill. Or used the rowing machine. I'm not going to aspire to do a half marathon, but I am going to try to get healthy and finally lose the weight. Needless to say, I have a lot of work to do.

Again, I apologize for regaling you with my own guilty pleasures and New Year's resolutions. I have never been one to hesitate to throw my friends under the bus and expose their guilty pleasures. Again, they have caught on to me. When I put out the call for New Year's resolutions, I did not have a single taker. Not even one. So, I may be resorting to bribery for the next column. Again.

*February 2013*

## From Capital Defense to Managing Capital: Student Loan Expert Heather Jarvis Helps Attorneys Get a Grip on Student Loan Debt

In 1998, Heather Jarvis graduated with honors from Duke University School of Law with a law degree and $125,000 in student loan debt. "No one ever told me that I couldn't afford to go to Duke, even though, um, I couldn't," says Heather. "My mother was a modestly paid executive assistant, and my father was a mostly unemployed Shakespearean actor."

Heather didn't know she couldn't afford an expensive education until after she got one. Facing monthly payments of $1,200 for thirty years, Heather had two choices: "I could take my dream job representing people facing criminal prosecution, which paid $25,000 per year, or I could take a job where I made a boatload of money." Thanks to Duke's generous loan repayment assistance program, Heather was able to take her dream job without defaulting on her student loans. "I will always be grateful that Duke enabled me to continue ignoring my own financial security in pursuit of my irresistible urge to stand up for people in trouble," says Heather.

Heather realized, though, that other young attorneys weren't as lucky. She turned her passion for helping those facing criminal prosecution to those facing overwhelming student debt. "I wanted people to realize that higher education is not just for rich kids," states Heather.

After working as a public interest attorney for the Center for Death Penalty Litigation and the Death Penalty Information Center, Heather went to work for a nonprofit organization in Washington D.C. in 2005 with the desire to break down the financial barriers to practicing public interest law. During her time at Equal Justice Works, Heather had the opportunity to master the complex labyrinth of student loan policy and student debt relief programs. Because of her knowledge, she had the opportunity to contribute to student loan debt relief policy for the House Education Committee and other committees in Congress. Also, she was asked to serve as Chair of the Committee on Government Relations and Student Financial Aid for the ABA Section on Legal Education and Admissions to the Bar.

Heather has dedicated her professional efforts to advancing public service loan forgiveness which allows recent graduates to dedicate their careers to the greater good. Using her knowledge of the law as it relates to student loans and debt forgiveness, Heather has helped public interest-minded law graduates and attorneys across the country to break down the financial barriers to entering public service careers. "I've based my career on the belief that student debt should not force people to choose between a career helping others and a higher-paying job."

Heather has become widely recognized by law school professionals and media representatives as an expert source of information. The recipient of the 2010 Award of Distinction for Leadership from NALP (the association for legal career professionals) and the 2012 Inspire Award from the Benjamin Cardozo School of Law, Heather is a highly sought-after and nationally recognized speaker. Says Kashyap Choksi, Senior Director of International Advancement at Harvard University, "Heather is a super-articulate, smart, and conscious lawyer with great teamwork skills. Her national expertise and mastery on issues related to student debt and public policy, particularly related to law schools, is unmatched. Her customer-focused approach and poise, coupled with her substantive knowledge, has made Heather a much sought-after speaker."

Susan Feathers at Teach for America echoes that sentiment. "Heather's work is at the forefront of the movement to educate and empower law students about pragmatic ways in which they can manage student loan debt, while pursuing positions in low-paying public interest fields. Her expertise in the area of student loans (particularly in the law school context) is truly unparalleled."

With the support of sponsors, Heather launched her website, askheatherjarvis.com in 2011 with the goal of sharing her knowledge with others. "I am expanding my ability to provide free educational resources and training for high-debt graduate and professional borrowers. It has enabled me to broaden my focus to include more students, more graduates, and more campus visits," says Heather. Through her website, online seminars, and speaking engagements, Heather is working to inform borrowers, schools, and employers about how to benefit from available debt relief programs, as well as continuing to champion efforts to expand student debt relief programs.

The KBA is lucky to have Heather Jarvis as a guest speaker at the Law Practice Today Expo. Don't miss the exciting opportunity to learn more about whether you can benefit from President Obama's newest program for student loan borrowers and to hear Heather Jarvis—the Student Loan Expert—share her tips for managing debt while pursuing your dream career.

*April 2013*

# GUILTY PLEASURES

## For True Guilty Pleasures, Regret Not Required

I've said it before. It's not the first cupcake, it's the second. And the third. On the same day. It's the purchase of the pair of high heels that you affectionately call "sit-down shoes" because no woman in her right mind would try to walk in them.

"Big G" guilt, as USA Today journalist Cathy Lynn Grossman termed it, is heavy and incites us to ask forgiveness, but guilty pleasures are, again in Grossman's words, "guilt with a wink." I've confessed a multitude of my own guilty pleasures, and I recently got to indulge in another one.

As a law student, I acquired the nickname "Imelda Marcos" because of my penchant for shoes. Lots of them. My law school roommate started a game with some of my classmates called "Guess the number of shoes in Angelia's closet." I'm not sure what the number was, but it was a lot. I think I had a pair to match every outfit that I owned. I had shoes with high heels, low heels, and in every color of the rainbow (and some in colors never found in nature). For those of you who remember the eighties, you understand what I am talking about.

Shoes were my comfort (figuratively, not literally, mind you . . . some were anything but comfortable). No matter how much my weight fluctuated, my shoes always fit. Until I had a baby at thirty-seven. As my girth expanded, so did my feet. I recall wearing flip flops to court while very pregnant . . . men's flip flops (because nothing else would fit). At that point, I knew that life and footwear would never be the same. So, all of my pretty shoes were given to new homes.

Comfort replaced fashion as my key to finding good footwear. My shoe selections were much more practical, and my colors were confined to black, brown, and athletic. And then, like magic, I found shoes by Donald J. Pliner. Fashion met comfort, and I found love.

My first DJPs were a pair of kitten heel pumps that were perfect for work found on the clearance rack at Proffitt's. I wore them several times a week for nearly eight years. For our anniversary, my husband bought me a pair of Pliner riding boots, which I wore with everything (including my pajamas) for about a week. It was my twelfth pair of Pliner shoes in eight years, and it was the best gift he could have given me. (He wrapped them in a Hickory Farms sausage and cheese box, but that is another story for another day.) I recently received an invitation to meet Donald J. Pliner at Dillard's at West Town. I'll swear, I was like a teenage girl meeting Harry Styles from One Direction. I was in heaven. I asked Mr. Pliner why he chose emerald green for the bottoms of his newest Signature Collection. He said that he chose the color because, when he first met his wife, he thought she had the most beautiful green eyes that he had ever seen. Great shoes. And a romantic.

He reminded me of that cute kid selling lemonade on the side of the street. You can't pass without buying some. With a designer so charming, I could not walk away without new shoes. I walked out wearing new patent leather flats. He signed the bottoms of them, and I proudly show off my autographs every chance I get. I was certain that I was not the only person with a penchant for shoes.

My dear friend Jessica Shafer (who, coincidentally, introduced me to www.people.com) confessed that her guilty pleasures are celebrity gossip and shoes. Says Jessica, "Shoes are fabulous because they can really spice up an outfit, and they always fit . . . except when you are pregnant." Tasha Blakney agrees. "I'll have to agree with Jessica on the shoes. You can never have too many of them." In addition to impeccable taste in clothes, Darsi Sirknen has amazing taste in shoes. I've seen her design an entire outfit around a pair of fabulous shoes.

Men are not immune to this guilty pleasure. My husband owns seven or eight pairs of shoes. He is particularly attached to two pairs of them . . . a pair of cordovan loafers he got in the eighth grade (which was 1980) and a pair of Chuck Taylor high tops that were white at one time (probably 1985, when they were purchased). I hate those shoes, and I have begged him to get rid of them. To no avail. I was horrified in Nashville when he wore the Chuck Taylors to a hockey game with one of my clients. (The client was amused, thankfully.) When we moved from Nashville to Knoxville eight years ago, he became panicked when he couldn't find them, emphatically stating to me, "I know you are pregnant, but I swear I'll divorce you if you threw away my shoes."

Guilty pleasures are things that bring you joy and give you a bit of escape from the real world. I think I need a bit of escape today . . . maybe I'll do a little sole searching.

*May 2013*

# GUILTY PLEASURES

## Cake v. Pie: **The Ultimate Showdown**

In our house, I often tell Hugh that I am good for one meal a week. That meal is usually on Sunday, and there are usually enough leftovers that he and Trace are forced to eat them until Wednesday. That one meal usually does not include dessert. In fact, other than the occasional Oreo, the only dessert you will generally find at my house is the Olive and Sinclair chocolate I have hidden in our liquor cabinet. Until a holiday rolls around.

Hugh often says that I am good with big holidays and large gatherings, kind of like the athlete who does horribly in practice but then "brings it" for the big game. I have a notebook full of holiday menus. I will read cookbooks for weeks, trying to meld the perfect blend of foods so that all of the dishes (and spices) complement each other. I'll brag a little and say I do a pretty good job . . . that is, until it comes to dessert. I never know exactly what to fix.

For Thanksgiving last year, I did a Bourbon Apple Pie, which included six pounds of various sorts of apples (peeled, sliced, and cored), two cups of pecans, and a cup of Jim Beam's finest (or, more likely, cheapest). It was a big hit. With the men in the family. The women, on the other hand, preferred the poached pears with ice cream but wondered if I had also made cake.

When Christmas rolled around, I took a poll. The men in our family preferred pie (and specifically, the Bourbon Apple Pie). The women wanted Peppermint Red Velvet cake. So, we had both.

I thought it curious that all of the men preferred the pie, while the women wanted cake. I wondered if this might be universally true, so I did a very unscientific poll to see if all men truly preferred pie while women preferred cake or to see whether my family was some weird anomaly.

Ed Smith, Doug Blaze, Keith Burroughs, and Debra Poole fall firmly into the "pie" category. Doug prefers berry pie like his grandmother made, and Ed Smith agrees. Says Ed, "A good fruit pie beats cake any day because it has fruit in it. The fresher the fruit, the better. Apple, cherry, berries, peach . . . doesn't really matter. We celebrate birthdays in our office, usually with cake, but they always buy me fruit pies." Ed goes on to praise mango key lime pies. "One of the highlights of our family's annual Florida panhandle beach trips is always mango key lime pie from Publix. We will drive from Publix to Publix if necessary to find the mango version. The regular key lime pie is fabulous, but the mango key lime makes your eyes close as in prayer. Now, thankfully, we can get them in West Knoxville."

Keith Burroughs, likewise, tends toward pie and, in particular, homemade butterscotch meringue pie in a pastry crust. "This is not the kind made from melting the morsels sold by Nestle' or made from Jell-O pudding mix, but rather a made from scratch custard filling cooked and blended together in a double boiler with brown sugar, milk, egg yolks, butter, flour, corn starch, and vanilla extract," says Keith. "My birthday is in late June, and my mother would make this pie for me on an annual basis. It makes your tongue so excited, it nearly causes a concussion."

Debra Poole prefers pie because she almost never has it. "I like pie that has a squishy meringue topping beaded with drops of sweetness. There are pies you could almost roll around in—chocolate and coconut being the best."

Katrina Arbogast, Eric Setterlund, and Kyle Baisley are firmly in the "cake" category. Katrina says cream cheese pound cake is her favorite. "It was my mother's go-to recipe to serve as dessert for impromptu company, to console a neighbor or fellow church member over the loss of a loved one, or just for a family Sunday dinner. I have a copy of it that she handwrote for me framed in my kitchen."

Eric Setterlund is a fan of coconut cake. "It was my grandfather's favorite, and it always reminds me of him. And it's delicious, of course." Kyle Baisley agrees that cake is king. Says Kyle, "Cake every day of the week. It is more filling. Chocolate Bar Cake from Grady's back in the day was the best. I grew up on that stuff!"

Kelli Thompson and Judge Debbie Stevens have a hard time deciding. Although Kelli rarely eats dessert, she likes both cake and pie. "I associate desserts with my grandmother (Chocolate Meringue Pie) and Joe's mom (German Chocolate Cake, Fudge Pie, Pecan Pie). My favorite cakes are decadent chocolate gooey cakes, a la Mississippi Mud Cake or Tiramisu, because who doesn't like chocolate?!? My favorite pie is Key Lime Pie because it is so refreshing."

Judge Stevens' tastes depend on the season. "Nothing says spring like strawberry shortcake, summer like lemon meringue pie, fall like apple or pumpkin pie, Christmas like . . .. Well, there are always cookies." Debbie goes on to say that she shuns cake and pie in the winter because she is always on a diet at that time of the year!

My research has shown that my family is just a weird anomaly. Men are NOT universally pie eaters, and women do not prefer cake. When we were in California a number of years ago, Hugh and I toured Chandon, which is famous for its sparkling wines. The tour guide said that we should not save sparkling wine for special occasions . . . since every day of life is a special occasion. I have a refrigerator magnet that says, "Life is short. Eat dessert first." There is something to be said for that. Dessert just because it's Tuesday. Or Wednesday. Or because I responded to all of my emails today.

Come holiday time, though, I may try to make it easy on myself. I understand that Southern Living has an excellent recipe for Pecan Pie Cake.

*August 2013*

# GUILTY PLEASURES

## Cars: Guilty Pleasures or Necessary Evil?

After nearly ten years and almost 200,000 miles, it finally happened. My trusty Volvo S-80 bit the dust. On the way home from a meeting in Atlanta, my colleague Eric and I stopped at the Chick-fil-a in Dalton. As we were leaving, the Volvo died. I restarted it and, after a couple of tries, soon realized that the car would die if I let up on the gas. We made it back to Knoxville in record time, and I barely slowed down to let Eric out at his house. Needless to say, Eric will likely never ride with me again.

I drove straight to the Volvo dealer to leave the car. As I slowed to enter the lot, it died again. At that very moment, I spotted a beautiful new SUV. As I navigated the dying S-80 toward the garage, the new car was calling my name.

I didn't know whether to be happy or sad the next day when the mechanic called to let me know that he could fix the S-80 for $1,200. Frugal Hugh could barely hide his excitement. "Now, we have time to evaluate whether we even need a new car. If we do, we can take our time and get the right one."

Trace, ever the optimist, smiled, "Like a Jeep Wrangler with the Army star on the side or a Ferrari." Hugh's retort, "Way too flashy. I'm thinking a station wagon or a minivan." Hmm.

Obviously, no one in my house is on the same wavelength. Some of my fondest childhood memories revolve around cars. I recall countless Saturday mornings spent "kicking the tires" on new cars with my dad. I also loved going to car shows with him and listening to him brag about the 1962 Chevrolet Super Sport that he called "Maybelline," which had been stolen in 1974. Suffice it to say, I'm a big fan of cool cars (and trucks). I love the "new car" smell. I love the way it feels to drive a fast car down a curvy country backroad.

Hugh's philosophy on cars is quite different. He believes a car is nothing more than something to get you from Point A to Point B, and he does not believe that a car needs any frills. Suffice it to say, he calls power steering "over-engineering." But for the fact that he seems to wreck a car at least once every couple of years, I would venture to guess that he would never buy another car.

I thought I would take a poll to see what some of our colleagues thought about cars—and whether I could get some ammunition in my battle with Hugh.

Brad Morgan and Adrienne Anderson fall into Hugh's camp. Says Adrienne, "I do not like cars. They are only good to get from point A to B and to carry your people and your stuff. After over ten years of driving a huge SUV in order to carry football players and lacrosse players and their stuff, I downsized to a Subaru Outback, which can accommodate a bike rack and a kayak rack and gets twenty-seven to thirty-seven miles per gallon. My husband says it is too small for people over six feet tall, but I am only five foot six. I'll keep driving it until it falls apart, although I am not sure that ever happens with a Subaru."

Brad Morgan agrees with Adrienne. "My favorite car is one without a note," says Brad. Brad says that he would keep a car forever, but that he has had to replace his cars about every three years "because my wife keeps getting into accidents."

Darsi Sirknen and Josh Ball fall firmly into my camp. Josh says, "I love cars. In my opinion, a car is a thing of beauty. A car is much more than a way to get from point A to Point B. I am thirty-eight, and I still vividly remember getting my driver's license the day I turned sixteen and the freedom that it represented to me. I understand from people I know and recent articles that young people are not rushing out to get their licenses on their sixteenth birthday as my generation did. I think that the 'car culture' of worshipping muscle cars probably ended with my generation."

Josh goes on to state, "I like all types of cars—especially fast ones. I used to drive a sports car—and then along came kids. Now I drive an Acura TL. It is a four-door sporty car with plenty of power, and it is fun to drive. I also have a mid-size SUV, and it is also sporty and fun to drive. Josh tends to keep vehicles a long time. "I develop somewhat of an attachment to them, and I keep them until it no longer makes financial sense to do so. If I had a larger garage, I would keep three or four vehicles (there are only two drivers in my house). One day, I hope to have enough garage space to keep a small, fast convertible to drive around on the weekends."

Darsi Sirknen agrees. "A car is a thing of beauty. I was raised by a car lover and have inherited that trait. My parents gave me a 2005 limited edition Thunderbird (the 'throwback' style) for law school graduation, and it is my pride and joy. I had wanted one since they started making the Retro Birds in 2002 but, as I was in school, figured I would never be able to buy a new one. 2005 was the last year they were made, which is one reason why that car was such an awesome surprise for me (I didn't graduate until 2006). To this day, she has barely 2,300 miles on her."

Darsi goes on, "As far as my daily driver goes, it still has to be a thing of beauty, but it needs to be functional as well. I prefer to buy a nice car brand new and drive it until it dies. I like knowing it's always been 'mine' and has been well cared for all its life. You never know what kind of problems other people are going to leave you. I currently have a 2008 Lexus ES350 that I bought new at Thanksgiving 2007 (still going strong at 125,000 miles, and the car wash guys always think it's new when I take it in). I love the lines of that car and have never had any problems with it mechanically, but I'm not a fan of the front end on the new ES. If I had to buy a new car today, my current fascination is with the Porsche Panamera, but that's a significant step-up in price. As you can imagine, there's also a 'difference of opinion' in our household as to whether it's worth it (there's actually a difference of opinion in my own head as to whether it's worth it). In all likelihood, I would end up with something more reasonable like the Lincoln MKZ."

So far, it looks like both sides are even, and Hugh is not budging. In the meantime, please wave when you pass a silver Volvo S-80 over the next decade. Chances are, it will be me.

*October 2013*

# GUILTY PLEASURES

## Biking on the Virginia Creeper Trail

During our car debate, Hugh suggested that I get something practical—like a station wagon or minivan. My exact words in response were "I would rather ride a bike." I have eaten those words with a fork and spoon.

This year, Hugh agreed to be a Cub Scout leader. Their first adventure of the year included a bike ride down the Virginia Creeper Trail. Hugh convinced me that moms were going too, and that he had signed the three of us up for the trip.

Having not been on a bike in ten years, I was apprehensive. "It is easy." "No one has ever NOT completed the ride." "You will love it." These were the things I heard the morning of our ride.

The morning of our ride, it was "see your breath cold," which was not what I expected. While other parents had long pants, jackets, and gloves, I set out in yoga pants and a t-shirt. Big mistake. I was freezing.

As we started down the trail, Trace remarked, "If you lost control and went down one of these hills, you could die." This attitude dictated our speed for the day, which meant that I was constantly holding the brake on my bike. At about mile six, I realized that my right hand was completely numb. While I initially thought it was from the cold, it quickly became apparent that the cause was a pinched nerve from holding the brake so tightly.

At mile eight, we were attacked by gnats. Hugh said they were a good source of protein and that I shouldn't be concerned about inhaling them. Frankly, I would have preferred a granola bar.

At about mile ten, I thought it could not get any worse. And then it did.

For whatever reason, I looked down, only to see something long and green with an orange tongue and triangular head. And then I hit it. A snake!!!

Hugh says he heard a scream and then heard me utter words he didn't know I knew. I was convinced that I had seen a glimpse of hell, and it was the Creeper Trail. I kept praying that it would end, but it didn't.

I had seven miles to go, and there was no way out. At various points, I could see a stream at the bottom of the hill and the road just past. I was tempted to cross the stream to get to the road and then beg a passerby to pick me up. But for the thought of snakes, I probably would have.

The last seven miles were marked with intermittent tears and cursing. And I was convinced if I heard one more person say, "To the left. To the left," my head would explode. It wasn't the Creeper Trail; it was Creeper Hell.

That day reminded me why I like to view nature from behind glass. And that I really don't like to ride bicycles. I was convinced that other people probably felt the same way, so I started asking my friends who had done it what they thought.

Doug Blaze had this to say. "What is not to love? Seventeen miles all downhill to Damascus through beautiful country. Lunch and ice cream in

Damascus then you can keep going all the way to Abingdon. Which is another cool town with beer. If that is hell, my past and future transgressions don't worry me so much."

Rick Carl agrees. "Jeepers Creepers the Trail is awesome! Son Rick and I rode it several years ago on the anniversary of Lynn's death—first half is downhill practically all the way; we stopped and ate at the little restaurant on the side of the trail. Met interesting folks—two girls from New York City who were spending the summer interning in Richmond; we fixed the chain for a young woman from somewhere in Europe who spoke no English; and had a great memorable day. The only knock on it is it is too popular—we were there on a weekday in August so it wasn't too crowded, but it was still busy. Hiking, biking, and the great outdoors are what is special about East Tennessee. Imagine if you lived in Ohio, or Kansas for crying out loud."

Brian Lapps, Mary Miller, and Adrienne Anderson offer some helpful hints for those wanting to ride. Says Brian, "I did a fifty-mile ride on the Creeper with a Boy Scout troop in October 2011. In order to put yourself in the appropriate mood, I suggest you spend the night before your ride in a tent in the downtown Damascus Park (advance permission required). If the temperature is going to be in the mid-thirties, take only a sleeping bag liner, not the actual sleeping bag. You can tell your child that you're setting an example in how to be tough. If, on the night after the ride, you get asked, 'If you're so tough, why are we going to Dollar General to buy blankets,' you can answer, 'In case you need them tonight.' I would do most of it again, but I could probably be convinced to stay in Abingdon."

Mary Miller says, "I have the good, the bad, and the ugly with the Creeper Trail. We did it two years ago with our son, Will (just the downhill part of course). And of course, we did not dress warmly enough. By the time we finished, I looked like a cross between Minnie Pearl and Phyllis Diller between the gloves, hats, sweatshirts, and jackets we pieced together to stay warm. My reward was that my son painted a beautiful picture of one of the railroad trestles for me. It is really good, and it does make me laugh though it is not supposed to."

Adrienne Anderson also has some good advice. "For a wedding anniversary (somewhere around the fifteenth anniversary), Jeff and I decided to spend the weekend in Abingdon. We planned to stay in a quaint little bed and breakfast, see a play at the Barter Theater, and ride the Creeper Trail. On the morning of the bike ride, the van dropped us off at the top of the mountain, and we told the driver we were riding the whole trail all the way back into Abingdon. The first eleven (or so) miles are downhill and the last eleven (or so) miles are only a one to two percent average grade uphill, so what was there to worry about? The scenery is absolutely beautiful, and the trail only slightly bumpy on the first half, but if you are just a casual, occasional cyclist with a cheap bicycle YOU MUST STAND UP on your pedals. Trust me. Halfway through the trail, I pulled off, went into a shop in Damascus, and bought an overpriced gel-filled bicycle seat cover in order to complete the ride. It is the best investment I have ever made in my entire life. (I note that the store had many of these gel seat covers in stock, and the lady at the cash register said they did a brisk business in that particular model). I share my experience so that average women like me do not have to wince when settling into their seats at the Barter Theater."

I am still not convinced. At the end of the day, Trace got a merit badge. If he can get a merit badge for cooking, housecleaning, or party planning, I'm game. But I will NEVER ride the Creeper Trail again.

*November 2013*

# GUILTY PLEASURES

## Turkey, Traditions, and Other Fun Things

I was recently speaking with a friend about the holidays. He intimated that his family's favorite holidays were generally "The Eating Holidays, you know, Thanksgiving, Christmas and Easter." I've always loved The Eating Holidays myself—especially Thanksgiving.

I've always been fond of the month of November. The Vols have traditionally done pretty well in November. My dad's birthday was in November, which always meant really good German chocolate cake (his favorite—homemade by my grandmother). My wedding anniversary is in November. And, of course, there is Thanksgiving.

As a child, Thanksgiving was always great fun. It usually began with watching the Macy's Thanksgiving Day parade, followed by lunch at my Mamaw and Papaw French's house (always at twelve o' clock sharp, which included our immediate family and food that would rival any Cordon Bleu chef), which was followed by "lunch" (usually around four thirty because she kept on schedule about as well as my eight-year-old) at Grandmother Morie's house. Thanksgiving was always a day of non-stop eating. And non-stop fun.

Grandmother Morie's house was always full of people—lots of relatives, lots of family friends, and the "randomers" who were quickly taken into the family (as long as they didn't eat my dad's birthday cake). It was a day I looked forward to all year, and it never disappointed. I had lots of cousins who were close to my age, and we always managed to find some mischief in between the actual sitting down to eat and going back through to pick at the leftovers.

After Hugh and I got married, we became Thanksgiving drifters. For the first couple of years after we were married, we had dinner with Hugh's mom (my mom was usually either working or traveling). After his mother died, we spent a couple of Thanksgivings in restaurants. One year, we traveled to London (anniversary trip), where we enjoyed Indian food on Thanksgiving Day (one of the best meals I have ever had). A couple of years after that, we went with relatives on a Disney cruise and spent Thanksgiving Day drinking mojitos on Disney's private island. All of these were great holidays, but we seemed to be lacking "tradition."

A couple of years ago, Hugh and I decided to make our own tradition. We picked up the Williams-Sonoma Thanksgiving cookbook and decided to make every dish in there for Thanksgiving and share with (a) any relatives in town who wanted to come and who were brave enough to try my cooking, and (b) any friends who may not have any family in town. To us, we were creating our own family traditions.

When I recently asked Trace if we had any Thanksgiving traditions, however, he promptly informed me that we do not. He said that Thanksgiving is usually just "you fixing a bunch of fancy food—mostly good, except for butternut squash soup—and then me watching television while you wash dishes all day." He then suggested that we needed a new tradition: the family football game. I did not have the heart to tell him that (1) the average age of the adults at our Thanksgiving is usually somewhere north of seventy, and (2) all of his cousins are girly-girls who will not want a family football game (a family dance party, maybe—but not a football game).

He and I agreed that we do need our own traditions, but we were at a loss as to what they should be. Since we came up with nothing, I solicited some input from friends as to traditions that we might copy.

Troy Weston said, "Last year, I started the tradition of eating supper alone at the Chef Ben Chinese restaurant in Fountain City." I don't think we will try that one—but Troy will be receiving an invite to our Williams-Sonoma food fest.

I loved Sherry DeCosta Alley's suggestion that we watch the Macy's Thanksgiving Day Parade. "My Thanksgiving tradition is to have the Macy's Thanksgiving Day Parade on the TV all morning. I just love watching all of the giant cartoon-character floats, marching bands, and Broadway musical numbers. I have memories of watching that parade as a little girl at my grandparents' house while my mom and grandma cooked Thanksgiving dinner. I don't think I've missed one yet. Whether I'm cooking that morning or visiting at my in-laws' house, it simply would NOT feel like Thanksgiving without watching that parade! To me, it marks the start of the Christmas season, and I cannot begin decorating for Christmas until after that parade. I am sooooooo very thankful Macy's has continued that parade and I hope my children have fond memories of it when they are adults."

Trace was a bit more interested in Joshua Ball's Thanksgiving tradition. "I take every Thanksgiving week off to spend with my family and to hunt deer. I enjoy sitting in the woods in solitude and watching the sun come up through the trees. I enjoy hearing nothing but the sounds of nature as the woods come alive, as opposed to the telephone, fax machine, and dings of email and text notifications that accompany every workday of the year. Of course, I enjoy spending the week with my family, but my guilty pleasure is slowing down from the frantic pace of everyday life, spending several hours in the woods up in a tree stand just enjoying being outside and taking in God's wonderful creation."

Chuck Young may have the Thanksgiving tradition that we can all agree on. "I like to catch a movie Thanksgiving night if possible. (Same goes for Christmas night.) There are usually good new movies out then, and it's a welcome tonic after a day of interaction. This year, I'm eyeing *Catching Fire* at Thanksgiving and *The Wolf of Wall Street* at Christmas."

No matter what the choice, I am certain that we will love whatever "tradition" we make. Although it may be "borrowed," the experience will be uniquely ours. And, hopefully, Trace will remember it fondly (or even carry it on) for years to come.

*December 2013*

# GUILTY PLEASURES

## Holiday Style

I've always been a big fan of Christmas. Even as a kid, I remember turning the Fisher Price Little People barn into a Santa's workshop diorama. I remember spending countless hours every year decorating the Christmas tree with my mom while my dad, a.k.a. Scrooge, stood in the background and said, "If it were up to me, we wouldn't bother with all this mess. What's the use of putting up all these trees if you are just going to take them down in a few weeks?"

It really should come as no surprise that my obsession with all things Christmas continues to this day. Every year, on the day after Thanksgiving, I drag out boxes and boxes of--- to quote my husband, a.k.a. Scrooge Jr. – "Christmas crap." Like my dad, he often remarks, "If I have to get one more thing out of that attic, there won't be Christmas around here." He makes fun of the fact that I photograph all of the decorations every year so that I can remember exactly how they looked (and so I can duplicate them the next year).

Decorating is one of my holiday "guilty pleasures." I absolutely love to decorate, and I turn on the trees every morning as soon as I get out of bed. I have even been known to leave the trees up until well into February. Sometimes, I just cannot bear the thought of the house without them.

As much as I like decorating, I also like Christmas movies and music. From the day after Thanksgiving until Christmas, the radio in my car is firmly set to the twenty-four-hour Christmas music station. And our television watching is limited to ABC Family's *25 Days of Christmas* and *Fa-la-la-la Lifetime.*

I absolutely love all of the Christmas movies—everything from old school *Rudolph the Red-Nosed Reindeer* to Mario Lopez in *Holiday in Handcuffs.* One of our family favorites, though (and perhaps because it hits pretty close to home with our crazy family), is *National Lampoon's Christmas Vacation.* To quote Clark Griswold, "The most enduring traditions of the season are best enjoyed in the warm embrace of kith and kin. Thith tree is a thymbol of the thpirit of the Grithwold family Chrithmath." In the Griswold family tradition, our house looks like—to quote Hugh – "it puked Christmas." I wouldn't have it any other way.

Certain that we aren't the only family with over-the-top decorations and wacky traditions, I asked a few friends to share their own holiday "guilty pleasures."

Darsi Sirknen prefers another type of decorating. "Instead of tacky sweaters, my sister and I do tacky gift wrap. We compete each year to see who can wrap the other's gift in the most tacky, ugly, and sometimes gross items. We've used buckets, baling twine, beer cases, horse feed bags, junk mail, cotton balls – if it looks awful, we've done it."

Ashley Lowe says, "I have five words for you—Mayfield's Peppermint Stick Ice Cream. I cannot wait until it hits the grocery store shelves every year, and I eat it as often as possible until it disappears from the shelves. Fat and calories don't count at Christmas, right?"

Regina Lambert enjoys the creativity—and craziness—involved in creating the perfect holiday card. "My fun holiday tradition is the annual Christmas card photo shoot. I am one of those 'crazy dog people' and have a picture taken with all of them in front of the Christmas tree every year. It was much easier in past years when I only had two or three pups, but I am now over the top (way over the top??) with four standard poodles and one toy poodle. Last year two of the standards were puppies, so they could be held. This year Russell Rain weighs in around fifty-five to sixty pounds and his twin sister Daisy Dance is forty to forty-five. My old girl Morgan Stanley can't stand anymore, so she had a bed covered in a red fleece. Parks (my first poodle of color—named after Rosa) behaved surprisingly well this year, but my ten-pounder Lilli Mac would rather avoid the paparazzi. So ... It is always quite an adventure to try to get five dogs and two people in one decent picture. We wear matching outfits (normally sweaters—this year pajamas), and the experience is usually as funny as the final product!"

We all have traditions that make the holiday season special. Our own little guilty pleasures become holiday treasures, creating memories that will last a lifetime. And to quote Clark Griswold, have the "hap, hap, happiest Christmas since Bing Crosby tap-danced with Danny Kaye."

*January 2014*

# GUILTY PLEASURES

## Cats v. Dogs: The Ultimate Showdown

I have always been a "cat person." It has been rare that I have not had at least one cat. Sometimes, two. I've never been a fan of dogs. They jump, lick, chew on things, and bark. And they are smelly. Cats, on the other hand, smell really nice. They use a litter box, don't have to be walked, and are generally low maintenance.

I was lucky enough to be "owned" by Alexa, a small, black long-haired cat, for over a decade. I will forever believe that she was the best pet to ever live. About six years ago, Alexa became very ill. During that same time, Hugh had broken his shoulder playing hockey and was in an immobilizer, which meant that I did pretty much everything for him for about twelve weeks. One day, while flossing Hugh's teeth, I received the call that Alexa had been diagnosed with a brain tumor and that the feline neurosurgeon wanted to operate. Hugh's response was, "How much is this going to cost me?" After reminding Hugh that I had Alexa long before I had him, I authorized the surgery.

When Alexa died during surgery, I was devastated. Afterwards, although Hugh (a "dog person") really wanted a dog, he settled for Max, the Maine Coon show cat, who is dog-like in personality and who is forty-four inches long and weighs over twenty pounds. Between Max and Hugh's crazy cat, Possom, I assumed our pet family was complete. I should know what happens when I "assume."

The week before Christmas, after much debate, Trace finally agreed to see Santa (as long as there was no chance any of his friends would see him being photographed with Santa). When we finally reached Santa, Trace told him, "I want a dog for Christmas. Nothing else. Just a dog. Give toys to all the other children in the world. All I want is a dog. If I get a dog for Christmas, it will be the merriest Christmas ever."

Much to the surprise of both of us, I looked at Hugh and said, "It looks like we are getting a dog." Having never owned a dog, I thought I would ask some friends which were better: cats or dogs.

Anne McKinney, a fellow "cat person," is firmly in the "cats" corner. Says Anne, "Definitely, definitely CATS! A cat can be trained (believe it or not) to act like a dog, but a dog will NEVER be a cat. All the cats we have ever had learned to fetch, but there was no slobber or gross stuff on the toys they dropped back into our laps. Of course, if they want to fetch in the middle of the night when you want to sleep, you have a serious problem! Show a cat one time where the litter box is, and you never have to spend time potty training again. (Unless they get really mad at you . . .)"

Anne continues, "Cat owners don't stroll through the neighborhood with plastic bags in tow, praying there's not a hole in the bag they failed to detect. You can leave a cat alone in the house for a weekend. The cat will remember this slight, sneak up and bite you on the toe during the nap you desperately needed upon returning home, but you didn't have to spend money for a cat sitter while you were away. Also, you can't smell a cat's breath from across the room (though it's pretty bad sometimes close up!). Cats (like dogs) can sense when your heart is broken, and for a wonderful brief moment, they will come close, purr and comfort you. Then they walk away because you've had your chance to get over it."

Kyle Baisley and Kristi Davis are in the "dogs" corner. Kristi advised, "Definitely dogs. I don't trust cats. One minute you're petting a cat, then the next minute it bites you for no reason."

Kyle Baisley agreed. "I have to go with a dog. The only cats that I get along with are cats that have personalities more like dogs (or cats that are bigger than most dogs, such as your Maine Coon). Cats are too moody and demanding. My dog Chloe is the one being on this planet that is guaranteed to be happy to see me and cheer me up every time. She loves me at my best and my worst. In general, dogs are way more happy-go-lucky and forgiving animals. Cats, not so much. My mom has two. They are almost always in a foul mood and not very eager to go out of their way to be a companion or cheer anyone up, which, in my opinion, is the whole reason for having a pet."

Troy Weston and Cheryl Rice are a bit more diplomatic. Says Cheryl, "I've had both. I love dogs (usually), love certain cats (many fewer than dogs), but really at this stage of life prefer to have responsibility for NEITHER! That said, we have two cats, at the moment."

Troy added, "I have had both cats and dogs, and I have never been able to resolve this question. My most recent dog, Blanche, was very similar to a cat in her daily habits. Also, she did her own thing and didn't really pay much attention to what other people and animals were doing. My most recent cat, Rocky, was very similar to a dog in that she would come running up to you when you came home, and she wanted constant attention. So, that really changed my perception. I prefer them both to rattlesnakes." His best advice, though, was this. "Most importantly, everyone should go and adopt an animal, whatever their preference."

And we did. On December 21, Spanky, a three-pound Cavachon puppy, joined our family. He is a lot of work—much more than I expected. But he is, without a doubt, the cutest, sweetest puppy in the world. As Hugh said that night, as we watched Trace sleeping in a chair with the puppy on his lap, "I feel like our household is complete."

*February 2014*

# GUILTY PLEASURES

## The Best Part of Waking Up

I was a late adapter to coffee. I never quite understood the hype. Then I met Hugh while we were both living in Nashville. When we first met, Hugh was in sales with Disney, which meant he had lots of early mornings, late nights, and long trips in the car. He was, without a doubt, addicted to coffee. He was a regular at Starbucks and seemed to know every barista in town. On average, he visited Starbucks (or one of the independent coffee houses) at least twice a day. I quickly realized that, if I ever wanted to see him, I had to at least pretend to enjoy coffee. "Meet me at Starbucks" was a common phrase in our relationship.

Then, a funny thing happened. I actually started to like coffee. A lot. I found myself going to Starbucks when Hugh was out of town. My week was never complete unless I had at least two Venti Skinny Peppermint Mochas. I found my grandmother's old hand-me-down Mr. Coffee and started making my own coffee (Dunkin' Donuts with French Vanilla Coffee Mate) at home *before* I went to Starbucks.

While planning our wedding, Hugh and I discovered a chicory blend coffee that was amazing. It was full-bodied, yet lacked the bitterness you find with some coffees. It was especially good with sugar. It was even better when made in the programmable Cuisinart coffee maker we received as a wedding gift. Every morning, a fresh pot with an amazing aroma greeted me when I awoke. My couple of cups of joe every morning soon turned to an entire pot. Nearly a decade later, little has changed.

A few years ago, I traded in all of my regular coffee cups for twelve-ounce mugs. My mornings don't begin until I've filled one of those mugs at least twice with the coffee of the week, plus a little sugar-free hazelnut creamer. I'll admit that I am addicted.

Recently, I've been traveling to Nashville frequently for work. Generally, I stay at the Hermitage Hotel for one reason. The coffee. I cannot get enough of that delicious French press. It has a rich flavor and an aroma that has to be close to the scent of heaven. On my last trip, I ordered room service breakfast. In addition to my standard egg whites and fresh berries, I requested a pot of French press for two. When the very sweet lady from Food and Beverage arrived with the tray, she said, "Oh, you are traveling alone. I think they've made a mistake with your order. This is a pot of coffee for two people." I replied, "Not at all. Coffee for one just isn't enough. I need this whole pot." And then, I drank it. It was a wonderful way to start a very early day.

If I could have only one beverage for the rest of my life, it would be coffee. I really cannot get enough. It is my morning guilty pleasure. And I am not alone.

Donald Farinato says, "I can't say I love coffee, but I don't think I can live without it. Each weeknight, I get the automatic coffeemaker set with Dunkin' Donuts so that hot coffee waits for me while I get up. (I like skipping that task on the weekends.) And each weekday morning on the drive in, I stop at Starbucks. I don't like the time that stop takes – including driving a bit out of my way – but it is better than being a zombie all day."

Dave Fielder agrees that coffee is a morning "must have." "I started drinking coffee in the Army over forty years ago when there was nothing else available. I was with a field artillery unit in Germany, and they made coffee when we were in the field by bringing a fifty-gallon pot to a boil, pouring in coffee grounds, and then poring cold water on top to make the grounds sink to the bottom. They would then re-heat the coffee and serve. When it is below zero and you have been firing artillery rounds through the night, it actually tastes OK. I have not gone without morning coffee since then, and I drink any type of coffee except decaf and flavored coffee."

For Kacie McRee, coffee is a good way to ease into the day. "I love coffee, but it's not an 'I can't live without it' kind of item. I enjoy taking my time drinking coffee in the morning before the madness of the day begins. There's no particular type of coffee I like more than others, but I do have to have particular creamer. It's the Hood creamer they sell at the Fresh Market. It makes all the difference."

Adrienne Anderson enjoys the "social" aspect of coffee. "I like the smell of coffee much better than the taste. I love the smell of fresh brewed coffee! (Almost as much as the smell of frying bacon.) When I drink coffee in the morning, I drink half a cup of hot milk (from the microwave) with half a cup of coffee, kind of a low-brow latte. When I have really enjoyed coffee, I think it has had more to do with the circumstances than the drink – cappuccino in Italy, café con leche in Little Havana in Miami, strong black coffee with really sinful desserts at fancy dinners, and most importantly, when someone I really like has invited me to sit for a while and talk over coffee."

Coffee is a "guilty pleasure" for a lot of people. Every person that I asked admitted to a love of coffee for one reason or another. For some of us, it is the caffeine jolt the first thing in the morning. Others preferred the joys of drinking the coffee, as opposed to the coffee itself. No matter the reason, I think Folgers got it right in their commercials. Coffee is "the best part of waking up."

*March 2014*

# GUILTY PLEASURES

## Don't Wine ... Just Drink It

A number of years ago, I started collecting cocktail napkins. One of my favorites says, "Wine improves with age. The older I get, the better I like it." For me, this is most definitely true. I was a late adapter to good wine. In law school, my drink of choice was either (1) boxed wine (I had not mastered the opener), or (2) for really special occasions, Martini & Rossi sparkling wine. This started to change when I met Hugh.

A few months after we met, I made an offhand remark that I thought hot air balloons were beautiful. When my birthday rolled around, Hugh surprised me with a balloon trip over the Sonoma Valley. He did not realize that I am deathly afraid of heights, so I was relieved to learn that the trip started with mimosas and ended with lunch and sparkling wine. I kept a death grip on the inside of the basket for the entire trip (in spite of having a mimosa), and I was thankful for the wine with lunch.

As cool as the balloon trip was, the highlight of the trip was our tour of the wine country. I started to develop an appreciation for the craftsmanship that goes into winemaking. I also learned how to pair different wines with foods to really bring out the flavors in the wines. I also realized that I like good wine.

My favorite wineries were Sterling and Domaine Chandon. To get to Sterling, you had to ride a chair lift up a mountain (again, something involving heights), so I was ready to sample when we got to the winery. While Hugh loved their cabernet, I was a huge fan of the Malvasia Bianca, which is a slightly sweet white that goes great with spicy foods. We purchased a couple of bottles and vowed that we would purchase more when we returned home.

Unbeknownst to us, Sterling only sells the Malvasia Bianca at their vineyard or through their wine club. Suffice it to say, I was delighted a few years ago when Tennessee relaxed its restrictions so that residents could receive shipments of wine. I am like a kid at Christmas every month when my shipment of two bottles arrives.

I also enjoyed Domaine Chandon, which is renowned for its sparkling wines. I had always been a huge fan of sparkling wine, but I considered it a "special occasion" wine.

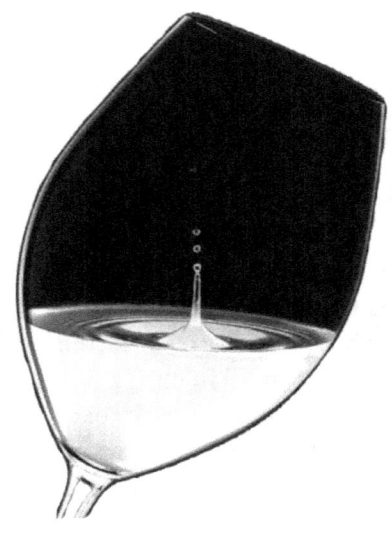

The sommelier read my mind when she said, "People often save sparkling wines for special occasions. I think you should drink it every day because every day is a 'special occasion.'" I've taken that to heart, and I often find myself opening a bottle for small occasions, like a clean house or because the laundry is finished.

I'm not alone in my love of wine.

Bill Maddox says he has not always loved wine. "I didn't think too much of it in middle school," laughs Bill. On a more serious note, Bill relayed, "The fewer years I have left on the planet, the less patience I have for bad wine. I particularly like big reds, especially from Argentina, Australia, or California." Bill also enjoys pairing good wine with food. "I like a big, bold red (like The Prisoner from Orin Swift or Scout's Honor from Venge) with a giant, rare ribeye, a loaded baked potato, and a salad with bleu cheese chunks the size of your fist."

Annette Winston says, "I love wine, and have since I was about sixteen, I mean, eighteen. I used to drink mostly whites, but now I prefer reds today because of the health benefits. I still like a good chardonnay now and then, but I usually stick to pinot noirs, cabs. And I like them with great food, of course."

"I love, love, love wine," says Darsi Sirknen. "Like many people, I assume, I started with super sweet whites (Riesling was a fave for a long time). Then, the strangest thing happened. One day it was like a switch just flipped, and I couldn't stand the sweetness anymore. My favorite Riesling suddenly made my mouth turn inside out. So, I set out to find a drier wine and thought I might just move to Chardonnay or another less-sweet white, but I didn't find my new happy place until I had migrated all the way to a Cabernet Sauvignon. Talk about a drastic difference. I also love a good Cab Franc paired with some horseradish cheddar or another spicy cheese. Ben and I enjoy wine in a variety of settings, but our favorite thing is to sit back in an outdoor setting and listen to some live music while sipping wine (I still prefer white wine if it's hot outside, but nothing as sweet as I used to drink). We actually just got back from a weekend at Biltmore, which has always been one of our favorite places. You can buy bottles of wine from their winery (they even have chilled white wine for purchase), take it out to the open space in their Antler Hill Village, and sit around drinking it while you listen to the music they have out there just about every afternoon. If you're going to do that, though, I highly recommend staying at the Inn on the Estate, which provides shuttle transportation between the winery and the Inn for its guests. You don't want to have to drive after an afternoon of those wine bottles piling up."

Regina Lambert also enjoys a good wine. "For some reason, I have always preferred whites. My favorite had always been a Pinot Grigio—until this past summer. Last June I was in the South of France to celebrate my big 5-0 with family and friends. It was there that I discovered my love for rosé. We spent one day touring Provence wineries, including sampling several great wines. The rosé was by far my favorite. Now whenever I enjoy a glass of rosé it takes me back to an incredible day spent in paradise with family and friends."

Good wine is meant to be shared with good friends. If you are a wine lover, please make plans to attend the KBA's Blind Wine Event honoring Don Paine, which will be held at the hangar at Island Home Airport. To quote Amye King, "I like my wine with lots of friends and little pretense." I hope that you will be one of those friends on May 15.

*May 2014*

# AROUND THE COMMUNITY

## Jack Neely: "Explainer" Of Knoxville

Like most great writers, *Metro Pulse* associate editor and Knoxville historian Jack Neely did not set out to write about Knoxville. Sometimes, things just happen.

After graduating from Webb in 1976, Neely attended Millsaps College for two years before returning home to UT. "I bounced around a lot and studied different things. I studied Business for a year and then tried Journalism, but I hated the electric typewriter, which led me to Liberal Arts," says Neely. Not planning any particular course of study, Jack took classes he enjoyed, including classes in U.S. Foreign Policy. One day, recounts Jack, "My advisor said to me, 'Congratulations. You are about to graduate with a degree in history.'"

While at UT, Neely began writing for the *Daily Beacon*, also serving as "wire editor." He also worked at the Knoxville News-Sentinel at night to finance a post-graduation trip to Europe. Upon returning from Europe, he was hit with the harsh reality of a soft job market in a struggling economy. "I worked temp jobs ... as a truck driver ... in a factory at Forks of the River."

Sometimes, though, things just happen. "I got lucky that the World's Fair came along," says Jack. After working in brochures and telephones, he took a job with crowd control, which allowed him to see the entire Fair site every day. As the crowds began to dwindle and faced with a lay-off, Neely saw an opening for a guide at the Egyptian pavilion. "I went to the library and checked out every book I could find on Egypt. I learned as much as I could and presented myself as an Egyptologist. I got the job," says Neely. "I loved it."

More than a job, the World's Fair was pivotal in shaping Neely's career. "That was my first introduction to dealing with people from out of town and hearing their ideas about Knoxville. It became interesting. I was amazed at how many Americans had no idea what Vols were and to hear their perceptions of Knoxville and East Tennessee."

While giving a tour, Neely met Howard Lumsden, who worked in Placement at UT. Lumsden introduced him to Bob Ritchie, who was looking for an investigator for criminal defense cases. Thinking that this would build his resume when applying for law school, Neely took the job. While three-fourths of the job was clerical, one-fourth was drawing detailed maps of crime scenes and interviewing the accused and witnesses. Soon, he realized that what he really loved was more akin to journalism than the practice of law.

While working as a legal investigator, Neely began writing for a lifestyle monthly, *Knoxville Lifestyles*, which became *Citytimes*. He also started writing columns about Knoxville history. Soon, this became his full-time job.

Sometimes, though, things happen. When the principal investor withdrew and the magazine closed, Neely went back into the legal profession, working with Wagner & Myers as a proofreader. After the birth of his son, Jack made the decision to stay at home and do freelance work.

While freelancing, he was offered a job as editor of a coal marketing weekly, which featured inside information about the coal and gas markets. *Northerncoal Newsletter* was a Xeroxed publication that was produced on a shoestring budget, but Neely learned a valuable lesson. People would pay top-dollar for reliable information.

During this time, Neely had also been applying at Whittle Communications. After "sending at least ten resumes," he got a job as an editorial assistant, writing jokes for a publication called *FUNNIES*. He went on to serve as an editor of *Special Reports*, a bi-monthly publication of six separate magazines, one of which included fictional stories.

While at Whittle, Neely realized that most Whittle employees were not from Knoxville. Accordingly, he became the "explainer" of Knoxville, entertaining his co-workers with stories about Knoxville and the characters from Knoxville's more colorful past. He also realized that people who were not from here were more "fearless" about where to go and where to live. He realized that outsiders were more inclined to frequent out-of-the-way places and that they were more likely to eschew the more traditional neighborhoods for places "off the beaten path." Through his association with his Whittle co-workers, he began studying Knoxville's "hidden gems" like the Old Gray Cemetery, Harold's Deli, and the old Bill Meyer stadium. He quickly realized how much was actually happening in his hometown, thanks to fresh eyes showing him around.

When Whittle began phasing out publications, Neely was contacted by two friends who were starting a magazine called *Metro Pulse*, which was to feature the "happenings" in Knoxville. As a result, Neely began writing stories about Knoxville. He also started hearing from people who read his columns. "It was a big revelation that people were interested in Knoxville. My family had traveled growing up, but we had never explored the city where we lived. It was interesting because Knoxville is older than a lot of places, and its history is certainly more complex."

In 1995, Neely did a compilation of his Knoxville stories, and the first *Secret History* book was published. Neely is now working on his eleventh book related to Knoxville—a coffee table book about the history of the Tennessee Theatre. When asked about the most interesting tidbit of information he has found, Neely said that he is amazed at the number of famous people who performed here, including Desi Arnaz, Fifi D'Orsay, Danny Kaye, Even Arden, and Roy Acuff.

Neely is also working on a history of the Old City. He said that it is a bit more challenging because, unlike Market Square, not a lot is written about the area. It appears, though, that the Old City was at one time home to a very diverse immigrant population, including Lithuanian Jews, Greeks, Irish and Italians.

Neely has studied Knoxville's past and has seen firsthand the resurgence of downtown. He attributes it in part to dumb luck and in part to an interesting combination of people, who include an aerospace engineer, a hairdresser, convicted felons, and a Christian charity, among others. Amazingly, they all exist harmoniously. Says Neely, "In the 1990s, someone asked about downtown. I said it would be revitalized, but that it would not look like it did in the past. There would be no live-audience radio shows, movie theaters, or department stores. Now, we have it all. Plus a fantastic Farmer's Market." Sometimes, things just happen.

*August 2014*

# GUILTY PLEASURES

## Weekend Getaways

My dad used to say, "If the wheels are rolling, Angelia is going." I have always loved to travel, and I am especially fond of a quick getaway. I am usually game for an adventure (as long as it does not involve "rustic" accommodations or the Virginia Creeper Trail). When I met Hugh, I found a kindred travel spirit.

Pre-Trace, in what we now refer to as the "Go-Go 0-0's", Hugh and I were masters of the weekend trip. During his days with Disney (and in the days of $35 Southwest airfares), we went to Orlando fifteen weekends in one year. When Trace was born in 2005, our travel became less frequent in large part because of the amount of "stuff" required for a baby. As he got older, we returned to our traveling ways. And then Spanky, the Christmas puppy, joined our family.

We have officially become "those people" that treat the dog like an additional child. Having never had a dog, I did not fully appreciate the travel restrictions that come with dog ownership. I quickly learned that (1) dogs cannot be left alone for more than a few hours, and (2) boarding a dog costs as much as hiring a babysitter for a child. It became apparent that, if we wanted to travel, we would need to travel with the dog.

A couple of weeks ago, we got the "guilt trip" from Trace—"I've done so much summer homework that I really haven't even had a summer." Since he had been asking to visit Biltmore for the past eight months, we decided that a quick trip to Asheville was in order.

There are websites specifically for people who want to travel with a dog—and Asheville is particularly dog-friendly. Based on reviews at dogfriendly.com, we booked a room at Asheville's four-bone hotel, the Hotel Indigo. We were greeted with water and treats for Spanky. Our room was large and well appointed, and it had laminate flooring, which was a bonus with the dog.

Downtown Asheville is particularly pet friendly. We saw as many people with dogs as without, and most businesses had water bowls for four-legged patrons. We stopped in to no fewer than three pet-related businesses and dined outside at a couple of fabulous restaurants where the service for the dog was as good as the service for us.

We also learned that Biltmore is dog friendly. While dogs are not allowed in the house and gardens, they are welcome in Antler Hill Village and the surrounding area. While Trace and I toured the mansion, Hugh and Spanky visited Antler Hill Village, where Spanky enjoyed the petting zoo and walking around the farm property. He even enjoyed visiting the pub named for Cedric, the Vanderbilt's Saint Bernard.

Our trip to Asheville with Spanky was a success, so much so that I (a sucker for the upsell) bought season tickets to Biltmore. We have officially become "those people" that treat the dog like an additional child. I was curious as to whether other people were like us and traveled with their pets.

Regina Lambert is a frequent weekend traveler with her dogs, and she is especially fond of Folly Beach. "Folly is one of the friendliest dog-welcome beaches I have ever visited. The Tides (the only hotel, which is right on the beach and has the best restaurant, Blu) has no limit on dog size or how many you bring along. It is always hard for us to decide which of our Standard Poodles get to join (we have four but can only manage two on the trip), but my Toy Poodle, Lilli Mac, always goes. She can lose up to two pounds chasing birds on the beach! It is like a fitness camp for her as her normal preference is to be carried everywhere. Folly brings out the dog in her!"

Per Regina, "My favorite part: the outdoor restaurants that line the main strip all welcome pets. When you are seated, the wait staff brings the humans a big glass of ice water, and the dogs are welcomed with a big bowl of ice water and a biscuit. Also, dogs are welcome on the beach (during hot summer months—June through September—they are not permitted from ten through six; otherwise, no limits). The town has clean-up stations all over, and people are happy to keep up with their dogs, so it is a really clean and tidy city, too."

LeAnn Mynatt likes to get away to Kiawah with Sugar Dog. Says LeAnn, "Why is it that the best stories are never funny at the time they're happening? My parents, two nephews and I left a day early for a 4th of July holiday weekend to the beach at Kiawah. We were fine until the car started shaking as we pulled into the Asheville Farmer's Market. We spent the next four hours at Harry's Buick Cadillac dealership. Fortunately, there was a Subway just down the hill and, importantly, free Wi-Fi in the service department waiting room. The nephews watched Netflix and played video games, and Mom checked emails. I walked Sugar dog around the car lot. When we loaded up and pulled out of the service bay, I asked the service manager if he remembered the movie *Vacation* with Chevy Chase. He started laughing and said, 'Yes, and you even have the dog!' We made it to Wally World (i.e. Kiawah) thirteen hours later (normally a seven-hour drive) including Sugar dog, and the rest of the trip was postcard perfect."

Mary Miller enjoys weekend getaways with her non-furry children. "We love to go to Fontana Dam and Fontana Village. Believe it or not, my kids love it because there is no wireless service. They get Mom and Dad to themselves. I love it because at fifty-three, I can still go there and water ski with my brother and sisters. But you have to be careful what you imbibe. A few years ago, my brother received a ticket for "SWI" – skiing while intoxicated. A new challenge for the criminal defense lawyers out there!"

*September 2014*

# GUILTY PLEASURES

## Tennessee Football Game Day Traditions

There are two things in life that you don't mess with around me. The first is my kid. The second is Tennessee football. One of the worst arguments Hugh and I have ever had occurred when he gave away our tickets to the Tennessee-LSU game a few years ago. At that moment, he learned the depths of my devotion to all things orange. And that you don't want to get into an argument with a lawyer.

Come every August, the only reason I don't go into a deep depression over summer ending is because I know what is coming. The tailgates, the bright lights, ESPN College Game Day, the Pride of the Southland playing "Rocky Top," and 100,000 of my closest friends yelling "V-O-L-S, V-O-L-S, V-O-L-S, Go, Vols, go!" There is something majestic about Saturdays in the South, and Tennessee football is my "guilty pleasure." Other than a loss, there is very little about Game Day that I don't enjoy.

My enjoyment begins long before Saturday. I often find myself perusing local stores or the internet for the perfect game day attire. As someone who does not naturally look good in orange, this is sometimes the difficult task. The older I get, the more comfortable I want to be. Still, I love dressing up for games. You will almost always find me in orange and white (although sometimes accented with black, brown, or Smokey gray). To me, pulling that off without looking like an orange and white construction barrel or a parade float is what separates veteran fans from novices.

My true "guilty pleasure," though, can be found on Game Day itself. I love walking across campus from my parking space at the Aquatic Center. And I know it is Game Day when I am greeted by that familiar smell. The frying onions at Hot Dog Heaven. For those unfamiliar, Hot Dog Heaven is the food vendor on the sidewalk across from the library and the Haslam Business building. While I'm normally a pretty health-conscious eater, I cannot resist Hot Dog Heaven. Every fall, it is like running into an old friend that you haven't seen for a while. And it is good.

I'm not the only one with a passion for Game Day and the traditions associated with it.

Tasha Blakney can usually be found clad in orange on any given Saturday (unless she loses a bet with her Georgia Bulldog husband). "My absolute favorite tradition is taking advantage of our fortunate ability to travel by water to UT games. The Volunteer Navy is such a great tradition that is very unique to Tennessee. You really just can't beat it!"

Although not originally from Tennessee, Cheryl Rice has been converted into a die-hard Tennessee fan. "When we moved here almost fifteen years ago, it didn't take long to notice the 'orange fever' that swept over Knoxville in late August and lasted through the end of the year. At first, we were concerned, as it was completely foreign to us and seemed as though it caused even the most conservative of those we knew to turn fanatical. However, it didn't take long for my husband, who has always possessed excellent leisure skills (just one of the reasons I married him!) to determine this was a party we needed to join. Flags for the car windows, magnetic stickers for the car, pom-poms and other symptoms of the fever appeared at our house. Even when we don't attend games, we often tailgate with friends. When not tailgating near the stadium or attending the game, our family still gets decked out in our orange-wear and we make it a family event to enjoy the game on the big screen with friends, and always with wings brought in from a well-known west Knoxville eatery and plenty of cold beverages. It's a great part of living in Knoxville."

Amye King enjoys Game Day . . . albeit in a different way. "I used to love UT football and went to every game for years. A few years ago, I decided I was OVER it. It might have been around the time of the Kiffin Experiment…. Anyway, my game day tradition now consists of running around town at record speed during the game because the stores are empty and I can do all my errands quickly."

Kelli Thompson's love of Tennessee football rivals my own. I recall a number of years ago when Kelli and her husband, Joe, purchased a ski boat. An orange boat. And they named it BOB, which was short for "Big Orange Boat." That is only the beginning. Says Kelli, "I enjoy both college and pro, but I absolutely love VOL football. My tradition is I have not missed a home football game since 1986. In 2004, it was in serious jeopardy. The last home game of the year was Kentucky the Saturday after Thanksgiving. On Monday of that week, I was put in the hospital with double pneumonia, and it was bad. I asked my pulmonologist on Tuesday when I would go home, and he said you will be here through Thanksgiving. I told him I didn't care about Thanksgiving (Joe brought me Cracker Barrel over the hospital's awful version of a Thanksgiving meal), but that I was going to the ball game Saturday. He said, 'No, you are not.' I said, 'Oh, yes, I am.' The next day, he was surprised when my friends had decorated my room in orange. So, we started working toward a plan. My uncle had a sky box and offered me a spot there, and I agreed to only stay until halftime. I was released at ten in the morning on Saturday and was at the game by noon. My doctor told Joe he was afraid I would just leave the hospital. He was right."

Volunteer football traditions can be a sacred thing. With each season, the cycle repeats itself. I, along with 100,000 other fans, flock to Neyland Stadium hoping for a big win. While we each have our own traditions and "guilty pleasures," there is one constant. We all yearn for the familiar sounds of a Saturday afternoon in Knoxville. Life, if need be, can be put on hold for a few hours. And we can all sing "Rocky Top."

*November 2014*

# GUILTY PLEASURES

## Holiday Treats and Eats

Anyone who has known me for any length of time knows that I have been on a diet for about the past thirty-five years. I have tried them all—Weight Watchers, Jenny Craig, Nutri-System, Atkins, Cabbage Soup, etc. And I have mostly failed at all of them. Last January, however, I vowed that 2014 would be different. Beginning on January 20, I gave up sugar, bread, pasta, potatoes, rice, red meat, and salt. I started drinking organic dandelion root tea and water instead of Diet Cokes. Amazingly, it worked. On November 8, I hit the half-century mark. I am down fifty pounds.

Anyone who has read this column with any regularity knows that I love to eat. A lot. I spend breakfast thinking about what I will eat for lunch and lunch thinking about what I will eat for dinner. I love great food. I prefer a good restaurant over most other forms of entertainment. I'm also a big fan of the "eating holidays"—Thanksgiving and Christmas. Given my propensity to eat, this has been a particularly difficult year.

In spite of the great odds (and the temptation of Chick-Fil-A), I have survived. Since it is the season of giving, I'm giving myself a reward—the gift of food. I have decided to pick one day to eat whatever I want. Since it has been so long since I have had "regular food," I have asked for some help. I have asked for suggestions of "holiday treats" to enjoy on my day of eating.

Tasha Blakney has suggested that I begin with something hearty and filling. "I think that you should start with sausage balls at the KBA Annual Meeting," says Tasha.

Regina Lambert suggests one of her family favorites. "My favorite holiday food is probably dry bread dressing," she says. My Mom used to break up bread the night before she made it so it could get "stale" overnight. The recipe includes celery, sage, butter, chicken broth, onion, and other spices. I love the crispy bites. I lost my mom in 2002, and dressing has never tasted quite that good since."

When I asked about dry bread dressing, she said, "I can tell you I was shocked after moving to the South and discovering that the dressing is different here. It is a debate I have every year: dry bread versus corn bread dressing. If it is my year to cook, I make both, but the dry bread dressing is my very favorite and brings back great holiday memories spent with my mom."

Other friends have suggested "sweet treats." Loretta Cravens has fond memories of her grandmother's dried apple stack cake. "Every year we would peel, slice, and dry apples in the sun. Then at Christmas, and occasionally if we were really lucky also on Thanksgiving, my grandmother would spend an entire day baking from scratch, thin, perfect, slightly spiced cake layers from her memory of her mother's recipe, and then I'd help her assemble several of these cakes. The worst part … she wouldn't let anyone have a slice for at least a full day so that the rehydrated apple filling she made from the apples we had dried could soak into the layers. At eighty-seven years of age, she now makes fewer cakes, but they are every bit as fabulous now as when I was a child."

Likewise, Katrina Atchley Arbogast has fond memories of holiday goodies from childhood. "You should definitely try peanut butter swirl candy—made with icing, powdered sugar and Peter Pan peanut butter." Katrina goes on, "My mom was an expert country candy maker. When I was law school in Syracuse, my mom would send copious amounts of it to me before exams. My northern classmates loved and affectionately called it 'candy crack.' It definitely has enough sugar and protein to keep you studying all through the night!"

Anne McKinney suggests another family-favorite delicacy. "My guilty pleasure is both in the process and the consumption of baklava (pronounced by my Arabic grandmothers as "ba' lau-wa"). First, you must gather together the mostly lovely ingredients: Lots of butter and Crisco (!), filo (or phyllo) dough (I admit I don't make my own), a combination of finely chopped almonds, pecans and walnuts with sugar, cinnamon and crushed zwieback. Set aside loads of honey, water, and lemon juice for later. Then you put on the soundtrack from "The Big Chill" and set it to repeat. It takes a few hours to brush the butter/Crisco on the layers of dough and intersperse with the wonderful filling. Finally, you cut up the sheets of deliciousness into triangles, bake (in the pan) in the oven, then ladle the honey and lemon over the top and let it sit for a while. Mmmmm, heaven!"

Carol Anne Long and Stephanie Daniel suggest beverages to complete my "day of eating." Says Stephanie, "Two words: Egg. Nog. I would never indulge in such a treat any other day, but love a little eggnog on Christmas Eve, especially the decadent Homestead Creamery brand!"

Carol Anne Long likes something a little less decadent—but equally as good. "My favorite guilty pleasure during the holidays is drinking Coke out of those little glass bottles. I think they're available all year, but for some reason, I'm only interested in drinking them during the holidays (maybe it's those cute commercials with the polar bears?). They just seem to taste better out of the glass bottles. We even leave one of the glass-bottle cokes sitting out with our Christmas cookies for Santa. We understand that Santa enjoys the Coke more than milk."

I have some great suggestions, and I am looking forward to my "day of eating." I look forward to trying all of these foods. Happy Holidays, or, better yet, Happy Eating. And pass the Alka Seltzer.

*January 2015*

# GUILTY PLEASURES

## Guilty Pleasures v. New Year's Resolutions

Several colleagues have said that they cannot believe that I am brave enough (or stupid enough) to admit to some of the things that I love. I've told you that I love soap operas, trash TV and *People Magazine*. I was more than a little delighted when Trace, who is now nine, encouraged me to purchase a *Soap Opera Digest* when we were at the grocery store "because I know that you love it ... and you can hide it from Daddy." (He then asked for a candy bar, sugar cereal, and a half-gallon of ice cream. I choose, though, to think that he was not merely trying to bribe me into buying junk food, but sincerely trying to be nice).

You also know that I love food. In my last column, I wrote about my weight loss journey and asked colleagues to give me some ideas so that I could choose one Christmas "treat." Unfortunately, I got caught up in the holiday spirit and tried every one of them. And then tried some other things that were not on the list. I learned that there is nothing like homemade baklava, that real Coke from bottles tastes fabulous, and that Stephanie Daniel makes the world's best cookies. I went down the path of sugary and carb-laden treats ... and watched the scales go up and up. By January 4 (the date that I picked as the "official end date" of the holidays), I was up five pounds.

The holidays have now given way to New Year's resolutions, another annual tradition. To my chagrin, two of this year's resolutions are opposites to my guilty pleasures. First, I vow to read at least one quality book a month and to go the entire year without purchasing a *People, National Enquirer* or *Soap Opera Digest*. In that vein, I have also resolved to watch less trash television and more documentaries and highly rated movies. So far, I am not doing so well. While my consumption of trash television has gone down (I have been too busy), I have read nothing of any value—not even the newspaper. Still, it is only January.

Second, my goal is to exercise more, eat healthy, and lose the five pounds that I gained in December, plus about ten to fifteen pounds more. While my diet is, for the most part, under control, I am not the greatest when it comes to exercise. I'm not a fan of sweating, and I don't like pain. I know what needs to be done, though. Thankfully, I have my husband's complete support on this one. He goes to Operation Boot Camp pretty much every day, and he continually encourages me to find the exercise regime that will work for me.

Hugh has suggested in the past that I take up running to lose weight. He suggested that I run a half-marathon a couple of years ago and then took the liberty to sign me up for one. I'm not sure if he meant to be encouraging – or if he just wanted my life insurance – but I didn't do it. I am not certain that I can do a marathon (or even a half), but I am going to try a sprint triathlon. Trace has done several of them, and he always gets a medal. Like a child, I am motivated by rewards. I love a good trophy.

When you see me, ask how it is going. Keep me accountable. Cheer me on at the finish line. And, if you have been frying bacon, please stand down-wind so I can savor the aroma.

Finally, I have resolved to take down my Christmas decorations prior to February 1. For someone who once took down the Christmas tree on St. Patrick's Day, this is a big deal. Last year, I made this same resolution and was able to get the decorations down by January 15. This year, however, my house still looks like a Christmas wonderland. Today, I drove through the neighborhood just to be sure that another family still had decorations on the exterior of their house. Thankfully, we are not the only family that looks like we are still waiting for the arrival of Old Saint Nick.

I will apologize for regaling you with my own guilty pleasures and New Year's resolutions. If you have read this column in the past, you know that I do not hesitate to throw my friends under the bus and expose their guilty pleasures. They have caught onto me. When I put out the call for New Year's resolutions, I did not have a single taker. Not even one. I may have to be sneakier next month …

*February 2015*

Note: In 2022, I'm still making these same resolutions, and I continue to fail miserably.

# GUILTY PLEASURES

## Snow Days (Or How to ~~Enjoy~~ Survive the Snowpocalypse)

I grew up with parents who hated snow. My dad was the UPS man, and my mom worked at a hospital, which meant snow was a four-letter word (both literally and figurately) in our house. As my mom would say, "People don't schedule being sick around the weather forecast, and packages have to be delivered." Secretly, though, I could not wait until snow was in the forecast. Although I am much older now, things haven't really changed.

I was like a kid at Christmas when the local meteorologists called for snow over President's Day weekend. Like everyone else in Knoxville, I loaded up on milk, bread, and toilet paper and prepared for a day or two of fun in the snow. By day three, any vestiges of healthy eating were gone. By day five, our "no television" restriction for Trace was out the window.

With his newly found freedom, Trace wanted to rent "On Demand" movies from Comcast. Of course, being the stir-crazed mom, I said, "Yes." Little did I know, Comcast now has a "buy" feature that shows up with the rentals. When I was looking at the "recent purchase" screen last week, I realized Trace had "rented" (i.e., purchased) twelve movies during the snowpocalypse at $15.99-$20.99 a pop. In spite of this (or because of it), we very much enjoyed the recent nasty weather at our house. Days were filled with movies, coffee by the fire, sledding, and eating various treats. Curious as to how others were faring, I emailed a few friends (since getting out of the neighborhood was impossible) to see how they were passing the time during Snowpocalypse 2015.

Chuck Atchley and Chuck Young were a little smarter than we were- their families enjoyed Netflix. Says Chuck Young, "The snow days have turned us into *Lost* junkies. We're obviously several years late to this particular party, but the kids – who were too young to watch when the show first aired – and I have been binge-watching *Lost* on Netflix. My daughter has written fan mail to Evangeline Lilly – and if you know the show, that's both sweet and kind of concerning."

Hanson Tipton likewise enjoyed watching movies. "We were fortunate to not lose power during all of that harsh weather, so on the snow days I was unable to get out of my driveway, we watched some of the movies we got for Christmas (including the *Godfather* trilogy) in front of the fire. I also got some sledding in with my daughter Maggie, who informed me that I "got massive air!" off the small ramp made by the neighborhood boys. Surprisingly, I was able to walk the next day."

Justin Martin also enjoyed being outside in the snow. He says, "Madeleine likes to 'make music' breaking icicles, and I like to toboggan on old school sleds. Snowball fights, snow angels, and snowmen. And pop-up neighborhood potlucks are great. Hot cocoa to top it off, of course!"

Tasha Blakney has enjoyed baking. "My snow day guilty pleasure is turning our kitchen into a bakery and baking sweets with our girls. Caroline and Katie created some masterpieces during snowpocalypse!"

Annette Winston and Dawn Coppock enjoyed the slow pace and solitude created by the snow and ice. Says Annette, "I mostly turn into a slug. I do try to get myself to exercise regardless of the weather."

Dawn Coppock enjoyed slowing down, as well. "I realized just how over booked and stressed I was when I had to come to a dead stop. I've been trying to pace myself better since the snow but looking at my calendar for next week I'm not sure how long that will last."

Says Dawn, "On several occasions I just sat and watched the bird feeder for well over an hour. Then, I looked up the birds I didn't know and put my observations into a science data collection site online. Nerdy, but really relaxing and oddly engrossing. I hand wrote some paper letters with stamps and everything. I was door keeper to the normally outdoor pets. The barn cat lived in a cage in my living room after she pooped in a plant when allowed to wander at large. The pets never did synchronize their potty breaks. Kind of like siblings on a car trip. I did not clean my closets and felt better when I allowed myself to stop thinking about such chores."

Dawn continues, "It is hard for high energy, high productivity people to be content as human BEINGS instead of human DOINGS. I'm working on it. That project apparently has something to do with the plumage of birds and the schedules of dogs."

Snowpocalypse 2015 was fun, and "guilty pleasures" ruled the day for many—me included. By the end of the fourth storm, though, I must confess I was ready for it to end and ready for things to go back to normal. I had cooked too much, watched too much television, and had eaten foods I normally would never eat (think Girl Scout cookies). In fact, at one point (after I had done the fourth load of wet laundry in one day), I remarked that I hoped to never see snow again. By next year, though, I am certain I will be wishing for snow again—and will be more than happy to indulge in "snow day guilty pleasures" once more.

*April 2015*

# GUILTY PLEASURES

## The Classics (Cars ... Not Literature)

I guess that I was always the son my dad never had. When I was three, my dad bought me a football and helmet. When I was four, he bought me an electric guitar with an amplifier. I always seemed to have a collection of model cars and tractors (which quickly became the preferred mode of transportation for my Barbie dolls).

Given this, it should really come as no surprise that I would grow up loving cars. Some of my fondest childhood memories revolve around them. I recall countless Saturday mornings spent "kicking the tires" on new cars with my dad at the local Chevrolet dealer. I also loved going to car shows with him and listening to him brag to me about the 1962 Chevrolet Super Sport that he had named "Maybelline," which had been stolen in 1974. I think he often hoped that he would find her, but he never did. My dad studied art in school, and he often talked of the beauty in the lines of an automobile and the craftsmanship in the manufacturing process. He instilled in me an appreciation of automobiles—as objects of beauty, of art, and certainly something more than a means to get from Point A to Point B.

I am still a fan of cars. I recall on our first date that Hugh and I discussed that his first car was a 1985 Firebird and mine was a 1986 Camaro Z-28. We discussed how cool we probably thought we were back then and whose car would have gone the fastest. (It would have been mine, by the way).

For our third date, Hugh asked me to meet him at his apartment so that we could grab lunch and then play nine holes of golf at the local golf course. When I arrived, he asked me to wait in the parking lot—he had a surprise for me. I was a bit confused, but I liked him, so I figured I would roll with it. I heard (and smelled) her before I saw her—the land yacht that was Hugh's daily driver for several years—and our mode of transportation for the afternoon. Hugh thinks I married him because he makes a mean tomato pie. Not true. I married him for his car.

Hugh's car is a 1975 Chevrolet Caprice convertible. Think Boss Hogg from *The Dukes of Hazzard*. On our way to lunch at The Pig and Pie, Hugh told me how he came to own this Detroit masterpiece (which was much cooler than the company-issued gold Buick LeSabre that he drove for work).

Before Hugh moved to Nashville, he was the resort manager for Disney's property on Hilton Head. When his lease was up on the BMW he was driving, he had to decide whether to purchase the car or lease another one.

The salesman was trying to convince Hugh that he needed a sports car and suggested that the backroads of Bluffton, South Carolina were perfect to "see what this car can do." (Anyone who has ever been in the car with Hugh knows this is laughable—because he never drives over 50 mph. But I digress).

"We were driving down the backroads when I saw her. She was parked in front of a restaurant named 'The Squat and Gobble' (or 'Gobble and Squat,' depending) with a very large 'For Sale' sign in the windshield," Hugh told me. "I knew then that it was destiny."

Hugh says he took the salesman back to the dealership, went to the Squat and Gobble, and drove away with the car. He calls her "Red Velvet" because "she looks like a big, delicious piece of red velvet cake." The car's exterior is painted white diamond, and it looks different depending on how the sun hits it. The seats are red leather, and the carpet and dash are red. She rumbles when she rolls, and she smells like gasoline and exhaust fumes. She is unique—a sight to behold. Red Velvet is Hugh's pride and joy, and, as much as he loves me, he has only let me drive her twice in the last fifteen years.

I'm not the only female lawyer in town who loves cars. Darsi Sirknen says, "A car is a thing of beauty. I was raised by a car lover and have inherited that trait. My parents gave me a 2005 limited edition Thunderbird (the 'throwback' style) for law school graduation, and it is my pride and joy. I had wanted one since they started making the Retro birds in 2002, but, as I was in school, figured that I would never be able to buy a new one. 2005 was the last year they were made, which is one reason why that car was such an awesome surprise (I didn't graduate until 2006). To this day, she has barely 2,300 miles on her."

LeAnn Mynatt also loves classic cars. "Dad was in the car business. When a '67 Camaro 327 RS convertible crossed his path, he jumped on it. Despite Mom's protest. That was 1974. When I turned sixteen, I got to drive it—some. I was sixteen, and never knew whether it was me, or the Camaro, which was attracting the boys, but I wasn't taking any chances. I still have the car today; of my three cars, the 1967 has the fewest miles. I love how it drives. I love how heavy the door is when it closes. I love listening to its AM radio at night, and pick up Cincinnati and Chicago radio stations. Mainly though, I love that connection with my dad."

For all of us, it seems that the appreciation for classic cars runs deeper than the car itself. It is the connection to the people that taught us to appreciate their beauty. Recently, Hugh and I missed Sunday School so that we could take Trace to a car show at West Town. Hopefully, Trace will remember that day as fondly as I remember those days with my dad.

*May 2015*

# GUILTY PLEASURES

## Donuts or "Do Nots"?

Many of my "guilty pleasures" center around food. I have a real weakness for bacon. I also cannot pass up anything with pecans. I'm a big fan of Cheetos. And I love vanilla ice cream. Fortunately, I am not tempted by donuts. Occasionally, I like a raspberry filled Krispy Kreme, heated, with a dollop of vanilla ice cream—but that is very rare. In a house full of donut lovers, I am known as the "do not."

Unlike me, Hugh is a connoisseur of donuts. When we first met, he told me how his mother would often cut stale Krispy Kremes into pieces and fry them in butter for breakfast. He also told me that he could eat an entire box of hot Krispy Kremes in the one and a half miles from Kingston Pike to his house after high school football games. He was proud of the fact that he purchased a house in Nashville that was within walking distance of the Donut Den.

Trace inherited Hugh's affinity for hot Krispy Kremes. I knew we were in trouble early on when, at the age of one, would wrinkle his nose and say "Mmm" every time we pulled into the Central Baptist parking lot because he could smell the doughnuts. Last summer, he wore a Speedo brief that said "Will Swim for Donuts" on the behind. He meant it.

Hugh's 48th birthday recently fell on the same date as Childhelp's biggest fundraiser. I wanted to surprise him with something special, but didn't know what to do at an event where there would over 500 people. A friend, knowing Hugh's love for donuts, suggested we make a donut tower. While I knew that I would not eat them, I also knew that it would be something he would love. And it was a bonus that Krispy Kreme currently has doughnuts with honeybees on them. (Hugh is a beekeeper, so this was perfect.) At the end of the event, over 300 doughnuts from the tower were consumed, but I remained a "do not."

Curious as to whether other people were pro-donuts or "do nots," I sought opinions from some of our colleagues. I found that, by and large, our colleagues are passionate about donuts.

Carol Anne Long is definitely pro-donut. "I LOVE donuts! They are pretty darn close to my favorite food. For me, it's Dunkin all the way. And definitely glazed over cake. My kids are donut fiends, too. Janie loves pink iced with sprinkles, and JR loves Boston cream. Jason is the lone wolf—he prefers Krispy Kreme."

Tasha Blakney is also a fan. "I just had the best donut I've ever tasted in Philadelphia at the Reading Terminal. It was glazed. Topped with vanilla. Then coated with Fruity Pebbles. Amazing. My hands start shaking just thinking about it again!"

Per Loretta Cravens, "There is really only one donut worth going out of my way for ... Ralph's Donuts in Cookeville. All Tennessee Tech Alumni will be familiar with this legendary local treasure that has been owned and operated by the same family for all of its fifty-plus years. While I don't know what their secret is, they make the best donuts—ever. Those who know Ralph's will fork over a couple of bucks for an apple fritter big enough to share, but which they will covet as if it were Gollum's "Precious" from J.R.R. Tolkien's *Lord of the Rings*."

Keith Burroughs disagrees. "Richy Kreme glazed are better than any other donut in the world. Located in Maryville. I think this is their 68th year in business. One location. Made by hand daily. Open until everything sells out (usually just after lunchtime)."

Doug Toppenberg prefers cake donuts. "My grandfather was a dairy farmer in rural Maine, and every morning he would get up at five AM and have what he called his "little breakfast," which consisted of coffee and a cake donut with peanut butter, before going to the barn to milk the cows. After he was done with his chores, he would come in for a big breakfast with the rest of the family. We are imprinted with memories and sensations at a young age, and to me the only real donut is a cake donut, not the puffy, glazed ones that Krispy Kreme makes."

Garry Ferraris, on the other hand, prefers beignets. "Although perhaps not technically a "donut," my hands-down favorite is a beignet served up hot out of the fryer at Dippin' Donuts on Kingston Pike."

Jim Cornelius and Heather Anderson prefer Krispy Kreme.

Says Heather, "I never knew about Krispy Kreme until I moved to Knoxville for college! Growing up, my favorite was donut holes from Shirley's Bakery in Jackson, which is still open for business! While I have grown to love the Krispy Kreme, or as we refer to it in my house, "Hot Doughnuts Now," my favorite kind is not hot doughnuts – I like it when the glaze has dried and is a little crispy."

Jim's love for Krispy Kreme goes back a little further. "When I was young, on several occasions, we sold Krispy Kreme doughnuts by the dozen to raise money for our Little League baseball team. We piled several team members into the back of various pick-up trucks and went door to door on Saturday mornings through the neighborhoods selling doughnuts. That was a long time ago, and it was a different era (riding in the back of pick-up trucks), but it is probably the reason I am a Krispy Kreme doughnut person today."

Says Jim, "My favorite is a glazed raspberry filled doughnut. My second favorite is the blueberry filled. But can someone tell me why they have to put powdered sugar all over the blueberry filled doughnuts?!? Why can't they make a simple glazed blueberry filled doughnut like the raspberry filled doughnut! The blueberry filled are really great, but the powdered sugar outside makes a real mess. My third favorite is chocolate glazed, and my fourth favorite is the plain glazed doughnut."

While a few of our colleagues were decidedly "do nots," most were pro-donut. Maybe my problem is diet-guilt. As Dawn Coppock said, "You can eat about eight glazed donuts without slowing down and without feeling full. Eight donuts are the calorie equivalent of a fork truck pallet of Cheetos."

*June 2015*

# GUILTY PLEASURES

## The Playlists of Our Lives

I recently attended a memorial service for a dear friend. One of the opening speakers talked about music as a part of life and the influence of music on my friend's life. In between the very moving tributes from his friends and family that gave even greater insight to my friend as a person and the impact he had on so many lives, various musical groups performed my friend's favorite songs and other songs that had special meaning to him. In addition to songs like "Ubi Caritas," "My Soul is a River" and "Light at the End of the Tunnel (Aslan's Song)," it included songs like U2's "Beautiful Day," Billy Joel's "Vienna," and Kevin Abernathy's "Visiting." Each of the songs had some special meaning, and all of the lyrics talked about the appreciation of life. The service was a touching playlist of his life, and it summed it up perfectly. It was truly a celebration of a life well-lived.

Lyrics speak to us, can be about us, and ultimately bring us together.

It also really made me think about playlists … what is on my playlist … and what would be included in the playlist of my life. I recall an old Clint Black song from the 1990s where the chorus included the line, "Ain't it funny how a melody can bring back a memory / Take you to another place in time / Completely change your state of mind." No truer words have ever been spoken. At least in my opinion.

I tend to associate certain songs with events in my life, and certain types of music tend to lend themselves to whatever mood I happen to be in. If I am feeling melancholy, I tend to listen to something like Joni Mitchell. And I may or may not have been caught speeding on one or more occasions while listening to Journey's "Separate Ways / Worlds Apart."

I'm certain this probably explains why I have 2,128 songs downloaded onto my phone (hence no more room for photos). I love music – and always have, and my musical tastes tend to be a bit varied. I was recently traveling with a much younger colleague, who was subjected for 10 hours to the songs from the playlists on my phone. They included everything from Nicole C. Mullen to Kid Rock, beach music to Southern rock, country to indie rock, Elvis to the eighties classics, and more recent tunes like Carly Rae Jepsen's "Call Me, Maybe," Idina Menzel's "Let It Go," and

Meghan Trainor's "All About that Bass." At one point on the trip she remarked, "Your musical tastes are probably the most – shall I say – ADHD that I have ever heard."

I prefer to think of my rather diverse musical tastes as the sign of a complex thinker, and I was certain other lawyers are much the same. I polled a few of our colleagues to see whether their musical tastes are varied or whether they tend to listen to music in one genre.

I learned that Darsi Sirknen's musical tastes very much mirror my own. "My music taste is all over the place," says Darsi. "I love everything from Rachmaninoff to Tupac, from Hank Williams, Sr. to Def Leppard. It's not uncommon for my iTunes playlist to switch from Taylor Swift to George Strait to Stone Temple Pilots to a song from a Disney movie. People who don't know me well might be surprised to see me driving down the road, bass thumping, engaged in an epic karaoke rendition of 'California Love.'" Heather Anderson agrees. "I love Biggie Smalls, which surprises A LOT of people. And Ludacris, too!"

Cheryl Rice can likewise relate to a diverse musical playlist. "I love music," says Cheryl. "I have very eclectic taste. The song that I can't get enough of is the Pharrell Williams' song, 'Happy,' which my youngest, Natalie (age twelve), and I would turn up loud and sing at the top of our lungs every time it came on the radio last year (when it was relatively new). She and I labeled it "our song" and, still to this day, when we hear it, we can't help but join in. It's become a family thing, too, so it's on everyone's playlist, and if it comes on when we are cooking dinner or are on a family road trip or other outing, everyone joins in and sings a part. It is infectious!"

I'm glad to know I am not the only one with eclectic musical tastes. And I am not the only person who associates songs with certain life events and great memories. Lyrics speak to us, can be about us, and ultimately bring us together. If I had to put together my own playlist, I would hope that it is diverse and varied because that would indicate I live a life that is full. And it certainly would include "Happy."

*August 2015*

# GUILTY PLEASURES

## Lawyer Musical Playlists, Part Two

No doubt, you have heard about the Lawyerpalooza Music Festival that will be held on September 24. At Lawyerpalooza, you will get to hear some of your favorite lawyers (and others) displaying their musical talents— sharing favorite songs and a wide variety of musical styles. While this lawyer will not be taking the stage (my son remarked that I have a voice that can make dogs howl), we have lots of talented musicians in our midst. Although I cannot sing, I love music—I always have and always will. Last month, I wrote about my own personal playlist and the songs that seem to define certain moments in my life.

Music seems to be a common theme for me as of late. I just returned from our annual vacation to Pawley's Island, staying in a house with 14 Nystroms and honorary Nystroms. Every year, Hugh's brother, Frank, develops the "Nystrom Family Playlist," which includes songs that become "our songs" for the week. In years past, we have been treated to such musical gems as Telly Savalas' "Who Loves Ya Baby?," Maria Muldaur's "Midnight at the Oasis," and Charlene's "Never Been to Me." The song that Frank chooses as "the song" for the week is played from sunrise until well into the night so that, by the end of the week, everyone (including the children) knows every word to the song. And, oftentimes, we hope that we can go until Christmas without hearing "the song" again.

This year, instead of one song, though, we had an entire playlist. Frank chose a medley of Carolina beach tunes, including songs like "Myrtle Beach Days," "Carolina Girls," and "Holy Moly." He also included tunes by The Carpenters. If we didn't know the words to their greatest hits before the week began, we do now. Trace's personal favorite was "Close to You." Instead of singing "you" in the chorus, though, Trace (whose actual name is "Hugh III") sang to all of the little girls "Just like you, they long to be close to Hugh." It was a kinder, gentler musical week. And Trace learned the meaning of the eyeroll.

Music plays an important role in our family. We have the songs we love, the songs we play ad nauseum, the songs that define us, and the songs that make us smile. After last month's column, I heard from a lot of you and realized that we are not alone.

Amelia Crotwell, too, enjoys music. Says Amelia, "This is pure confession, but I love to listen to Yanni's live music. It is a total guilty pleasure and embarrassing to admit. I listen in the car or on walks, generally alone, when I want to be uplifted. I love the emotional qualities." Annette Winston also prefers calming music as of late. Annette says, "Lately, I listen to anything that will calm down my newest grandson, who was born on April 9. I turn on the Sonos and put on classical, and sometimes Crosby, Stills for him. It's amazing how much he likes music!"

Kim Burnette's musical tastes are a little more "rock and roll." "I still love classic rock and soul: Beatles, Stones, Chicago, Temptations, Four Tops, Blood, Sweat & Tears, The Guess Who, etc. I also have a tremendous appreciation for great singers like Roy Orbison ("Oh, Pretty Woman"), Art Garfunkel ("Bridge Over Troubled Water"), Dionne Warwick ("Walk on By"), Carole King ("So Far Away") – just to name a few. My favorite listening spot is in the car – you can listen as loud as you like – and sing along if you want."

Kyle Baisley's musical tastes are likewise a little more "old school;" however, his "old school" is 1990s-early 2000s. "I would say the music that makes me the happiest would have to be something like Hootie & the Blowfish or Dave Matthews Band. It takes me back to high school/college and fond memories. One song that I could literally put on repeat for the rest of my life would be "#41" by Dave Matthews Band. It always calms and relaxes me."

Kyle goes on to state, "Something that my choice of music for studying throughout might surprise people is college/law school. I wrote some of my best papers and outlines with Nirvana's Unplugged album playing on a loop in the background. I used to joke with people that it was about the only thing more depressing than whatever I was studying/writing! For some reason it just got me in the zone."

Sherri Alley is decidedly more current in her musical preferences. "My music guilty pleasure is anything by Taylor Swift. I feel it is a bit immature of me to love her music so much, but I can't help myself. In particular, her song "Shake It Off " makes me break into an exuberant dance much like that of my pre-school son."

While our musical tastes may vary, music unites us. Again, I hope that you will plan to attend Lawyerpalooza on September 24 at The Standard. Whether you like the classics or whether your tastes tend to run toward the more contemporary, there will be something for everyone. It promises to be a night you won't forget.

At Lawyerpalooza, you will be delighted to hear some of your favorite lawyers (and others) displaying their musical talents—sharing favorite songs and a wide variety of musical styles. Don't miss it!

*September 2015*

# GUILTY PLEASURES

## Those Things We Cannot Live Without

I never understood the appeal. Growing up, our house was filled with the aroma of freshly brewed coffee. My dad fired up the old Mr. Coffee at promptly five o' clock every morning. He and my mom would then split a full pot of Folgers (the kind that came in the really big can). When the first pot was gone, my dad would make a second and then fill a large green Stanley thermos. And when he arrived home at night, he would make yet another pot of coffee, which was his beverage of choice with dinner. He truly believed "the best part of waking up is Folgers in your cup."

In law school, a number of my classmates would drink coffee like water in order to pull an all-nighter. I enjoyed the caffeine buzz from iced tea (and Diet Coke) but never really got into the coffee craze. It smelled nice but never tasted quite as good as it smelled. It really didn't have much appeal to me. And then I met Hugh.

Hugh is a coffee fanatic. When we first met, he traveled for Disney and practically lived at Starbucks. Every weekend, he would ask me to meet him at Starbucks near where I lived. Often, he would surprise me at work during the week with a cup of coffee. And I pretended to like it because I liked him. And then, one fateful day, I decided I did like it. A lot.

Trace is proof that coffee does not hurt a developing baby. Before I knew that I was pregnant, I drank an entire pot of Cuban chicory coffee every morning before work. Now, I make sure I am up at least an hour and a half before I have to leave for work. I spend my first hour every morning on the sofa with my dog, the local news, and my coffee. It really starts my morning off right.

My current favorite is Iron Brew Sticky Bun coffee, which I purchased in bulk in South Carolina during our recent vacation. My morning is not complete unless I have two twelve-ounce cups of it, with a little Coffee Mate Sugar Free Sweet Cream creamer added in for good measure. It is my guilty pleasure and truly is the one thing I cannot live without.

I am not alone. Scott Griswold agrees. "I'm with you. The one thing I cannot live without is coffee."

Amanda Busby also laments that she cannot live without coffee. "Mine is coffee too, but my husband says a close second would be my cell phone.

I could text him right now and argue with him about that, but that would really just prove his point. But I would definitely say coffee is the top of my list. It is just about the perfect beverage. It wakes you up, and it is warm. I probably like it so much because it reminds me of my mother and grandmother who spent a lot of time together talking and drinking coffee. My grandmother told me that I could not drink it unless I drank it black and that is still how I like it the best. I remember signing an agreement with one of my mother's friends when I was about twelve agreeing not to drink alcohol, smoke, or drink coffee before I was twenty-one in exchange for her friend's agreement to pay me $100. This was probably one of my first experiences with contracts. In any event, I did not get the $100."

Zach Farrar's guilty pleasure—and the one thing he cannot live without—is culinary. "The Cheeseburger, French Fries, and a Milkshake at Hoskins Drug Store in Clinton, Tennessee is one of my favorite things. Hoskins Drug Store is a local drug store with a full-service soda fountain. It truly is a step back in time. It is a place where the community gathers daily to meet, visit, and seek the refuge that only a homemade milkshake can provide. Lawyers, politicos, small businessmen, county farmers and their children can all be found at Hoskins at any given day. We all know that we can go to Hoskins for a cheeseburger, fries, and milkshake and for just a moment we can forget the worries of the day and enjoy something that we all crave … good food and good friends. The connection that Hoskins provides is a strong one. Despite our differences we gather together in a local drug store and have a simple milkshake, talk about the local high school football teams and if we are lucky the local celebrity, Freddie, may even stop by to assure us the Clinton Dragons will win that week. My faith in humanity is restored daily from this time-honored ritual at Hoskins and the friends that meet at Hoskins whether I've just met them or I've known them for years feel the same."

While some of us enjoy food and drink, others cannot live without technology. In response to the query as to what she cannot live without, Katie Lane says, "It's such a cliché. It is my smartphone."

Robyn Jarvis Askew enjoys another form of technology. "I cannot live without SiriusXM Channel 20 – E Street Radio. I do not really need to explain why, everyone knows Bruce is the Boss."

Ruth Ellis had a rather unique response when asked about the thing she cannot live without. "I keep my gardening asparagus fork with me (in my car) almost all the time. I love gardening and don't like weeds at my house or at my children's houses. Thus, I am always ready!"

We all have one thing that we cannot live without—that thing that makes life a little more enjoyable, no matter what it may be. Mine happens to be coffee … and I hear Starbucks calling my name.

*October 2015*

# GUILTY PLEASURES

## Turkey, Traditions, and Other Fun Things

I've written about the fact that I love November. The football Vols have traditionally done pretty well in November. Tennessee basketball begins in November. My dad's birthday was in November, which always meant really good German chocolate cake (his favorite, and especially the ones that were homemade by my grandmother) and pecan pie (made by one of his favorite cousins). My wedding anniversary is in November. And, of course, there is Thanksgiving.

Growing up, Thanksgiving was always great fun. It began with watching the Macy's Thanksgiving Day parade, followed by lunch at my Mamaw and Papaw French's house. My grandmother was a fantastic cook. My plate was always loaded with perfectly cooked turkey, cornbread dressing, and maybe one or two tablespoons of green beans – just so I had something from the vegetable food group. Dessert always included chocolate pie and my favorite – banana pudding. When the Detroit Lions took the field, we usually headed for the car and off for round two.

"Lunch" at my Grandmother Morie's usually started around four thirty p.m. (because she kept on schedule about as well as my ten-year-old). Grandmother Morie's house was always full of people – lots of relatives, family friends, and the "randomers." It was comforting because it was always the same. Our celebration was our own family tradition.

Several years ago, Hugh and I decided to create our own tradition. We picked up the Williams-Sonoma Thanksgiving cookbook and decided to make every dish in there and share them with (a) any relatives who happened to be in town and (b) any friends who were brave enough to try my cooking. Those recipes have become some of our favorites and have become staples in our holiday meals.

We tried to create our own "tradition" with these meals; however, according to Trace, we had no real "Thanksgiving traditions." I solicited some input from friends as to their own traditions in hopes that we could copy them.

My friend Sherri touts the merits of starting the season with the Macy's Day Parade. Chuck Young suggested the Thanksgiving movie. We decided to give their ideas a try. For the last two years, we have watched the Macy's

Thanksgiving Day parade from start to finish. Hugh and I had fond memories of it from childhood, and we hoped that Trace would enjoy it, too. He wasn't sold on it at first, but quickly changed his tune. We told him Hugh's friend, Matt, works as a handler with the Disney balloon, and "Where's Matt?" became our own "Where's Waldo?" Trace also was amused when he realized Justin Bieber (who he constantly ridicules) was actually lip-synching (and very badly). For the past couple of years, we have watched the parade from start to finish, and I was a tiny bit excited when, on a recent trip to New York, Trace was pointing out things he recognized from the parade.

We have also tried making a movie a Thanksgiving tradition. This one has been a bit harder, as my taste in movies and Trace's taste in movies is as different as night and day. (Case in point: He took me to see *Paul Blart, Mall Cop 2* for Mother's Day.) While the movies may not be great, I do enjoy creating our own "traditions."

*November 2015*

# GUILTY PLEASURES

## The Anguish of Good and Bad Books

Reading is a guilty pleasure for me. It is also the source of great anguish. A book – good or bad – is like a bag of Lay's potato chips. Once I start, I cannot stop. I become so engrossed in the stories and the characters that I tune everyone and everything else out. For that reason, I hate to read.

When I was heading to Orlando for a business trip a couple of years ago, Hugh encouraged me to read the first of the *Hunger Games* trilogy. He knew that I had seen the movie, and he told me, "The books are so much better than the movie." Reluctantly, I took the first book with me. On the flight from Atlanta to Orlando, I read half of it. Because I was certain I would finish it before the week was over, I ran into the bookstore in the Orlando airport as they were shutting the doors to purchase *Catching Fire* (even though Hugh had it at home). During that week, I read every chance I got—during breaks in the conference sessions, at night after the conference ended, and into the wee hours of the morning.

On the last day of the conference, I finished the second book. Then, I checked out of the hotel and headed to the airport three hours early … to purchase *Mockingjay*. I gladly sat in the airport for three hours so that I could read. When my plane landed in Knoxville at midnight, I drove home … and then continued to read. Until I finished the book the following morning.

I notice that my little apple has not fallen far from the tree. Trace received the latest *Diary of a Wimpy Kid* book on the day it came out. He literally would not put it down. I had to forcibly remove it from his hands so that he would do homework. I confiscated it when I found him reading in his room at midnight. He read it until he got out of the car for school the next morning. And he finished it later that evening.

I've wondered if other people have the same issues. Do they become so engrossed that they cannot stop reading once they start? Or do they read like me on a normal day, choosing only lighter fare that requires little concentration?

Kacie McRee is much like me when it comes to larger books. "I like to read suspense thrillers at night. They can become a 'guilty pleasure' at times. Sometimes, I know I should be doing something else, but I just have to read because the book is so good."

Cheryl Rice agrees. "I love to read – always have! I read sporadically now; it's either feast or famine for me. I really enjoy fiction, mystery, history, and historical fiction. No sci-fi or fantasy, please! The best book in a long time was *Unbroken* by Laura Hillenbrand which was, believe it or not, recommended to me about three or four years ago by my husband's grandmother (who is now ninety-two)."

Justin Martin likes books in series and similarly cannot put them down. "I've really enjoyed the *Outlander, Hunger Games* and *Insurgent* series. That's of late!"

Reading is a "guilty pleasure" for Tasha Blakney, as well. "I love to read, and I'm always reading something. Over time, my tastes have changed, and I read a lot more nonfiction than I used to. But honestly, I read a little of everything. From young adult (I want to know what our girls are reading, and they have great taste!), to sci-fi, to bestsellers, I am all over the map. Which reminds me. I love reading travel books too!"

Heather Anderson and Mary Beth Maddox have reading habits that are more in line with my normal reading habits. Says Heather, "I'm not sure I should share this, but I used to hide my *People* magazines and only read them on airplanes, then I noticed that Pam Reeves is an avid *People* reader and I decided I shouldn't hide it. She's done pretty well!"

Mary Beth Maddox agrees. "I don't have time to read – except for the million magazines I subscribe to which cover anything from culture to cooking to fashion to home. After reading all day, it is hard to delve into something else. However, the two best books I've read at the beach in the last few years are *Gone Girl* and *Girl on the Train!* While I prefer something with less of a time commitment, Bill, on the other hand, literally reads a book a week."

*December 2015*

# GUILTY PLEASURES

## Guilty Pleasures Reversed: Holiday Bah-Humbug

I love holidays. All of them. I have decorations for Valentine's Day, Easter, Memorial Day, the Fourth of July ... and the list goes on and on. Hugh says that if there were decorations available for Labor Day and Arbor Day, I would have those, too. My absolute favorite, though, is Christmas.

I love Christmas. Really love Christmas. I spend days on end after Thanksgiving decorating at our house. I had a closet built in our bonus room to hold all of my Christmas decorations. On the first pretty day following Thanksgiving, you are likely to find me hanging out of our second story windows, attempting to affix Christmas wreaths to the windows. Hugh says our house "looks like it puked Christmas."

I love everything about Christmas. Almost. Nothing turns me into Scrooge quicker than The Elf on the Shelf. That cute little stuffed toy is my own personal nemesis. I hate him. Despise him. It didn't start out this way, though.

I first saw The Elf on the Shelf about fourteen years ago at Junior League's Tinsel and Treasure, and I fell in love – so much so that I purchased elves for each of my nieces and goddaughters. When Trace was born, Hugh and I immediately purchased our very own Elf for Trace. Like about ninety percent of all families with an Elf, we named our Elf "Buddy."

Life with Buddy was good for the first five years. Buddy would make an appearance when the Christmas decorations were removed from the closet, would perch himself on a high shelf in our family room next to a jar of moonshine and would remain there until the Christmas decorations were put away. We told Trace that Buddy stayed there because he could see the entire room. The fact that Buddy stayed next to a jar of moonshine was Hugh's and my own little "inside joke" about "Buddy the Drunken Elf." Trace was happy with this … until he started school.

When Trace started kindergarten, The Elf on the Shelf became a regular topic of conversation in the weeks between Thanksgiving and Christmas. Trace would come home, telling me how the other children's elves would move around their homes and would get into all sorts of mischief. He would regale me with tales of elves that fished in the toilet, ate candy in pantries, rode in Barbie cars, and did all sorts of other fun things. For the first couple of years, we had Trace convinced that our Buddy was much better behaved than other elves and that he liked the comfort of his "spot." Of course, that only worked for so long.

For the past couple of years, Trace looks every day for Buddy to see where he has moved and whether he has gotten into some sort of mischief. When I was out of town for work last week, Buddy did not move, which caused great distress in our house. Trace was sure that something was wrong with Buddy and that he needed to be "cheered up." This weekend, we purchased Buddy a suitcase full of t-shirts from the "Claus Couture Collection," as well as a Cousin Eddie bathrobe and slippers. Trace is certain that these will inspire Buddy to engage in a little holiday mischief. Every time Trace asks what I think the Elf will do, I cringe. When I read Facebook posts about elves that have met their ends at the hands of the family dog, I secretly smile. That smiling stuffed toy has officially turned me into The Grinch.

I was certain, though, that I was not the only "holiday junkie" who could be turned into Scrooge by a tradition that should be fun but somehow had become anything but. I quickly realized that I am not alone.

A number of our colleagues turn Grinch-y when the holiday music starts. Says Ian Hennessey, "No other song seems to be able to cancel out Christmas cheer for me quite like the Beach Boys' 'Little Saint Nick.' Specifically, the line repeated many, many times throughout the song: 'Christmas comes this time each year.' Really? A holiday with a specific date occurs … annually? Is this supposed to be profound? I'm gonna need to run, run reindeer all through the mall if I have to hear this one. more. time. Plus 'Oooo Little St. Nick' (over and over again) is just sappy sweet awfulness. Baby Jesus needs to sleep, not hear you croon over Santa's hot rod sled."

Lisa Hall, Alicia Teubert, and Nick McCall go Scrooge when "Grandma Got Run Over by a Reindeer" hits the airwaves, and Lisa particularly dislikes "Blue Christmas" with Porky Pig. Brian Lapps hates "Christmas music played on mall organs (the kind that used to be sold in shopping malls)." In that same vein, David Eldridge is not a fan of "the endless sappy jewelry TV ads."

Cindy Wagner, LeAnn Mynatt and Susan Fendley are not fans of holiday traffic, particularly around the malls, while Justin Martin hates pine needles. Donald Farinato is not a fan of Christmas lights. He lists, "Setting up Christmas lights. Working on getting all the timers to work properly. Trying to figure out why some are blinking … and some are out … and where the receipt is so that I can take it all back to the store. In the traffic."

Brad Morgan goes batty over certain holiday attire. Says Brad, "I hate Christmas Jammies pictures. Christmas Jammies videos. Christmas Jammies songs. Plastered everywhere. By everyone. All of the time. Without respite."

Heather Anderson is not a fan of holiday cards, or rather ill-timed holiday greetings. "I hate getting Christmas cards before it's even December (I like to mail mine on Christmas Eve from the airport!); Christmas decorations for sale in stores immediately after Halloween; perfect Christmas day photos."

Others share Heather's sentiment for the rushing of the holiday season. Says Tasha Blakney, "I hate Christmas decorations out in store BEFORE HALLOWEEN. Come on, people. One thing at a time." Nick McCall agrees. "I absolutely hate Christmas decorations in place well before Thanksgiving – e.g., at Halloween or earlier; really, people?"

Zach Farrar hates the timing for another reason. "The most annoying thing for me during Christmas is the idea that Christmas ends December 25. There are twelve days of the Christmas season in the liturgical calendar. Christmas is not over December 25, it is only beginning. So, leave those Christmas decorations up, make a joyful noise, and continue the merry making and the cups of cheer for the entire twelve days of Christmas!"

My fellow Grinches, may your hearts grow three sizes this holiday, and may all of you have holidays that are merry and bright.

*January 2016*

# GUILTY PLEASURES

## Baking Fun and Pinterest Fails

Since I was a kid, one of my guilty pleasures has been baking. In 5th grade, I was the Dandridge Elementary School 4-H biscuit baking champion (although Hugh says he has been waiting nearly two decades for me to make real biscuits for him). By middle school, I graduated to cakes. I took the Wilton cake decorating classes that were offered through our local Extension office and learned how to decorate pretty much any character cake that could be made. (If the legal career did not work out, I had always said that I would decorate cakes in the bakery at Food City.) My love of baking continued into high school, and I always made chocolate yule log cakes for our French classes (and even took orders for them from my friends and their parents).

Baking has always been fun. It's not an art ... it truly is a science. I put my skills (and ability to follow a recipe) to good use in college, as I majored in chemistry for a very long time. I didn't love the lectures or the theories. I loved the experiments...the measuring, the combining, the heating everything to just the right temperature. It was really just like baking, and I was good at it (at least that portion).

Although my time for baking has decreased, my enjoyment has not. I delight in making cakes and pies, and breakfast at my house is often a "straight-from-the oven" mixed berry pie. I read cooking magazines and collect cookbooks, always looking for new cakes and pies to bake. My favorite things, though, are the features on the internet called "Pinterest Fails."

I'm not a Pinterest fan. It's a little confusing and a bit overwhelming, but Yahoo (which I can navigate) often has Pinterest Fails. Pinterest Fails are photographs that have been submitted after a reader has tried to bake something that was posted on a Pinterest board. The original is always some grand and glorious creation, and the reader's interpretation is always something absolutely abysmal. The photograph usually says "Nailed It," but it should more aptly be titled "Failed It." I am so meticulous when it comes to baking that I never had a Pinterest Fail. Until I did.

My office was recently planning our Christmas party, and I volunteered to make my famous Peppermint Red Velvet cake. I've made this cake so many times that I can almost make it in my sleep. Since I now work for the Institute of Agriculture, I decided that the cake that I was making would be made with all locally sourced and organic products. I visited several local markets, where I purchased organic cake flour, organic sugar, Cruze Dairy Farm buttermilk, and a host of other ingredients. In fact, the only thing "unnatural" that I purchased was the red food coloring, which was a rare and precious commodity on a Saturday afternoon in the middle of December.

I whipped up my cakes (I usually do three or four layers per cake) on Sunday afternoon before we had to go to a church function. My plan was to come home from church and frost them with the peppermint cream cheese icing. I was so far ahead of schedule that I did not think twice about going out to dinner before we came home after the church function. Big mistake.

I should have known that I was in trouble when I tried to place the first layer on my red Le Creuset cake stand. When I turned the first layer onto the stand, the layer fell apart, and the top of the stand separated from its pedestal base. I thought I was going to cry.

I actually think I did cry when the succeeding layers, too, crumbled when I removed them from the pans. Hugh suggested that I use the frosting to cement them. "Nobody will notice," he said. And he was wrong. (Too bad you cannot see the photo!)

Hugh asked what I was going to do in the face of such a disaster. It was, after all, eight o' clock on a Sunday night. He suggested that I go to Ham and Goody's the next morning, purchase a cake, and then put it on my newly repaired cake stand. He said I could just smile when people said it was good. I was not going to be defeated, though. I headed out to the grocery and purchased all new ingredients for the cake (albeit the regular flour, regular sugar, etc.)

I ran into a little hiccup, though, in trying to find red food coloring. It is pretty much impossible to find red food coloring on a Sunday night two weeks before Christmas. But you can't have red velvet cake without it. After visiting five different stores, I finally found some ... and proceeded to buy every single bottle they had. Driving home, I also saw lights on in the Bed, Bath & Beyond. I knew that I needed an extra cooling rack. While I was there, I spotted some "professional" cake pans, which apparently have a rough surface to keep cakes from sticking. I bought three of those, told the cashier my disaster story, to which he replied, "Ma'am, that will be the most expensive red velvet cake ever made."

I started Peppermint Red Velvet Cake Part Two at about midnight. Thankfully, they turned out beautifully the second time around. In the end, the cake stood as tall as a wine bottle (when on the stand) and weighed about fifteen pounds. *(See photo.)* The icing had about four pounds of sugar, and I lost count as to the number of sticks of butter that I used. People at my office said it tasted great (I wouldn't know because I was so disgusted with it that I really did not want to eat it).

But I had a great story and a beautiful cake!

*February 2016*

# GUILTY PLEASURES

## Sweet Temptations

As a general rule, the Nystroms try to adopt healthy eating habits. We have been known to eschew bread for weeks on end, and pizza and fried chicken are a thing of the past in our house. But we have not always been successful when it comes to bypassing dessert. When sugar is present, our collective willpower goes out the window.

I recall making a chocolate trifle a couple of years ago. It included chocolate brownies with chocolate chips, chocolate pudding, whipped cream and English toffee bits layered in a trifle bowl. Hugh called it "heaven in a bowl," but I called it "chocolate sin" because it was sinfully good. I had made it for a dinner party, and unfortunately (or fortunately), the bowl was not empty at the end of the night. Hugh put the leftovers in Tupperware and placed them in the refrigerator. Try as I might, I could not sleep ... for the leftovers were calling my name.

"One bite," I told myself, as I crept down the stairs. Sometime later, Hugh found me, sitting on the floor in front of the refrigerator, with an empty Tupperware container and a spoon. I may or may not have even licked the container clean. Needless to say, desserts are one of my guiltiest pleasures.

Although I am not a fan of Crème Brulé or cheesecake, almost everything else is fair game. I love coconut pies and cakes, and I never pass up banana pudding. Hot blackberry cobbler with vanilla ice cream is always a hit with me. And I even like fruitcake.

I am happy to report that I am not alone

Esther Bell says, "I don't just 'like' dessert. I LOVE dessert. Favorite part of any meal. Or all by itself. Anytime. Day. Night." Esther continues, "Picking a "favorite" is really challenging for me. But cookies are probably the one dessert I'd wish for if I were stranded on a desert island. Wade's Bakery thumbprint cookies were the best! Wade's was a grand and wonderful bakery in the ooooooooold Oak Ridge mall, back in the day when that mall was a robust square-shaped strip mall, and Walgreen's had a fountain counter, and life was still magical at Christmastime. This tiny girl toddled along with her mother and siblings in her frilly anklets and patent-leather shoes, because back then, going to Oak Ridge to go

Christmas shopping was a BIG DEAL. And we always ended the day by visiting Wade's Bakery with everyone getting one thumbprint cookie apiece. It was SO delicious, partly because of the anticipation as we strolled by the bakery numerous times while shopping and the scents rolling out of that place were delicious beyond description! YUM!"

"Alas, Wade's closed down when the Oak Ridge mall became an "indoor" mall, but the good news is, some years ago the Knoxville News-Sentinel was allowed to PUBLISH the Wade family's secret recipe for thumbprint cookies, and my mother clipped that recipe. Now it is one of my most treasured documents in the house! I make them only on special occasions because they are so tempting to me. I confess I have absolutely no control and will eat two dozen in a day without the slightest twinge of guilt! HAHA!"

Esther is also a fan of a dessert that could be classified as healthful (pumpkin is a fruit, right?). "UT Bakery's pumpkin bread is in my top ten. I've loved that bread since college and always enjoy a slice whenever the opportunity arises to be close to a retail outlet that sells the pumpkin bread on campus."

Heather Ferguson is also a fan of desserts. "Sadly, I love sugar. My favorite cake of all time is Litton's Strawberry Cake. I could just die thinking about it right now. Of course, there are family favorites that I could think of if I took the time, but my top dessert of all time is their strawberry cake! What makes it great is the dense, moist texture of the cake; the real strawberries buried in the cake layers and the frosting, and the perfect balance of sweet and tart all in one forkful."

Cindy Wagner is also a cake fan. "I love Ham and Goodies Red Velvet Cake. I once ate the entire cake for my birthday and ate my sister's entire cake for her birthday (in the same month ... lol)."

While some of us are "cake fans," Joanie Stewart is an ice cream fan. Joanie says, "I love a caramel sundae with no whipped cream. I tell myself that since I don't get the whipped cream, the calorie count is minimal. Keith will go to Sonic and get these for me. Best. Husband. Ever. My dog, Elvis, always hopes I will share it with him. He is an eternal optimist."

Annette Winston is an "equal opportunity" dessert eater—she likes both cake AND ice cream on occasion. She also cannot say "no" to pie. Says Annette, "Lately I watch my sweets so much that I reserve my sweet calories for one very special ice cream from Cincinnati. It's Graeter's Black Raspberry Chocolate Chip. It is phenomenal. As far as around town, I have quickly come to love the bundt cakes at Nothing Bundt Cakes. But my favorite restaurant dessert has to be the coconut cream pie at Litton's."

It's good to know that I am not alone when it comes to dessert. I try not to keep them in the house, but sometimes I cannot resist. This year, when the option presented itself, I bought forty boxes of Girl Scout cookies (mostly Thin Mints, which are safely in my freezer). But I think I may need one—or two, or a sleeve—now. As the old saying goes, "Life is short. Eat dessert first."

*April 2016*

# GUILTY PLEASURES

## Memorial Day Traditions

Memorial Day. The "Unofficial Start of Summer." And a day's guilty pleasures can suddenly become new traditions.

Hugh and I never really had any Memorial Day traditions. Sure, there had been years where we went to the random cook-out, saw a movie, or even cleaned out the garage. But Memorial Day took on a new twist a few years ago.

Several years ago, we were home on Memorial Day, with no plans. Coincidentally, several of our neighbors with kids about Trace's age had no plans either. We decided to create our own fun – a "progressive party."

Our fun started down the street, with a cereal bar and pancake buffet for the kids and mimosas and Bloody Mary's for the grown-ups. For several hours (and until it got hot), the kids played a massive game of "hide-

and-go-seek" through the neighborhood. When the weather warmed up and the kids wore out, we took the party to another house so that the kids could swim. Each family brought a hodge-podge of snacks, but the hit of the party was the key lime pie. While I am certain that the key lime pie was good by itself, the kids got the bright idea to use Doritos as spoons and treat the pie as a dip. A new sweet/sour/salty treat was born.

After several hours, the water-logged kids headed to our house for grilled hot dogs. Knowing that I was cooking for a friendly crowd, I decided to add a twist to the hot dogs – bacon. I wrapped the hot dogs with thinly sliced bacon and threw them on the grill. If you have never tried this, I highly recommend it. The hot dogs were perfect and really didn't need chili or condiments. And calories and fat don't count on a holiday.

As the years have passed, our tradition has morphed a little, but the spirit of the party has not changed. Now, we spend the Saturday of Memorial Day weekend with the Toqua District of the Boy Scouts placing flags on the graves at the Tennessee Veteran's Cemetery on Lyons View Pike. Our progressive party may or may not happen on Memorial Day, depending on what is going on. Instead of just a few families with children, our party now includes the entire neighborhood. Hot dogs are a staple for the party, and we always include key lime pie and Doritos (although we now have a kid's pie and an adult's pie – too much double-dipping by the kids with the Doritos). The grown-ups look forward to getting together with our neighbors every year, and the kids – who go in a million directions during the school year – get the opportunity to "reconnect" as summer begins. The weekend is a great reminder of those we have lost defending our freedom and a blessed celebration of our freedom.

While I love our traditions, I love hearing about my friends' traditions as well.

Nick McCall's traditions have also morphed throughout the years. Says Nick, "Until five years ago, Memorial Day was spent visiting my late mother in Franklin, Tennessee. For the last five years, though, Memorial Day Monday – or at least, several hours of it – have been spent at the East Tennessee Veterans Memorial located in World Fair's Park near the L&N STEM Academy. Beginning shortly after dawn, a group of volunteers read each of the names – all 6,222 of them, from 35 counties – slowly and with dignity. This small gesture seems a very appropriate way to commemorate the reason why the holiday exists. I hope to participate again this year."

Mary Ann Russell's celebration has also changed through the years. "As 'empty nesters,' for years we went to the beach with three other couples on Memorial Day; and, while we haven't gone to the beach in a while, we try and do something, whether it's go to the mountains for the weekend, or just get together at one of our houses. We're continuing the tradition this year, with those that can going to the home of one of the couples in North Carolina," says Mary Ann.

LeAnn Mynatt is changing it up this year. Says LeAnn, "Usually, I'm headed to the beach with my family. Memorial Day in South Carolina on the beach is perfect: not too hot, not too crowded (think 4th of July). But this year, I'm headed to Grand Teton and Yellowstone national parks with two of my cousins. We're celebrating a cousin's birthday, and we wanted to do something different. I've never been, and I can't wait."

Memorial Day is the "Unofficial Start of Summer." It is also the official day to remember those who fought, defending our nation. As you enter this Memorial Day weekend, I hope you take the opportunity to pay respects to our war dead by enjoying the freedoms they fought to preserve.

*June 2016*

# AROUND THE BAR

## Pursuing Justice and Promoting the Public Good: Former U.S. Attorney Doug Jones' Prosecution of the 16th Street Baptist Church Bombing Cases

By the early 1960s, Birmingham had earned a national reputation as a tense, violent and racially segregated city, in which even tentative racial integration of any form was met with violent resistance. The city had no African American police officers or firefighters, and few of the city's African American residents were registered to vote. Violence was a regular occurrence, and the city had earned the nickname "Bombingham."

By 1963, Birmingham was a powder keg, ready to explode.

In the spring of that year, the famous "children's marches" were organized by Dr. Martin Luther King, Jr., and others to integrate the public facilities of downtown Birmingham. Civil rights leaders and marchers protesting segregation faced Birmingham Public Safety Commissioner Bull Connor's high pressure fire hoses and police dogs. Dr. King delivered his "I Have a Dream" speech. That same summer, the U.S. Court of Appeals for the Fifth Circuit ordered Birmingham's public schools to integrate, and a federal judge approved Birmingham's desegregation plan. On September 10, 1963, two African American students enrolled in Graymont Elementary School in Birmingham.

On September 15, 1963, hate prevailed over everything at the 16th Street Baptist Church.

In the early morning hours that day, four members of the Ku Klux Klan – Thomas Edwin Blanton, Jr., Herman Frank Cash, Robert Edward Chambliss, and Bobby Frank Cherry – planted a minimum of 15 sticks of dynamite under the steps of the church, close to the basement. Five young girls – Sarah Collins, Addie Mae Collins, Denise McNair, Carole Robertson, and Cynthia Wesley – were in the ladies' lounge, preparing for a youth-led worship service. At approximately ten twenty-two in the morning, the explosion from the home-made bomb blew a hole measuring seven feet in diameter in the church's rear wall and a crater five feet wide and two feet deep in the ladies' lounge where the girls were preparing for the service. At ten twenty-two in the morning, four innocent lives were brutally snuffed out. Only Sarah Collins survived.

On that day, Doug Jones was a nine-year-old, living in the suburbs of Birmingham.

The shockwave created by this senseless tragedy was felt around the world and proved to be a pivotal point in the struggle for civil rights in this country. "Once that happened, I think so much of America's consciousness woke up and said, 'Oh, my God – this is not just a question of culture anymore, it's a question of hate.' When you remember those deaths and the bombing, what you really think back and do remember is the changes and the catalyst. I think it was one of the things that caused Congress to act and caused the American people to start changing their hearts and minds," says former U.S. Attorney Doug Jones.

Although the identities of those involved were widely known among law enforcement, witnesses were reluctant to talk, and physical evidence was lacking. Consequently, the first prosecution did not occur until 1977, when Alabama Attorney General Bill Baxley brought charges against Chambliss for the murder of Denise McNair. Chambliss was found guilty by the jury and sentenced to life in prison. Doug Jones saw the trial unfold.

"As a second-year law student, I cut classes and watched from the balcony of the courtroom as the trial of Robert Chambliss unfolded. It was one of the most amazing things I've ever seen. The history, the power, that the law can change things for good, that public-service lawyers can have an effect on the world around you. I never imagined that twenty-four years later, I would stand in the same courtroom as the United States Attorney for the Northern District of Alabama and finish prosecuting the 16th Street Baptist Church bombing cases," says Jones.

In the early 1990s, the FBI discreetly re-opened their investigation into the bombing, resulting in the unsealing of some 9,000 pieces of evidence previously gathered by the FBI and which had been unavailable to Bill Baxley. In May 2000, the FBI publicly announced their findings that the bombing had been committed by Chambliss, Cash, Blanton and Cherry. At the time of the announcement, Herman Cash was deceased; however, Blanton and Cherry were still alive. Both were arrested.

U.S. Attorney Doug Jones was the prosecutor. The Blanton and Cherry trials took jurors on a journey through history. Some of the jurors had lived during the time of the bombing, while others had only learned about it in school. The prosecution used black-and-white video footage and photographs to walk jurors through the black-and-white world of

1960s Birmingham, a constant, albeit subtle, reminder throughout the trial of a once-segregated city.

The juries' historical journey started in Birmingham in 1957, when Rev. Fred Shuttlesworth attempted to enroll his children in the all-white Phillips High School. He and his wife were met by an angry mob, about ten of whom proceeded to attack Rev. Shuttlesworth in front of the school, all of which was captured on film. Witnesses identified one of the attackers as Bobby Frank Cherry, then a near-thirty-year-old Ku Klux Klan member who resorted to violence to stop integration. Jurors then learned through photographs and testimony that 1963 and the months leading up to the bombing were pivotal times in Birmingham.

The Blanton jury heard evidence of the defendant's hatred for blacks and his membership in the KKK. Tapes were played of conversations between Blanton and an informant in which he joked about "bombing my next church." Blanton and Chambliss were identified as holding some type of satchel next to the steps of the church in the weeks leading up to the bombing. Finally, the jury heard Blanton himself, on tape, admitting to being part of the meetings where the bomb was planned and made.

In the Cherry trial, there were witnesses, including an ex-wife, a granddaughter, and a former co-worker, who gave compelling testimony about his admissions to them over the years.

In both trials, the prosecution's case concluded with their most powerful witness – Sarah Collins Rudolph, the lone survivor of the bombing. She testified about going into the ladies' lounge. She stated that, as she went to wash her hands, she turned around and saw Addie Mae tying the sash of Denise's new dress. The explosion then trapped her beneath the rubble, unable to move and see.

While testifying on the witness stand, Jones asked what happened after the explosion. "I called out for my sister … Addie, Addie, Addie," she said, her words echoing in the courtroom.

"Did she answer you back?" "No," she said softly.

"Did you ever see her alive again?" "No," she said as she wiped back tears. The prosecution rested.

On May 1, 2001, the jury convicted Thomas Edward Blanton, Jr. of murder for his role in the bombing. A year later, on May 22, 2002, another Birmingham jury convicted Bobby Frank Cherry, who was the last surviving suspect in the crime.

Reflecting on the cases, Doug Jones says, ""It is impossible to express the emotion felt by the prosecution team and the satisfaction gained from being a part of these cases. I have said many times that I wish every lawyer, at least once, could work on a case that meaningful to so many people. The Blanton and Cherry cases remind us that we as lawyers work in a service profession."

The Birmingham bombing holds a special place in civil rights history because of the randomness of its violence, the sacredness of its target, and the innocence of its victims. Because of the work of investigators and the prosecution team led by Doug Jones, the killers of four innocent little girls were brought to justice.

Doug Jones reflects, "Our job is to seek justice for our clients no matter what the obstacles or delay. Justice delayed does not have to mean justice denied."

We will welcome Former U.S. Attorney Doug Jones as the keynote speaker at the KBA's Annual Supreme Court dinner on September 7. You will not want to miss this very special evening.

*August 2016*

# GUILTY PLEASURES

## Finding Adventure in the Great Outdoors

Ralph Waldo Emerson once wrote that "the health of the eye seems to demand a horizon." For many lawyers, the horizon line extends only as far as the office door. And some of us have been fine with that.

As a kid in Jefferson County, summer weekend days were spent picking up sticks that had fallen from the pecan trees in the backyard (and if you know anything about pecan trees, you know they lose a lot of limbs) and working in the gardens at various relatives' farms. (My dad had a saying, "If you don't pick it, you don't eat it.") It was hot. It was dirty. And I hated every minute of it.

At twelve years old, I vowed that I would someday have a job where I had continuous air conditioning and would never have to go outside again. The practice of law seemed like a good option; and for a number of years,

I shunned the Great Outdoors. In fact, my only foray into the Great Outdoors was a bike trip down the Virginia Creeper Trail, which I not-so-affectionately dubbed "The Virginia Creeper Hell." As I have gotten older, though, I've started to need a horizon—a sight line that goes beyond the office.

Recently, Hugh and I were invited on a five-day sailing trip around the Abaco Islands. We were told that we could bring no more than a duffle bag, would not have air conditioning or Wi-Fi, and that we would be responsible (at least somewhat) for catching our own food. Although I was excited to spend a week with friends, I approached the trip with a bit of trepidation. While the website for the charter company suggested that you "take a photo on each day to watch the stress melt away," I wasn't quite sold on the idea. I had no idea what to expect.

As it turns out, though, it was one of the best trips I have ever taken. It was everything that was promised ... and then some. The ocean was clear (you could see all the way to the bottom), and it was so calm that we were able to paddleboard from the boat to the neighboring islands. We visited sparsely inhabited islands, where our footprints were often the only ones that were visible. We did catch our own food (although not every day), and it was some of the best seafood I have ever eaten. My favorite part of every day came in the afternoon, when we lifted the anchor, hoisted the sails, and moved to a new location. Each day, I would sit on the top of the boat, with the wind blowing on my face and basking in the beauty of the sand, sea, and sky.

I spent an entire week without makeup and without ever drying my hair. If I had on shoes, I was over-dressed. And it was bliss.

While I found peace in the ocean, Annette Winston says that she finds peace in the beautiful mountains that we call home. "This year, 2016, has been my year to renew my appreciation for the Great Smoky Mountains National Park. I have taken on the Superintendent's Challenge, and currently have fifty-seven miles on my log. Spending time outdoors every day became a habit when I got a dog in 2010. Our hour- long daily walks have reminded me, though sometimes in itchy ways, that it is restorative to one's soul to be outside."

Annette continues, "Something else happened that took me back to the Smokies. A new friend decided she wanted to try hiking; and since I had some experience, she goaded me into going with her. We started with an easy hike, Rainbow Falls. She immediately was hooked. Whenever both of us are available on the weekend, we will drive to Sevier County, find a trailhead, and start walking. We try not to let anything (other than grandchildren) interfere. In these few short months, we have added another hiking buddy and taken my niece and her boyfriend with us when they were visiting over a weekend. Lately we've started discussing planning how to do all the trails. Our longest hike so far is a mere eleven miles, but neither of us were very taxed by that, so we will be doing longer ones, I'm sure. I've discovered new trails already and look forward to discovering many more I have yet to traverse."

"There is an inner peacefulness you feel in the woods that extends into your week after you return. It is hard to explain to someone who hasn't tried it. The effort of slogging up a mountain (really, up and down and up and down and up and down) reinvigorates one in a way that most other types of exercise cannot do. Work harder and the relaxing is all the more rewarding," says Annette.

It has been rewarding to get out—to step outside and seek adventure in the Great Outdoors. Whether you expand your horizon in the mountains or on the sea, I've learned that you can find peace and happiness along the journey to that horizon.

*August 2016*

# GUILTY PLEASURES

## Outdoor Fun

For months, Hugh, Trace and I have been running around our house, yelling, "The British are coming! The British are coming!" Although Trace is quick to point out that Paul Revere likely did NOT say that, the British are coming to our house. Our friends Rob and Claire, along with their two children, are visiting Tennessee from Bristol, England. It will be Claire and the children's first visit to our fair state, and we want to make it memorable.

Trace has suggested activities like Dollywood and Hillbilly Golf; however, Hugh thinks we can do much better. Given that we live in the shadows of the nation's "Most Visited National Park" and that this area is known to be one of the most beautiful in the world, I'm certain there are lots of activities we can do that show off the beauty and the culture of our region. But I have been at a loss as to what to do.

Those who know me well know two things: one, I am a planner and get very antsy when there is no plan in place, and two, I am not outdoorsy at all. My outdoor activities are limited to gardening and the occasional round of golf. I refer to the Virginia Creeper Trail as the "Virginia Creeper Hell," and I have never been on anything remotely resembling a hike.

Given those two things (and the fact that I really want our friends to have a great experience here), I have solicited some advice as to relaxing and fun outdoor activities.

Rick Carl, an avid outdoorsman, suggests that even those of us who do not regularly enjoy the great outdoors can have a great time in the mountains. Says Rick, "Ever since my days at Maryville College, I have been a lifelong backpacker, canoe, fly fishing, bicycle kinda guy. When my wife, Joanna, moved down here from the Washington DC area, the first time she ever laced up hiking boots in her life was a hike up LeConte. She then gracefully waited for me to catch up at the top. We take an evolving group of twelve up there every year and spend the night. Great memories – many, many sunsets at Clifftops. Son Rick made his first trip at age eight. We also enjoy biking the greenways in Knoxville and along the Little River in Walland and Townsend. And, for the past year, Jo and I have gotten into kayaking – so far this summer, we have been on Calderwood Lake in the Slickrock Creek area, floated the French Broad and are eyeing the Little

River. The thing I find fascinating is being able to pull out of the driveway, take a hike, bike, or float in another world, and still make it home in time to grill salmon. That is a perfect day. Along with some Ibuprofen."

Crista Cuccaro also enjoys outdoor activities. "My husband and I enjoy outdoor activities immensely. We feel pretty lucky to have such great amenities in our backyard. We like to hike, paddle board, swim, and mountain bike (and my husband road bikes). Hiking looks different depending on how much time we have. Sometimes, we just head over to Ijams for a short walk, and sometimes we make a day of it and head out into the Smokies. Just recently, my husband went on a long road ride, and I met him in the park with a picnic. We convened at the Wye and went swimming. That was a great way to cool off when it was super hot in town."

Continues Crista, "We also love paddleboarding in Meads Quarry. As for mountain biking, we just tried this recently for the first time and took advantage of the awesome trails in South Knoxville. I find outdoor activities to be refreshing – it gives me a sense of renewal. And trying mountain biking was exciting! It was also meditative – as odd as that sounds, I was so focused on the trail (and not falling!), that I couldn't think about anything else."

Heather Anderson has a practical view. "I enjoy outdoor activities as long as there's a REAL bathroom (no porta-potty) – and a place with air conditioning for cooling off. The national parks in the U.S. only have porta-potties – they look like real facilities but are not. Just a structure over a porta-potty. But I do like to hike – in fact, before having children, I would often hike a different trail in the Smokies every weekend. I even biked Cades Cove! Now, I don't even get to shop in Sevierville because I am racing go-carts or in an arcade spending all of my earnings. But it's worth it, and when they are a little older, I hope they will enjoy hiking or at least shopping with me. If not, I can leave them home alone."

Robyn Askew's outdoor activities hit a little closer to home for me. "My outdoor activities consist mainly of screened-in porches, with a door very close to an enclosed climate-controlled room. I find such porches relaxing, especially with friends who are lethargic."

These are some great suggestions, and I am looking forward to seeing our friends. Wish us luck as we show off East Tennessee's finest!

*September 2016*

# GUILTY PLEASURES:

## Tennessee Football Game Day

I dread the end of summer. Thankfully, the University of Tennessee football relieves my doldrums. This year, gameday has been a little bit more fun. Team 120 has been tremendously entertaining (and maybe slightly frustrating), and I have been on the edge of my seat at every single game. They've been called the "Cardiac Kids," and I am pretty sure that I will suffer a heart attack before this year is over. But my own cardiac event will have nothing to do with the team ... and everything to do with my newfound love. Gameday food.

For years, I have loved walking across campus from my parking lot because I have always been greeted by that familiar smell ... frying onions at Hot Dog Heaven. For those unfamiliar, Hot Dog Heaven is the food vendor on the sidewalk across from the library and the Haslam College of Business. While I am normally a pretty health-conscious eater, I cannot resist Hot Dog Heaven. Every fall, it is like running into an old friend that you haven't seen in a while. And it is good.

This year, though, I've found a few other culinary treats that make gameday extra special.

The season opener on a Thursday night was a real treat. UT was closed, which meant that I had the day off, which was good. Hugh was sworn into Knox County Commission, which was even better. And the Vols were taking the field with a Top 10 ranking. It was a day for celebration. The day was so busy we literally forgot to eat. Until we got to the game. At basketball games, Trace often gets the Calhoun's pulled pork nachos. They always smell great, but I have been able to resist. But September 1 was a day for celebration, and I decided to celebrate with Calhoun's nachos. For the uninitiated, the pulled pork nachos are tortilla chips smothered with pulled pork, baked beans, beer cheese and jalapenos. They are every bit as good as they sound ... truly a culinary delight.

The next week, we played Virginia Tech at the Battle at Bristol. It was billed as the largest college football game in history, and it was quite the spectacle. Hugh called it "Football Meets NASCAR Meets County Fair." It was a once-in-a-lifetime experience, and I vowed to take it all in. Literally. Between the three of us, we tried turkey legs, wood-fired pizza (with chicken, wing sauce and bleu cheese), pork rinds, barbecue pork rinds, and funnel cakes. But we hit the Holy Grail with the deep- fried Oreos. I had always heard that they were good, but I was skeptical. Suffice it to say, I had no idea what I was missing. The deep-fried Oreo was like a beignet filled with gooey cookies and cream—unlike anything I had ever tried ... and utterly fantastic. Weeks later, Hugh and I are still talking about them. We can't wait to find them again.

On the weekend of the Florida game, we celebrated Ag Day at the Institute of Agriculture. I've always said that I love working for the UTIA because, among other things, we eat very well. Ag Day is no exception, as the students always prepare ribeye steak sandwiches and chocolate milkshakes for the attendees. I'm always glad to indulge because "it's for the students," after all. This year, we were blessed with great weather, resulting in a huge crowd at Ag Day. By the time I made it to the food area, we were out of steak sandwiches. We were also out of chocolate milkshakes. I was left with two choices: (1) don't eat, or (2) find something at the stadium. It was an easy choice. I was delighted to find that one of the concessions stands serves foot-long corn dogs. I have always loved a good corn dog, and this one was especially good. I was not disappointed.

As we head to the back end of our schedule, I am sure that I will find more culinary treats. To combat my new-found "guilty pleasures," I recently purchased a Fitbit, which I hope will stave off the need for a defibrillator.

Volunteer football traditions can be a sacred thing. And the "Cardiac Kids" are making it exciting. While we each have our own traditions and "guilty pleasures," there is one constant. Life, if need be, can be put on hold for a few hours each Saturday afternoon in the fall. And we can all "Eat, Drink, and Sing 'Rocky Top.'"

*November 2016*

# GUILTY PLEASURES:

## Turkeys, Trees, and Treats

The Nystroms are not talking turkey this year. Literally. The Thanksgiving turkey has received an official pardon for 2016 – we are skipping Thanksgiving. Yep – We have gone straight from Halloween to Christmas, and I could not be happier.

I am a holiday decorator. Every year, the pumpkins, ghosts and goblins are followed by the turkeys and pilgrims. This year, though, we are going directly from Halloween to Christmas since we will be heading to Hawaii for the festivities surrounding the seventy-fifth anniversary of the attack on Pearl Harbor the first week in December.

While I will miss the great Thanksgiving food, I'm not terribly disappointed otherwise. I've always been a big fan of Christmas. Even as a kid, I remember turning the Fisher-Price Little People barn into a Santa's workshop diorama. I remember spending countless hours every year decorating the Christmas trees (we usually had at least two) while my dad, a/k/a Scrooge, stood in the background and said, "If it were up to me, we wouldn't bother with all this mess. What's the use of putting up all of this crap if you are just going to take it back down?"

In the past, I have always started Christmas decorating on the day after Thanksgiving (because it takes me that long to do the Thanksgiving dishes). Every year, Hugh – a.k.a. "Scrooge II" – complains about the "Christmas crap." This year, though, we were both singing "Mele Kalikimaka" on November 10, when the first of the decorations made their appearance.

Decorating is one of my holiday "guilty pleasures." I absolutely love to decorate, and I turn on the trees every morning as soon as I get out of bed. I have even been known to leave the trees up well into February (on one particularly crazy year, they stayed up until St. Patrick's Day). Sometimes, I cannot bear the thought of the house without them.

As much as I like decorating, I also like Christmas movies and music. My car radio is now set to the Sirius XM Christmas station, and I have already been watching Christmas movies on Comcast's On-Demand. I'm anxiously awaiting the Freeform *25 Days of Christmas* and *Fa-La-La-La Lifetime*.

I absolutely love all of the Christmas movies – everything from the old school *Rudolph the Red-Nosed Reindeer* to Mario Lopez in *Holiday in Handcuffs*. (Confession, I've already watched that one twice, and it is only mid-November.) One of our family favorites, though (and perhaps because it hits pretty close to home with our crazy family), is *National Lampoon's Christmas Vacation*. I'm a big fan of Cousin Eddie, Aunt Edna, and the whole Griswold clan.

Once again, my friends and colleagues volunteered their own holiday "guilty pleasures." Ashley Lowe says, "I have five words for you – Mayfield's Peppermint Stick Ice Cream. I cannot wait until it hits the grocery store shelves every year, and I eat it as often as possible until it disappears from the shelves. Fat and calories don't count at Christmas, right?"

We all have traditions that make the holiday season special. Our own little guilty pleasures become holiday treasures, creating memories that will last a lifetime. And to quote Frank Sinatra, "Mele Kalikimaka is Hawaii's way to say Merry Christmas to you!"

*December 2016*

# LIFE HACKS

## Mele Kalikimaka and Mele Vacation: Life Hacks to Make Travel to Paradise Even More Heavenly

My mind is still in Hawaii ... even if my body (and laundry) are in East Tennessee. Last night, our family returned to Knoxville from what I can only describe as the "trip of a lifetime." We have been fortunate enough to visit some incredible places and meet some fabulous people, but nothing quite compares to Oahu.

Last year, Hugh and I decided that we would travel to Oahu for the seventy-fifth anniversary remembrance of the attack on Pearl Harbor. After booking our airline reservation and a room at Aulani (Disney's resort in Ko' Olina), we decided that, other than the Pearl Harbor remembrance, we would travel without an agenda. While that is a pretty daunting task for a type-A planner like me, it made the trip much more enjoyable. It is still hard to wrap my mind around such a grand adventure, but I wanted to share a few things I learned on this trip.

**1. Luggage scales are your friend.** Several years ago, I invested in a hand-held luggage scale (think scale attached to the top of a coat hanger) at AAA. Since then, I have always weighed my luggage before leaving home to make sure that I did not get an unwelcome surprise (overweight luggage fee) at the airport. For some reason, I decided to take the luggage scale with me to Hawaii. It is about palm-sized and fit in my purse. *This was a very smart move.*

**2. If you are on a very long flight, be sure that there are some "new release" movies that you have not seen.** I enjoy watching movies while I do paperwork and work around the house. Prior to our trip, I was able to catch up on all of my work from the office and home, plus decorate the house for Christmas. When we got on the plane for the eleven plus hour flight from Atlanta to Honolulu, the new movie selection included most of the movies that I had just paid to rent. *Very bad move on my part.*

**3. Although you can purchase tickets on your own through the Park Service, use a tour guide when visiting Pearl Harbor.** Hugh booked our initial visit to Pearl Harbor through a tour operator, who picked us up at the hotel and drove us to the Visitor Center. Along the way, he gave us interesting tidbits about the area surrounding Pearl Harbor, Hickam and Schoffield. He also gave us the history and took us to the Cemetery of the Pacific (a.k.a. Punchbowl...because it is in the crater of a volcano). He had our tickets to the Arizona Memorial (which are for a specific viewing time) and to the USS Missouri. While we ditched the tour at the end to stay longer at Pearl Harbor, the time with the tour operator was money well-spent.

**4. If your hotel offers cabanas for rent, do it.** Aulani is notorious for being crowded at the pool and on the beach and even has signs posted that you must remain with your belongings, lest the pool police remove them. Friends who had recently returned recommended renting a cabana. While Aulani was not crowded during our visit, I convinced Hugh to rent a cabana anyway. We had covered chairs (great for a redhead like Hugh), a cabinet to lock our belongings, and food service. It made a really great day at the beach even more enjoyable because we didn't have to worry about sunburn or leaving our belongings unattended. It was a little bit of luxury that has helped face the mountain of laundry that now greets me.

**5. Waikiki = Miami.** We spent two days of our vacation in Waikiki for the Pearl Harbor remembrance events. My preconceived notion of Waikiki was that it would be much like Myrtle Beach, with lots of tourists and souvenir shops. I could not have been more wrong. Although crowded, Waikiki's streets were lined with high-end shops like Gucci and Prada, and locals are glad to meet Tennesseans because Elvis is still revered there.

**6. If you get the chance to go to an event that celebrates our nation's veterans, do it.** We were fortunate to be able to attend a Gala that was hosted by Hawaii's governor to honor the Pearl Harbor survivors. The survivors received a "hero's welcome" and were treated like rock stars. Garth Brooks and Trisha Yearwood were in attendance, and they were lining up like the rest of us to be photographed with heroes from our nation's Greatest Generation. My "proud mom" moment came when Trace declined being photographed with Garth Brooks (one of his favorite country artists) in order to speak with more veterans.

**7. The remembrance ceremony on December 7 is something I will never forget.** We left our hotel at three in the morning to get in line for the parking lot, which opened at four in the morning. Along the way, we stopped the car twice for Trace to throw up (too much rich food and too little sleep). We got in line for the bus, which took the first 500 people there to see the ceremony live at Kilo Pier. Trace threw up again. I offered to take him back to the hotel so that Hugh could go to the ceremony. Hugh told Trace to "man up" and push through. I am so glad he did. The remembrance, which began at seven thirty and had a fly-over at the exact moment that the first bombs fell in the Harbor, was spectacular. The keynote was delivered by Admiral Harry Harris, Commander of the Pacific, who grew up in Morristown, TN. It was, without a doubt, the most eloquent and inspiring speech I have ever heard. We are in good hands with Admiral Harris in the Pacific. To quote the Hawaiians, I had "chicken skin" from the start to the end,

**8. Sometimes, the best discoveries are not planned.** During our trip, we drove to Oahu's North Shore to see Waimea Bay. When we got there, we learned that the Pipe Master's Triple Crown of Professional Surfing had just started. We were able to watch the pros practice with eight to ten-foot waves, and we even met Patrick Parker, the artist who did the artwork for the promotional materials. We also happened upon the Waimea Valley Botanical Gardens, where we hiked to see the waterfall (and where large portions of the *Hunger Games* movies were filmed).

**9. The locals recommend the best food.** While in Haleiwa on the North Shore, one of the locals we met suggested that we try Opal's Thai for dinner. He said that the owner would recognize us as "non-locals" and would suggest dinner options for us. The restaurant seated about fifteen people and didn't even have a restroom. It was, hands down, the best meal we had in Hawaii. The owner sent out five dishes, and each one was better than the last. And the total cost, including tip, was $80.

**10. Luggage scales are your friend.** When it came time to leave, we definitely had more than we had when the trip began. In the end, I was able to distribute clothing and souvenirs so that each of our three bags weighed exactly forty-nine pounds (including one that contained nothing but our dirty laundry). The rest of our purchases should be arriving back in Knoxville via UPS later this week.

We are tired and a little more than jet-lagged, and a mountain of laundry awaits. But our trip to Hawaii was indeed the "trip of a lifetime." I was worried that we would run out of things to do; but, in the end, we didn't do half the things we wanted to do. Along the way, I learned a few things that will make our next trip (*hint, hint, Hugh*) even better. Until then, Mele Kalikimaka!

*January 2017*

# LIFE HACKS

## Getting Fit and Eating Healthy in 2017

Despite the devastating fires in the Smokies, the civil unrest in our country and around the world, and despite the deaths of many iconic figures from my childhood (Prince, George Michael, David Bowie, Carrie Fisher ... and even Debbie Reynolds--- I was a fan of the VHS exercise tape "Do It Debbie's Way"), 2016 was a great year in the Nystrom house. Trace excelled in school and swimming. He was elected to Student Council. He even acquired some measure of acclaim with the Facebook videos, "The Trace Nystrom Show," which got over 30,000 views. Hugh continued to do great things at Childhelp and was elected to Knox County Commission after running a fantastic campaign. And I continued in a job that I love at the UT Institute of Agriculture, which Hugh describes as "the best lawyer job in all of Tennessee."

We were able to spend a week on a sailboat in the Bahamas with friends during the early summer, and we took the trip of a lifetime to Hawaii for the 75th anniversary of the attack on Pearl Harbor. We were blessed with good health and great happiness. It was an incredible year for our family. And it shows. It shows on my face, as I smile and laugh a lot. Unfortunately, it also shows on my waist, hips, and thighs.

While blessings were plentiful last year, so was good food. When the calendar rolled to January 1, I realized that I had gained a whopping twenty pounds in 2016! I knew that I needed to take action. My motto for 2017 is "The Year of Living Lean." To jumpstart my program, I decided to rid the house of the food that I deemed "bad." Cleaning the refrigerator was easy, as most of the "bad" food was well past its expiration date. The Christmas candy dishes were a bit harder. I made Trace eat the remaining chocolate covered cherries so that I would not be tempted, and I resisted the urge to eat the five remaining Lindor chocolate truffles that were in another one.

It's been a little more difficult, though, to find motivation to eat healthful foods and to exercise. It seems that I can always come up with the "I don't have time" or "we don't have any good food" excuses. Hugh says his favorite of my excuses is "It's a good TV night."

I'm trying to make healthy living a habit again, and I needed some "life hacks" to combat the excuses that always seem to get in my way. I sought out some advice from others who are much better at this than me.

Annette Winston makes good health a priority. Says Annette, "There are two rules by which I must abide to stick to healthy eating and adequate movement. For the food: Don't buy it. Leave it at the grocery store. Feel smug as you leave said grocery store without the junk food. For the exercise: Book it. I put every workout for the week on my calendar on Sunday afternoon. Then I do them. If someone wants that time for something else, I just reply, 'I'm sorry; I have a conflict at that hour.' It works like a charm."

Stephanie Daniel also has two great rules. "First, I try to eat the same things during the day every day and pack all of my breakfast and snack food for the week on Sunday nights. Second, I keep a packed workout bag in my car, so I can go out for a lunch or end of day workout if my schedule allows."

Rick Carl offered this advice. "My wife Joanna and I like (read: try when it's not nine degrees) to get up in the morning and walk down to the lake and back, about two miles. When I get home at night, Jo and I like to eat healthy and cook together – even on weeknights. Consequently, we tend to eat late, but it doesn't matter when we have music on the stereo, wine in healthy moderation, me on the grill and Jo on the sauté, and dance moves when we pass in the kitchen (we're active, right?). We like to think this keeps us from just getting pizza or tacos and watching *That 70's Show* reruns. We also try to hike/bike, etc., most weekends even if it's just a short trip. Disclaimer: our kids are college age and older, so we've thrown plenty of pizza and tacos down the basement staircase to the Zombie youth that used to invade our house every weekend, and we no longer have to attend sports, theatre, Scouts, concerts, meetings, etc. ten times a week. And, yes, we miss it terribly. Well, except for maybe Camp Buck Toms with the Scouts."

Alyssa Minge offers this advice. "For eating: I like to grab juice on my way out the door in the morning to avoid stopping for a sugar-filled coffee and/or snacks at Starbucks on the way in to work (so easy to allow yourself this indulgence, and so tempting ... mmmm ... Starbucks). It's all about convenience for me – grabbing an apple, orange, or banana so it's handy is so much easier than attempting to avoid candy jars around the office without a healthy alternative to put in its place."

She also says, "For stress, I have to get up and walk periodically. Getting ice water and moving even a little help break up the day and tension. Even if I don't take lunch, leaving the office for a few minutes can do a great deal to re-energize me! I also have a great group of friends who I don't see often enough, who I am trying to remind myself to meet for lunch or a drink periodically so as to allow time to take care of myself and my friendships. "

Finally, per Alyssa, "For health and sanity: Especially with billable hour requirements, very few people feel they can afford to stay HOME when sick. So, hand sanitizer (!!) stays near my desk, along with Lysol wipes and disinfectant. I tend to organize my desk at least once a week and wipe everything down at the same time – I get an idea of what is on my desk, create and update my "to do" list, and scrub everything down at the same time. (A bit OCD, yes, but it works for me.) I try to take the same approach at home ... With two little ones, I don't have much time to tackle what seem like big projects. This weekend, I cleaned out a few drawers in my kitchen. A little each day does a lot in the long run!"

Sherri Alley has found a way to make working out easier. "I found a gym close to my house that allows members to let themselves in between 5am and 11pm (Koko Fit Club). Its workouts take the hassle and guesswork out of training. An MP3 guides you through fifteen minutes of interval cardio on a treadmill or elliptical machine. It's low impact but the interval feature makes it as intense as a much longer session. Then, their SmartTrainer weight machines guide you through the workout program you choose by showing you what exercises to do, how to do it, keeping count of reps and keeping you on pace to complete the weightlifting portion in thirty minutes. I love it! I can easily make it in before the kids get up or after they go to bed and be back in my car headed home within the hour. (Sorry I sound like a commercial, but I really love this gym.)"

I've already incorporated some of these into my routine. These "life hacks" are helping me to get back on track. Here's to a healthy and happy 2017!

*February 2017*

# LIFE HACKS

## Keeping Organized and Keeping Sane

For as long as I can remember, I've had the motto, "Everything has a place, and it ought to be in it." From the time I was a child, I have been almost obsessive about being neat and organized. I recall being in the fourth grade and excitedly purchasing my very first Mead Trapper Keeper notebook at Gass Pharmacy in Dandridge. It was red and included separate color-coded folders for each of my classes. I got great joy out of organizing my classwork using the folders. It didn't stop there. Everything in my life was similarly organized, even at a young age.

That continued into high school. While I no longer used the Trapper Keeper, I was always neat and organized. And apparently, it didn't go unnoticed. Recently, a high school friend texted a photo to Hugh from our high school newspaper. It had photos of "Senior Superlatives." And I, in all of my 1980s big-haired glory, was pictured in front of an expertly organized locker with the caption, "Neatest."

Some thirty years later, other than the hair, not much has changed. When asked for a Mother's Day project at school what his mom liked to do for fun, Trace once remarked, "She likes to clean house." Sadly, that is not terribly far from the truth.

I seem to have cleaning and organization down to a science at our house. My closet is organized by type of clothing and then by color and fabric. It drives me batty for the khaki-colored pants to get mixed in with the black pants. And our pantry is organized by food type and then container type. I have dark-colored "snack bins" that contain the food that Trace likes to eat because I cannot stand to see the unorganized mess that they inevitably become when an eleven-year-old boy and his buddies get into them.

As organized as I am, I am also a creature of habit.

Every morning before work, I clean our house. I make sure that the coffee pot is cleaned and that the dirty dishes are loaded into the dishwasher before I go upstairs to get ready for work. I also clear the multitude of papers that inevitably land on the kitchen table or counter. Hugh likes to tell people that I will take the morning newspaper from his hands to put it in the recycle bin.

Also, I will not leave our house without making the beds each morning. To make it easier, I have a certain method for stacking the decorative pillows at night before we go to bed so that I can quickly make the beds in the morning. I have it timed so that I can make them all in under two minutes. It's a little bit crazy, but it works for me.

These are some of the "life hacks" that keep me sane. If the house is neat and organized, the rest of life will fall into place. At least from my perspective.

As neat and organized as I am, Hugh and Trace are polar opposites. I can generally keep the house in order when I am home, but it becomes a little more difficult if I am away. My job involves a decent amount of travel, and I'm always a bit scared when I have been out of town and then return home. I'm never sure what the house will look like. While Hugh tries hard to keep things neat while I am gone, he isn't always successful. And his attempt to create "life hacks" often go awry.

Hugh likes to say that he is responsible for all things nasty at our house. He cleans up after the dog and changes the cat litter. Once, when I was out of town, Hugh decided to experiment with cleaning the cat litter. Specifically, he decided that birdseed would be a more environmentally-friendly cat litter. His theory was that (1) the consistency of birdseed closely resembled cat litter and would be pleasing to a cat, (2) the birdseed lacked the "litter smell" that you get with traditional cat litter, and (3) instead of sending the litter to the landfill, he could dump it in the woods behind our house for the birds to eat.

I am certain that Hugh did this "experiment" while I was out of town because he knew that I would never approve. And he would have been correct. On the day that I returned home, I was met with the smell of cat poop and urine. While the cat did use the birdseed litter box, the birdseed did not absorb the odor. And Hugh didn't think about the fact that no bird would ever want to eat birdseed that had been used as a toilet.

Worse than all of this, though, was the fact that the birdseed stuck to the cat's feet, which meant that he tracked it through our house. And this was the thing that sent this neat freak over the edge.

Hugh's attempted "life hack" ended with a deep cleaning of our carpets and a thorough cleaning of the entire house by a professional cleaning team for good measure. On second thought, maybe it did work after all.

*March 2017*

# LIFE HACKS

## Hacking Stress Before It Hacks You

Attorneys are, as we are often told, stressed. We are engaged in a juggling act: trying to manage the needs of our clients and manage our practices all while shouldering family and other obligations. Stress is, at times, imminent. It is one of those things that we, as human beings, face on a daily basis. And it is one of those things we have to deal with on a daily basis.

It seems there are countless articles and websites that talk about ways to deal with stress. Pinterest even has an entire section of "life hacks" to cope with stress. It suggests meditation, exercise, and many other things. Unfortunately, none of those things really work for me.

If you read this column in last month's DICTA, you will recall that my "life hack" for dealing with stress is housecleaning. I love to clean house. A couple of years ago, someone asked Trace what his mother did for fun. His response, "Clean house." And when asked what makes his mom happy, he said, "When Dad and I clean house, too." It is no secret. I do love a clean and organized house. I find it strangely relaxing, and my stress level is greatly reduced when my personal space is in order. (Note: this does not always apply to my office.)

Every morning before work, I clean my house ... do the dishes, do any laundry that has accumulated, make the beds, and pick up Trace's toys. It relaxes me and really sets the tone for my day. I can feel my blood pressure going down, the stress being lifted, and it gives me time to think about all the things I need to do during the workday.

When I confessed this last month, I had some interesting responses to the column. A couple of people asked if I was available for hire. A couple more said I must be more than a little bit crazy. Still another said that Hugh must be a saint to put up with me and my neuroses.

It may not be the conventional way to deal with stress, but it works for me. I was curious, though, as to how other people deal with stress. I wondered if other attorneys had such unconventional stress management techniques, so I asked a few friends to tell me how they cope with the stresses that face us every day.

Adrienne Anderson has several coping mechanisms to deal with stress. "I really enjoy long distance flatwater kayaking and hiking. Both are relaxing and are the perfect way to deal with stress," says Adrienne. She also enjoys yoga to relieve stress. Her most interesting response was a bit more … unexpected, though. "Kickboxing/MMA training is a fantastic way to deal with stress. It is as fake as televised wrestling when I do it, but boy does it relieve stress!" says Adrienne. She continues, "I don't know why all these very different things work well to relieve my stress, but they do."

Kyle Baisley also enjoys a good workout to relieve stress. "I either go before daybreak to CrossFit Ktown and do a hero workout such as 'Murph' while blasting AC/DC's 'Live 1992' album (and hope to finish before the album finishes!), or I go late afternoon to a client's private range with one of my full autos and about thirty pre-loaded mags. Either one tends to clear my head fairly quickly!" says Kyle.

LeAnn Mynatt says that there is only one real way to relieve stress. "One word: running." LeAnn doesn't run in solitude though. "I need ear buds playing good music (sometimes Lady Gaga, sometimes Aretha singing spirituals) and a good, steady pace, enough to sweat." She doesn't take running for granted, though. "When I was sick in 2013, the one thing I needed to destress was what I couldn't do. Now, I do not take it for granted and dread the day when or if my joints take it away from me." She says, "You can tell from looking at me that I'm not fast, but I am avid."

Hanson Tipton prefers to find a little quiet – and a place away from middle school drama – to relieve stress. "I have a fourteen-year-old daughter, so when life gets stressful, I go to the office," says Hanson.

Annette Winston had the best response when I asked how she copes with stress. "Usually just send him to the golf course. (Bahahahahaha!)"

*April 2017*

# LIFE HACKS

## Making The Most of Meal Time

For several years, Hugh told people that Casa Don Gallo in Rocky Hill was our "second kitchen." Trace protested, stating that our "second kitchen" may actually be Tandur on Bearden Hill. It is no secret in our circle of friends that we eat out—a lot. With our work schedules and Trace's swim schedule and other school activities, it seems that my kitchen is used less and less frequently. One month, after an inventory of expenses, I decided it was time to cut back on the restaurant food and focus on eating at home. Unfortunately, our home-cooked dinners quickly became either pork chops or rotisserie chicken from The Fresh Market. I knew I had failed when Trace told me, "If I have to eat one more rotisserie chicken, I am going to sprout feathers and start clucking."

I know that we are not alone in the struggle. I asked a few busy lawyers to give us some ideas to make mealtimes easier and more economical.

Dawn Coppock says, "I like to cook, and I like to eat at home. Also, I live 'out' so going out to eat is a drive and not easier than cooking at home.

I cook on the weekends, and we eat leftovers for weeknights at least one or two nights a week. If I see I'm not going to get to leftovers in a timely manner (Does that sound like a lawyer?), I put them in the freezer so I have a quick lunch or dinner later. I often have spaghetti sauce and chili in the freezer for example. I cook things like pot roast and roast chicken that recycle to tacos, soup, and casseroles pretty easily."

Dawn continues, "Also, I have meat in the freezer that I can defrost while I'm working, and we grill whatever and make a salad. Last resort, rotisserie chicken from the grocery and a bag of salad. I'm pretty sure that chicken has hormones and other junk that is better consumed in moderation if you don't want to grow feathers. But better for us than Big Macs."

Dawn's final suggestion, "When it is just me for dinner, I get out the good cheese, make a fancy, little cheese plate with nuts, fruit, and olives. Five minutes. I can carry it out to the deck if the weather is nice. I love it, but that is just me."

Esther Roberts also lives 'out.' She offers these suggestions: "As old-fashioned as it sounds, this farm chic/lady lawyer still relies heavily on crock pots (slow cookers). I own three. My 'life hack' is to have all three simmering one weekend a month, with chicken and veggies in one, beef and veggies in another, and vegetable soup or pinto beans in the other. Once everything is cooked, I line up several freezer containers and fill each one and freeze. This provides at least a dozen suppers to quickly pull from the freezer and reheat during our busiest evenings. I am very fortunate that Hubs Greg doesn't mind 'one dish' suppers, and that he is easy to please."

Esther continues, "My second 'life hack' is the count my blessings that, while we live in a beautiful, rural setting, my farm is mere minutes from an Aubrey's, Puleo's, and Cracker Barrel. Speed dial and a quick pick-up run and voila! Dinner at home in fifteen minutes!"

Crista Cuccaro believes meal planning is key. "We plan our week's meals and purchase the groceries for those meals all at once. If it's a good week, we can even fit in prep in advance, such as chopping onions."

She continues, "We also alternate on who takes the lead for dinner. From time to time, we both have weeknight obligations, whether work-related or otherwise, so we always plan who will make which weeknight meals, too. We make enough dinner during the week so that we can take the extra for lunch the next day – this is a huge time and money saver!"

Jamie Ballinger-Holden agrees, "On Sunday, we always prepare something that has lots of leftovers and tastes better on the second day (such as a stew or a casserole). That way on Monday night we don't have to cook. Mondays are hard enough!"

Cheryl Rice says, "At our house we do a little of everything. When my kids were younger and less involved after school, we usually cooked two recipes on the weekend to do double duty (two nights.) Now, with more after school and evening activities to attend (and drive kids to/from), we work harder at being together than eating in. That said, we still try to plan ahead on the weekend for what the week looks like and cook one item that we can easily warm up during the week for a dinner or two. One of my favorites is when Bill grills marinated chicken tenders. We might eat them one evening with a salad, vegetable and roll, and another evening we enjoy a southwestern style grilled chicken salad, putting the reheated tenders on a bed of lettuce with corn, black beans, tomatoes, shredded cheese, tortilla chips, salsa, etc. Same goes for pork tenderloin—traditional one night, then use the leftovers with soft corn tortillas for a build your own taco night."

Heather Anderson enjoys taco night, albeit differently. "Some weeks I am better about thinking ahead (dinner-wise). Other weeks, I know that Mondays are $5 burger nights at Calhoun's … and we have Taco Tuesday (from *The Lego Movie*—every week, whether at home, on vacation or eating at a restaurant which serves tacos). Chick-Fil-A is a regular weekly staple, especially in the spring with baseball practice and games! And I love my Crock Pots! (Yes, I have more than one just like I have more than one dishwasher!)"

Annette Winston has a solution even easier than a Crock Pot. "I have recently discovered 'sheet pan recipes; and, man, are they are cinch. Google it; you'll see."

Katie Lane likes even more convenience. Says Katie, "There are two words for dinner: Trader Joe's!" Kristin Seabrook also likes convenience. She says, "We use Plated and love it!"

Brian Lapps, though, may have the most convenient solution of all. "Our kids are old enough that we can say, 'There's plenty of food in the pantry and fridge. If you don't like what's there, you know where the grocery store is.'"

*May 2017*

# LIFE HACKS

## Things to Make Travel Easier When There Is No Rest for the Weary

It is almost June. I am slightly alarmed by this. The year is zipping by, and I am wondering how I have squandered so much of the year with so many of my 2017 "To Do List" items still undone. It seems that the Nystrom family has gone in a million different directions this year. In the past month, Hugh has traveled to Washington, D.C. and to Nashville for work, Trace visited Colonial Williamsburg with his fifth-grade classmates, and I covered over 1600 miles of our beautiful state in a three-day stretch (which was just one of multiple trips in the past several weeks). Life seems to be happening at a more and more frenetic pace, and I feel a bit road weary at times. It has, however, given me an opportunity to hone my travel skills and learn a few tricks to make travel easier.

1. Never pass up the opportunity to purchase gas or use a clean restroom. A large portion of my travel lately has involved trips to beautiful small towns and more remote areas. While the scenery is beautiful and the people are lovely, gas stations and restroom facilities are often few and far between. If you have the opportunity to fill your gas tank and use a clean restroom, by all means take it. You never know when you will get that chance again.

2. Purchase a good scarf and keep it with you at all times. I was never much of a scarf person (I thought were for the Europeans); however, time and experience has changed my mind. The scarf is the Swiss Army knife of clothing. A good scarf can dress up an outfit, double as a blanket, and hide a multitude of sins (like Diet Coke down the front of your shirt).

3. Turn your suit jackets inside out and roll them up when packing. I laughed when Hugh did this on our trip to Hawaii and told him that he might be paying someone to steam his jacket when we got to Honolulu. He had the last laugh when his perfect looking jacket came out of the suitcase while my fancy dress looked like I had slept in it. If you are wondering how to do this, YouTube has great videos.

4. Use hotel laundry bags to hold your dirty clothes. When I return from a trip, I know which clothes are clean and which ones are dirty. I can

dump the dirty ones in the laundry room before I ever head upstairs to unpack.

5. When packing for kids, put individual outfits in large Ziploc bags and label as to which day/time the items should be worn. I did this for Trace's school trip, and he said it made getting dressed easier. Everything was together, and everything matched. Unfortunately for Trace, it also told me which days he *did not actually* wear clean clothes.

6. Use those shower caps from the hotel to cover the bottoms of your shoes in your luggage. In addition to walking through airports, parking lots, and public restrooms, my job takes me to farms and pasture fields. While I try to watch my step, things happen. Let's leave it at that.

7. Use glasses cases to carry your phone and other chargers, as well as headphones. It is a really easy way to keep them organized, and they don't get wound up in all of your other belongings in your bag.

8. If you are traveling by airplane, pack some luggage scales. This little trick has saved me numerous times. It only took one time of having an overweight bag at airline check-in (which meant opening my suitcase to readjust and reallocate, exposing my skivvies for all the work to see) to learn this lesson. When we returned from Hawaii in December, we had three checked bags. Each one weighed *exactly* forty-nine pounds. And we avoided overweight fees.

9. Always have snacks and drinks. And eat local if you get the chance. I recently purchased three Diet Cokes at a hotel in Jackson, Tennessee. When I got my bill at the end of the stay, I had been charged $3.50 per Diet Coke. Had I gone to the gas station that was within walking distance, I could have purchased them for $1.79 each. Although it wasn't much, it adds up. Also, if you have the option to eat at a local restaurant versus a chain, eat local. I've found some of the best food comes from the little hole-in-the-wall diners in these small towns. Caution: after you have eaten at one of these places, it might be wise to hit up the hotel health club. While the food is usually quite tasty, I am certain that it is also quite unhealthful. Almost everything that tastes good is.

10. Never speed in Putnam County, Tennessee. Ever. Enough said. Wherever your travels take you, I hope these tips and tricks are useful. For now, though, in the words of Willie Nelson, "I can't wait to get on the road again."

*June 2017*

# AROUND THE BAR

## GSMNP Superintendent Cassius Cash: Our Way Forward

Born and raised in Memphis, Cassius Cash admits that he didn't exactly grow up communing with nature – the closest he came to the wilderness was watching Marlon Perkins on Mutual of Omaha's *Wild Kingdom* on television. He attended college thinking he would become a doctor, but when recruiters from the U.S. Forest Service offered him an internship, he jumped at the chance to work with wildlife biologists. "I was always fascinated with animals," he says. "I just didn't see anyone who looked like me doing those jobs. It was like stumbling onto a dream."

His dream became a reality over two decades ago when he was hired by the U.S. Forest Service as a wildlife biologist in Washington State. As a wildlife biologist, Cash helped protect spotted owls and preserve public lands. He went on to serve in key leadership positions including as an administrative officer in Nebraska, district ranger in Georgia, civil rights officer in Mississippi, and finally as deputy forest supervisor in southern Oregon.

In 2010, Cash left the U.S. Forest Service to become the superintendent for Boston's National Historical Park, which links the stops along the Freedom Trail and African American National Historic Site, which is a collection of fifteen Beacon Hill businesses, churches, and homes along the Black Heritage Trail that were inhabited by Boston's free African American community in the 19th Century. Reflecting, Cash stated that the two parks shared a common theme: "When you look at the outcomes to each of the stories, the abolitionist movement or the Revolution, they both end in freedom." In 2012, when the new national park visitor center opened in Faneuil Hall, Cash began marketing the two as "Boston's trails to freedom," with the programming focusing on concepts from both trails.

In Boston, Cash used stories to rebrand the park and built impactful connections in the community. Superintendent Cash also took a deeper look into the historic stories most people know to find additional stories that included more people.

When the mountains of Tennessee called him home in February 2015, Cash realized that, while the Great Smoky Mountains National Park is the most visited in the United States, the key to operating the Park was not necessarily the millions of visitors who come from other places; rather, the key to operating the Park was connecting to the community. He felt that finding more inclusive stories is the key to building more interest and support for the Park. Inclusive stories connect parks to people of different backgrounds, interests and geographies. And they connect the Park to the community.

The understanding of the importance of connecting the Park to the local community has helped Cash face the challenges, weather the storms, and celebrate the successes of the Park during his tenure. Since his arrival in the Great Smoky Mountains in February of 2015, Cash has experienced many great rewards as well as great challenges.

A highlight of his tenure has been hosting the Hike 100 Centennial program that involved him hiking with more than 180 young people from the local community and encouraging them to become future stewards of the Park. Connecting with children is an important part of his mission at the Park. "I grew up in Memphis, and we didn't have national parks close to where I lived. I was that kid who grew up watching scary movies where bad things happened in the woods," he says. "I still see a lot of kids today that are scared of the woods. I want to change that."

He has also had to ensure that the Park met the demands of 11.3 million park visitors every single year. On the busiest days, the Park hosts some 6,000 visitors. He is tasked with balancing conservation and stewardship, making sure pristine woodlands stay that way for people to enjoy for the next one-hundred years, but also with making them accessible so that people can get outside and take it all in. This includes focusing on educating visitors to better understand how to interact with nature and minimize their impacts. "We have to step up our game from not feeding the bears to explaining what happens when you do feed them," he says. "You have to understand there is a sense of stewardship."

His biggest challenge, though, has been the management of the worst wildfire in Tennessee's history – Chimney Tops 2 Fire. While fire-related building and structural damage outside the Park is being repaired, areas that were scorched within the Park will recover naturally. In a few spots, that will likely be a century in the making. Only about ten percent of the 11,000 park acres ravaged by the fire were blackened or deadened. The recovery is going to vary depending on how many of the trees die and how high the severity was. In the areas that burned hottest, it will take a long time for those forests to recover. Cash is confident that the Park will be stronger than ever moving forward.

As Cash moves into his third year of service and the Great Smokies Park moves into its 101st year, his leadership message of getting back to the basics as the way to move forward rings with universal appeal. Cash has a passion about not only what we can do for our parks, but what our parks can do for us – in terms of health, peace of mind, and connection. He also believes that community is one of those key basics that often gets lost in the rush of life. Says Cash, "Our National Parks are about making a social impact as much as they are about making a scientific impact."

To learn more about his vision for the Great Smoky Mountains National Park, please join the KBA in welcoming Superintendent Cash at the Supreme Court Dinner on September 6.

*August 2017*

# LIFE HACKS

## Travel Tips with Little People (and Words of Wisdom from the Expert)

It is hard to believe it is July. Every morning, I look at Facebook to see photos of friends and their children lounging on the beach, taking trips to big cities, or enjoying grand adventures to national parks and other wildlife areas. And every day, it gets closer and closer to the day that my family hits the road for our annual summer vacation.

In the May issue of DICTA, I shared some of my favorite travel "life hacks"—those things that make travel easier for me. I received great feedback – and even a few requests for more travel hacks. Since I had pretty much given out all of my good tips, I contacted my dear friend and travel guru-extraordinaire, Heather Anderson, to see what she does to make travel easier.

For as long as I have known Heather (which is a long time), she has been on the road or in the air, traveling to some exotic locale. I thought that she would slow down a little when her children were born. She hasn't – and as a result, Charlie and Sophia have logged more airline miles than most people have ever driven.

I asked Heather to provide me with some of her top travel tips. She shared the following:

1.  Traveling by air with a baby? Always buy a seat for the baby – and secure the baby in a car seat. In 2014, the Wall Street Journal reported, "Safety investigators are raising warnings about in-flight turbulence, which is the leading cause of injury to children on airplanes and can sometimes catapult lap children into another row." Admittedly, infant deaths on airplanes are rare, but if it happens to you, the chance is 100%. https://www.wsj.com/articles/new-study-focuses-on-in-flight-risk-to-infants-1408574702. If you choose to fly with a baby in your lap, know that only specific seats are equipped with double air masks – so you are at the mercy of an airline employee to ensure you are seated correctly with the baby. Don't be cheap when it comes to the babies, especially if you are one of those parents who lug around one of those shopping cart covers for shopping. #firstchild #rookie

2.   Use a Go-Go Babyz to maneuver around the airport. The infant car seat straps onto it and becomes a stroller. You can also purchase a stroller with retractable wheels that converts into a car seat. They will also fit through the aisles in the larger planes; however, your kid may be in for a bumpy ride when you retract the wheels (which sometimes is no easy task).

3.   Check the stroller with the bags (unless you have the stroller/car seat in one gadget). See No. 2 above.

4.   For travel with toddlers, for years, we have used the Kid Cares Harness, which is the only FAA approved harness for kids. It provides shoulder support for the littles in turbulence or sometimes, something more serious. For years, the uneducated flight attendants have insisted on proof that it is FAA-approved. One flight attendant refused our use of it, and I was almost dragged from the plane (YouTube or cell phone video, anyone?) …. But I backed down. I reported the incident to the FAA and a Forbes magazine contributor wrote about it.

If you are interested in checking out the article, see: https://www.forbes.com/sites/johngoglia/2015/06/04/american-airlines-crew-still-unaware-of-kid-seat-rule-could-lack-of-faa-enforcement-be-responsible/#fb2c9879a592.

5.   Get the AMEX Platinum Card and check out the Centurion lounge at various airports around the country. With the Platinum card, you can get unlimited alcohol and food and quick complimentary spa treatments – and it has a kids' play area to boot. If you travel a lot, it is well worth the annual $450 fee.

6.   I pack by outfits/activities. You can use gallon-size Ziplock bags (one outfit per child per day) or reusable cubes for the more environmentally friendly option. If we are stopping overnight for a quick stay, I can grab two bags and the toiletry kits rather than hauling in all the luggage.

7.   Twitter is the best customer service option. Ever.

8.   Always, no matter what, travel with mini bottles of alcohol. You can get them through security without issue. For the record, you cannot (are not supposed to) open the bottles and drink them on a plane because, technically, it's a violation of federal law to drink an alcoholic beverage onboard an aircraft unless served by the airline. I'm not saying I have done it, but I have no prosecutions at this time.

9.   Any questions? See No. 8. Sometimes you do what you have to

do to keep sane while traveling, and especially while travelling with two littles who are under the age of six. One word of caution, though, don't clean out the empty airplane mini bottles post-trip at a mediation at Harry Ogden's office, because his runner will report the contents of the trash can to Harry.

Thanks, Heather, for the great "life hacks" for travel with littles. And Happy Traveling!

*August 2017*

# LIFE HACKS

## Coping With Grief and Worry When Times Are Tough

While there have many wonderful things that have happened this year (and while I have many, many things in my life for which I am eternally grateful), 2017 has been a year marked with profound sadness.

This year has brought the deaths of four very close cousins, all sudden and unexpected. People who I have known my entire life and who I never imagined would not be here are suddenly gone. I've experienced the loss of three of my former law partners. Several clients who were more like friends have passed away. A law school classmate died suddenly from a heart attack just days after his forty-ninth birthday. In one week's time, I attended four funerals.

My mom has had knee replacement surgery, ACL surgery, and has had major surgeries on both of her feet, each of which has necessitated long and complicated recoveries. My aunt, who is like a second mother, has had a third recurrence of cancer. Several of my close friends have been diagnosed or are suffering from serious illnesses. People I love are suffering, and I feel powerless to help.

I have seen several friends suffer through the end of their long-term marriages, and several more have children who are struggling. It is sad to see so many people I care about in so much pain.

Sometimes, it is hard to see the light at the end of the tunnel. And sometimes it feels like the light at the end of the tunnel is the front of a freight train bearing down on me.

So far, 2017 has been marred with grief, worry, and sadness, and it has been difficult on some days to cope. Thankfully, I have found some coping strategies that have made this year a little less stressful.

1. Support from others will help you heal from loss or deal with difficult situations. Take time to lean on the people who care about you, even if you take pride in being strong and self-sufficient. Rather than avoiding them, draw friends and loved ones close, spend time together face-to-face, and accept the assistance that is offered. Oftentimes, people want to help but don't know how, so tell them what you need – whether

it is a shoulder to cry on, help with a difficult task, someone to hang out with, or (my own personal favorite from Hugh) someone to mow your yard. If you don't feel as though you have someone you can regularly connect with face-to-face, it is never too late to build new friendships.

2. Draw comfort from your faith. If you are a religious person, embrace the comfort of your religion's traditions. Spiritual activities that are meaningful to you—such as praying, meditating, or going to church—can offer solace.

3. Cry if you need to. Crying is a normal response to sadness, but it isn't the only one. If you don't cry, though, it doesn't mean that you are not upset. Those who don't cry may feel pain just as deeply as others. They may simply have other ways of showing it.

4. Express yourself creatively. Writing is another excellent way to express yourself and alleviate grief and sadness (i.e., contribute a DICTA article). If you don't want to write for publication, try keeping a journal or writing letters, whether you send them or not. When words won't come, artistic outlets like painting or sculpting can help you to communicate what's in your heart and soul. Creative expression can bring clarity to the turmoil you feel and insight into feelings you weren't aware of.

5. Take care of your physical health. Grief and worry take a physical toll as well as an emotional toll. Rest, exercise, and proper nutrition are essential to dealing and healing. Counteract a poor appetite by eating small amounts of healthy foods rather than large meals. If you have difficulty sleeping, try taking brief naps or just putting your feet up and relaxing whenever you can. And while you may not be motivated to exercise, just taking a brief walk now and then can lift your spirits and help you to sleep at night.

6. Avoid using chemicals to numb your feelings. A glass of wine can be good for the soul and help to settle jangled nerves, but overdoing it can bring a host of new problems. Attempting to numb your feelings with alcohol or prescription medications will only prolong the pain. Eventually, one way or the other, you must come to terms with your sadness and worry.

7. Have fun. Grieving, whether it be over the loss of a loved one or the loss of life as you have known it, is difficult, but it doesn't mean you have to feel bad all the time; in fact, it's important to take a break from focusing on your grief and stress. Have fun when you can, whether it's

reading a good book, watching a movie, playing games, or resuming other activities you enjoyed before your loss. Don't feel guilty about it.

8.   Avoid making major decisions. Stress can cloud your judgment and make it difficult to see beyond the pain you're feeling at the moment. Impulsive decisions – to move or change jobs, for example – can have far-reaching implications for which you may be unprepared. If you must make an important decision, discuss your options with someone you trust, such as a friend or financial advisor.

It has been said that grief never ends – it just changes. It is a passage – not a place to stay. And we must deal with it in order to get through whatever the situation. Remember, grief is not a sign of weakness, nor a lack of faith. It is the price of love.

*September 2017*

# LIFE HACKS

## Turning Fall Failures into Fall Fabulousness

I have always loved fall. To me, there is no better time of the year. The air gets cooler, and the days get shorter. I get to wear my favorite clothes… and boots! The trees in our area put on their magnificent show, turning to beautiful shades of yellow, orange and red. I have a birthday. And Knoxville comes alive when we hear the words, "It's Football Time in Tennessee."

As much as I love it, though, I am best described as a "Fall Failure." Except for a few birthday parties for Trace (and, sadly, since he is now a middle schooler, he doesn't want any more of those), I really don't do fall well. My normally green thumb turns brown. The fall flowers that I plant usually die within days. My Halloween decorations leave much to be desired, and my deck and planters continue to wear the effects of fake blood that I used on the jack-o'-lanterns from Halloween a couple of years ago.

And, as much as I love football, I have never mastered the art of the tailgate. A few years ago (and before I started working at UT, necessitating my working before football games), Hugh and I planned an "epic" tailgate. I worked for days preparing just the right food… caprese skewers with balsamic vinaigrette, ham rolls, chicken tenders, spinach dip, blood orange brownies, and assorted other things. I got a set of orange dishes, with matching cups, and various football-themed serving platters. I purchased a UT-themed cornhole set. I got the magnetic Power Ts for the car. I even convinced Hugh to drive "Red Velvet," his 1975 Caprice Classic Chevrolet, to the game. Everything was perfect. Or so I thought.

Then, things got dicey. In the two decades that Hugh and I have been together, I have driven "Red Velvet" exactly twice. Hugh makes Trace and me put towels on the seats before we sit down so that our pants don't scratch the seats. To say he is particular about the car is an understatement. On that day, though, he let me back "Red Velvet" out of the garage so that I could load her massive trunk with our massive amount of stuff. Because of the car's age and size, it takes two people to lower the top. As the top went down, the crunching began. With the overloaded trunk, there was nowhere for the top to go… and the glass window shattered as it hit my meticulously prepared tailgate, leaving glass chards in all of my containers and in any food that was not inside a cooler. The game had not started… but I had already lost.

Undeterred, the next week I planned "epic tailgate – part two" but decided that Sweet P's could make it so much easier. I purchased barbecue, a bunch of great sides, and their famous banana pudding. At our tailgate, my cousin Todd wanted banana pudding, but he worried about eating the last of the banana pudding when others (including Trace, age four) had not had any. I told him not to worry… I had packed plenty. As Todd ate the last bite in one of the large containers, Trace decided he wanted some. Hugh started opening the remaining containers … all of which were potato salad. Trace still blames Uncle Todd for eating all the banana pudding in what our family affectionately calls "Banana Pudding-gate."

As much as I love it, I do not do fall well. I'm lousy with gardening. I'm lousy with tailgating. And I am always at a loss as to fun things to do with my family. I asked around for some ideas – some "life hacks" – to make my fall Pinterest-worthy.

Mary Beth Maddox insists that I am doing the tailgate wrong. "You know my tip – go to the tailgate, socialize, and soak up the atmosphere, and then drive home with no traffic as the game starts and watch it in your comfy clothes (unless you are sitting in the box!)"

Crista Cuccaro suggests an alternative to the football tailgate. "Our favorite fall activity is going to Tennessee Soccer games. The Regal Soccer Stadium is located off of Neyland, and the backdrop is the scenic bluff across the river. The games are free to attend and are very family friendly – plus, the team is off to a great start this season!"

LeAnn Mynatt suggests that fall is best spent enjoying our beautiful mountains. "As a native Knoxvillian, I've grown up going to Cades Cove in the Smokies, especially in the fall: camping, picnicking, hayrides. Fall is when the humidity's gone, when they exhibit how to make molasses, and when campfire smoke permeates the air. Now I take my nephews. We throw football, skip rocks in the creek, and grill burgers. There's nothing better."

Justin Martin, though, suggests that the best fall evenings are spent a little closer to the hearth. "My favorite fall evening is spent at home with a fire. Throw in chili, football, s'mores, and kids, and life is pretty much perfect."

These are some great suggestions. With a little luck and the helpful advice of friends, perhaps I will master fall this year. Happy fall, y'all!

*October 2017*

# LIFE HACKS

## Talking Turkey: Life Hacks for Thanksgiving

I am a huge fan of Thanksgiving. I love to cook, and I love to host our family and friends. A couple of years ago, though, I was a bit behind the 8-ball. I was busy at work and didn't quite get it together enough to shop and plan my menu until a couple of days before Thanksgiving. When I finally did make it to the grocery store, I quickly realized that my chances of finding a fresh turkey were about as high as my chances of winning the Power Ball.

Hugh suggested that I call Willy's Butcher Shop (which I love). Fortunately, Willy did have a couple of fresh turkeys. Unfortunately (for my wallet), they were heritage turkeys, which I learned are fairly rare (about 24,000 are sold each year) free-range turkeys that are naturally self-basting. It really was the best turkey that I have ever tasted… and, based on its price, it should have been. (As a side note, a couple of months later, I was visiting a farm with work and met Pete, a pet heritage turkey who thinks he is a dog. After meeting him, I will not be eating heritage turkey again).

Lesson learned: plan ahead. So that I'm not scrambling every year, I have come up with some "life hacks" to make Thanksgiving just a little bit easier.

1.    Set the table ahead a week before Thanksgiving. A couple of years ago, we were hosting twenty-two friends and family members for Thanksgiving. When I started setting the tables, I realized that my brown tablecloth for the kitchen had not come back in the dry cleaning from two years earlier. I spent about thirty minutes looking for it… and then about thirty more trying to figure out what sort of tablecloth I was going to use. Since then, I have started setting the table in advance. It lets me cross at least one thing off my to-do list on Thanksgiving Day.

2.    Let the salad bar be your sous chef. This may be my favorite tip. I can shave hours off my prep time by picking up ingredients from the supermarket salad bar that are already cleaned and ready to go—think chopped onions, sliced bell pepper and celery, hard-boiled eggs, and even crumbled bacon.

3. Learn how to carve a turkey by practicing on cheap rotisserie chickens beforehand. My carved turkeys have often looked like something out of a horror movie. With practice on rotisserie chickens, they now look much better.

4. Use your cooler as a fridge. In the lead-up to the big event, refrigerator real estate is precious. I clear out space-hogging bottles of ketchup, pickles, etc. and stow them in the garage in a cooler filled with ice packs. Another hack with the cooler: use it to brine the turkey overnight (but make sure to add plenty of ice).

5. Use a corkscrew as a guest-deflector. Ever heard the old adage about too many cooks in the kitchen? I have learned how to keep well-meaning family and friends out of the kitchen during the final flurry of cooking by coming up with a few tasks that they can do to help: opening the wine, filling water glasses (which are placed outside of the kitchen), hanging coats and herding children are all appreciated—and guarantee time to focus when I need it most.

6. Let the kitchen cabinets serve as a cookbook stand. I like to minimize clutter in the kitchen, eliminate flipping back and forth, and protect my laptop that I know (from experience) is going to get damaged in the cooking chaos by making copies of my favorite recipes that I will include in the feast. Then, on game day, I tape them at eye level to the doors of my kitchen cabinets. They are easy to read and follow, and I can even arrange them in order of my cooking prep.

7. Make dressing in a muffin pan for easier serving. Bonus: you get lots of crispy edges.

8. Use chicken broth as a turkey reviver. Overcooked the bird? Before you place that platter of dried-out breast meat to the table, drizzle it with a little warm chicken broth. It will help moisten the meat and add flavor. This is also a good trick for perking up slices that have gone from room temperature to cold.

9. Use a slow cooker as a mashed potato keeper. The only thing worse than lumpy mashed potatoes on Thanksgiving is cold, gluey ones. I keep my spuds warm when every burner of my stovetop is in use by buttering my slow-cooker insert, adding a little heavy cream, and then spooning in the potatoes. Set the temp to low and stir every hour or so to keep them smooth and silky.

10. Use a measuring cup as a fat separator. The secret to great gravy is skimmed – not greasy – pan drippings. If you are without a fat separator, pour your drippings into a large heatproof measuring cup and pop it into the freezer. As the drippings cool, the fat will rise to the top and solidify, making it easy to skim off with a spoon.

11. If you want wine with dinner (or just want to chill and watch football with a cold beer), chill it quickly in the freezer. Wrap it in a wet paper towel and place it in the freezer for fifteen minutes to get it cold.

12. When all else fails, go out to a restaurant. Last year, we were heading out of town the week after Thanksgiving. To make things easier, we decided to spend Thanksgiving at Brazeiros. It was one of the easiest and most enjoyable Thanksgivings I have ever had. I didn't have to cook, and I didn't have to clean up.

13. You can have leftovers without actually cooking. While I enjoyed dinner at the Brazilian steakhouse, I was a little bummed that we wouldn't have any leftovers. Hugh came up with a solution. We picked up some prepared Thanksgiving foods from Butler and Bailey, some William-Sonoma cranberry relish, and a turkey breast. It was just enough for the three of us to enjoy for a couple of days.

May these "life hacks" help to remove some stress and give you extra time to enjoy friends, family, and really good food. Happy Thanksgiving!

*December 2017*

# LIFE HACKS

## Making the Most of the Most Wonderful Time of the Year

I have always loved the Christmas season. I look forward to November 1 every year when XM radio starts its holiday music. I love to decorate and to drive around to look at Christmas lights. But this year, I've been a bit of a "bah humbug."

It's mid-December, and I have been feeling a bit stressed. In the past, I have always started decorating during Thanksgiving; however, this year, I started a small closet-cleaning project that ended up taking much longer than anticipated. Once I did start decorating (about two weeks behind schedule), I realized that my normally great "life hacks" for Christmas decorating had failed me. We always put up two trees – one on either side of our downstairs. I store them in the Frontgate standing bags in the garage, which means that they are assembled and ready to go when I get them into the house. Several years ago, I got the bright idea to leave the lights on them when I stored them so that I wouldn't have to re-string them every year. It has worked like a charm – until this year.

When I opened the first tree, it was perfect. The second one, however, was a different story. Our living room tree is eleven feet tall and about the same width, and it has over 2000 lights. When I unzipped the bag and plugged the tree into the outlet, I realized that about half of the lights were not working. Because the burned out/defective bulbs were scattered throughout, I had to take all of the lights off, purchase new ones, and then re-string the tree. In addition to taking several hours, I was covered in scratches. I looked like I was in a fight with a cat – and that I lost.

Once the tree lights were on, I started unboxing my ornaments. I discovered several years ago that the Harry and David fruit boxes are perfect for storing non-breakable ornaments and that the Hale Groves padded boxes are perfect for the more fragile ones. After I unpacked the ornaments and put away boxes, I realized that I was missing a number of ornaments. I drug out all of the boxes and went through them again. When I didn't find the ornaments, I had Hugh go through the boxes. After several hours of looking through boxes, I recalled that the padded boxes have two layers of padding and that I had put the ornaments between the layers.

After wasting way too much time trying to decorate, I complained to Hugh that (1) we had not made a shopping list and (2) that we didn't have a decent photo for a Christmas card. I was stressed out and feeling overwhelmed. I needed to clear my mind, so I logged onto Facebook. And found exactly what I needed.

Janet Strevel Hayes had posted the following, which was exactly what I needed to lift my spirits:

"In a move that was fairly out of character, I went Black Friday shopping (like got up in the wee hours of the morning and stood in line outside so I could get a forty percent off coupon). Much to my surprise, the people around me in line were fun and the time passed quickly. Although forty million of us were eventually crammed in a tiny boutique at an hour when it was barely daylight, the spirit in the place was amazing. "Excuse me," "please" and "thank you" were echoed throughout the morning- in harmony with "no, you go first." I watched people offer to hold packages for other people and save places in line. When I got home, I was not tired and frazzled. I was energized.

Last week, our church gave life to the biggest oxymoron ever invented: the FREE sale. Church members packed (literally packed) our gym with coats, toys, kitchen items, furniture, clothes, and everything else you can imagine. We then opened the doors to anyone in the community who needed or wanted something for free. The event was tirelessly organized by servant-hearted workers who could've been at ballgames or shopping for their own children. The members who donated items could have sold most of the stuff and made some extra cash. It was a labor of love, and the community was blessed. The generosity of those involved inspired me to do more.

Then, last week, I was a little grumpy at work-not feeling much holiday spirit. To get out of the office for a minute, I walked down to the post office. It turned into a walk around town--Market Square full of families eating near the ice-skating rink; Gay Street with Christmas trees and garland- I passed the old courthouse where I tried my first case on a cold December day. I remembered the bailiff who sensed my anxiety and gave me a wink and thumbs up when it was over. I ended at the post office, where I was greeted by a cheerful worker wearing a Santa hat. He reminded me of that bailiff--he winked and smiled as we talked about the craziness

of the post office at Christmas. He made me laugh. When I got back to my desk, my bad mood was gone.

Today when I came out of Sam's, it was a balmy thirty-three degrees, and the gray sky was spitting snow flurries. I heard the traditional jingle of the red kettle bell and the loudest, sweetest voice singing "Oh come all ye faithful, joyful and triumphant." The girl ringing and singing was bundled in a coat and gloves, and her smile was nearly as big as her voice. She was probably in her late teens or maybe early twenties. I thought of all the other things she could have been doing this cold morning. She paused only to look me in the eye and wish me what seemed to be the most sincere "Merry Christmas" I have ever heard. I got in my warm car and thanked God for that girl and prayed that I would be more like her.

Moral to this long story---I am so thankful that God still fills hearts with the joy that is Christmas. I am thankful that God uses other people to inspire us and to help us feel His love. If you are feeling less than festive, look around. I promise that, if you really open your eyes, you will see a reminder that this IS the most wonderful time of the year. In the darkness, there is light. May we see it. May we be it!"

I hope your holidays are merry and bright. And that 2018 is your best year yet.

*January 2018*

# HIDDEN KNOXVILLE

## Mighty Musical Monday at the Tennessee Theatre

We live in an area that is rich in history and culture and with abundant natural resources. No matter where I travel, I am always asked about my *distinctive* accent. Whenever people learn that I hail from East Tennessee (Dandridge, to be exact), people always share tales of trips to the Great Smoky Mountain National Park, Dollywood, and, for those who are around my age, the 1982 World's Fair. As a native, I will confess that I often take these things for granted. And don't experience them nearly as often as I should.

We live in an area that offers a plethora of activities and places to visit. With such an overwhelming selection, though, I find that I often overlook some of our region's more out-of-the-way places that offer a little something extra. Moreover, a lot of great things are happening in plain sight. This year, my column in DICTA will explore some of our region's "hidden treasures"—those places and activities that are well worth discovering.

Last month, my travels took me all the way to Gay Street to the historic Tennessee Theatre. Sure, I've been to the Tennessee Theatre many times, taking in a number of Broadway shows, productions by the Knoxville Opera, really great concerts and maybe even a *Thomas the Train* show or two. However, I am ashamed to say that I had never ventured out to the Mighty Musical Monday concerts. Sure, I had seen the Mayberry squad car with Barney Fife, as well as vans from local senior centers lining the street on various Mondays—but I never thought that I would enjoy spending my lunch hour listening to an organ. I was wrong.

Last month, my mom and several other relatives asked if I would like to meet them for the Mighty Musical Monday holiday concert. Normally, I would have politely declined; however, on this particular Monday, I had a morning meeting downtown, which meant that I would already be in the area. And my mom offered to buy the brown bag lunch (sandwich, chips, and drink, while supplies last), which is $5.00 at the event. She even offered popcorn, candy, and soft drinks. Not one to turn down food, I said "yes."

For those who are unfamiliar, the Mighty Musical Monday concerts are a free lunch-time concert centered on the Wurlitzer organ at the Tennessee

Theatre. The Mighty Wurlitzer organ was installed in the Tennessee Theatre in 1928, the time of the building's opening. Today, it is one of the few theatre organs still installed in its original location. Patrons of the performance are greeted by Sammy Sawyer, a.k.a. Barney Fife, in the lobby and then are treated to a performance by organists Dr. Bill Snyder and Freddie Brabson, along with various guest performers.

When asked how the idea of Mighty Musical Monday started, Becky Hancock, Executive Director of the Tennessee Theatre, says, "The organ was restored in later 2001, and the organ technicians told us that it was a good idea to play it regularly to give it exercise. We hadn't played it very often except for a few movies every year. So, Bill Snyder and I together came up with the idea of doing a standard concert. We picked the first Monday of the month and have been holding concerts since December of 2001."

On the day I attended, I arrived at approximately eleven forty-five (doors open at eleven thirty for the noon performance). The street was lined with buses and vans from local retirement centers, and the line to enter was extremely long. Thankfully, my family had saved me a seat. The concerts are attended by mostly seniors, and Hancock has a theory as to why: "So many of these people came to the theatre in the '40s and '50s, and they have such fond memories of being here when they were young. It's during the day, it's free and a lot of the music is what seniors enjoy. The daytime concert is really a great way for them to come back and enjoy the theatre and enjoy this beautifully renovated space."

The music, though, is not just for seniors. The Knoxville Swing Band played holiday favorites and Glenn Miller-era tunes at the holiday concert, and the performance also featured various soloists, a middle school show choir (with their own version of the Rockettes), a reading by WBIR anchor Robin Wilhoit, as well as the always impressive Webb School Madrigal singers. As I sat there on the front row, watching the organ rise from the orchestra pit and listening to the beautiful music, I could feel the stress of the day (and of the holiday season) melting away. For almost ninety minutes, I was transfixed on the beauty of the event and transformed by the magical melodies that were played. It was truly the best lunch hour that I can recall. And I wondered why, in all the years that I worked on Gay Street, I had never taken the time out of my day to attend this free event.

Of all of the holiday events and performances we attended this year (and we attended several), the Mighty Musical Monday event was one of the very best. If you have never attended (or if it has been a while since you last attended), please take time to attend one of the upcoming performances. You won't be disappointed in this hidden gem.

*February 2018*

# HIDDEN KNOXVILLE

## The McClung Museum of Natural History and Culture

If you know me well, you know that I am a bit of a germaphobe. I'm a huge proponent of handwashing, and I am even more particular when it comes to restrooms. When traveling, I have been known to make multiple stops in order to find a restroom that I deemed "clean enough." And I would almost rather die than use a porta-potty. It is that aversion to germs and porta-potties that led me to the hidden treasure that is the McClung Museum of Natural History and Culture.

A number of years ago, while tailgating at a UT football game, I was in need of the "facilities." Knowing my aversion to the outdoor toilet, one of my friends suggested that I go the McClung Museum because "It's open, and it has a bathroom." While I was glad to visit the restroom, I was even more delighted to discover the McClung Museum – and even stayed, visiting the exhibits, until it closed.

If you are unfamiliar, the McClung Museum is an amenity like no other in the region. A Smithsonian affiliate, the McClung Museum is a local treasure because of its vast and varied collections.

Although a museum of anthropology was first proposed in the 1930s when the University of Tennessee took a lead role in the excavation of Native American sites affected by the building of the TVA dams, the museum was not funded until years later. Funds for a permanent museum became available in 1955, through a bequest from prosperous attorney and world traveler John Webb Green and his wife, Ellen McClung Green. They named the museum project as a memorial for Mrs. Green's father, Frank H. McClung, a wealthy 19th century Knoxville merchant.

Using the directions contained in the bequest, the museum is designed to "… tell a simple connected story of the natural earth, and of the people on earth, particularly that part of the earth and its people that is the state of Tennessee." In addition to its campus purposes, the museum is intended to reach out to the people of the state and the nation.

Located on Circle Park in a Barber-McMurry designed modernist building, the McClung Museum is open to the public seven days a week (excluding holidays). Admission and parking are free, and visitors are greeted by "Monty," a bronze cast of an Edmontosaurus, which was a duckbilled dinosaur who once roamed North America. Monty's actual fossilized bones are owned by the museum and are sometimes on display.

Once inside, visitors can view The Vine, a large bronze statue of a dancer by the American sculptress Harriet Whitney Frishmuth, which is set in a fountain. They can also see the stained glass from the home of Henry Hudson, which was located on the site where the museum now sits.

The museum boasts a number of permanent exhibitions, including exhibits about geology, paleontology, evolution, ancient Egypt, and Native American culture. In recent years, the museum has also developed an emphasis on local history. A compact permanent exhibition now highlights Knoxville's role in the Civil War, with an unparalleled display of artifacts from the 1863 Battle of Fort Sanders.

Trace's favorite exhibition is "Ancient Egypt: The Eternal Voice." The exhibit includes original objects that shed light on the daily life, religion, and writings of the ancient Egyptians. It also features objects associated with mummification and burial. Visitors can view a coffin that once belonged to a priestess of the god Amun, as well as animal mummies (including a mummified cat!).

My personal favorite exhibition is "The Decorative Experience," which features 175 decorative and household items from the museum's collection that embody an aesthetic component. These items come from cultures and societies throughout the world and range in age from 2400 BC to the 21st century. Every type of medium is represented, including ceramics, textiles, stone, metal, glass, wood, paint, bone, shell, and a combination of these. In addition to objects from Africa and Asia, the exhibition also includes artwork from the indigenous people of the Americas. My personal favorite, however, is the area that includes decorative items from Europe and the United States, including articles by familiar crafters like Limoges, Tiffany, Wedgewood, and Lalique. Each piece in the collection is unique, and they are all truly beautiful.

Other permanent exhibitions include Tennessee Freshwater Mussels, Human Origins, Geology and Fossil History of Tennessee, Archaeology and the Native Peoples of Tennessee, and The Battle of Fort Sanders.

In addition to the permanent exhibitions, the McClung Museum also features special exhibitions. Beginning March 23 and running until August 19, the museum will feature "Pick Your Poison: Intoxicating Pleasures and Medical Prescriptions." This exhibition will explore why some drugs remain socially acceptable while others are outlawed because of their toxic, and intoxicating, characteristics. It will feature over forty medicines, advertisements, historic and popular culture documents and books, video footage and paraphernalia. Through these items, visitors will see some of the factors that have shaped the changing definition of some of our most potent drugs – alcohol, tobacco, opium, cocaine, and marijuana – from medical miracle to social menace.

The museum also features a wonderful gift shop. The museum store carries a wide selection of unique items, including local art, jewelry, books, one-of-a-kind gift items, stationery, and educational toys, including items that pertain to current exhibits. Proceeds from all purchases support the museum's educational programs.

The McClung Museum is one of our local treasures that is "hidden in plain sight." If you have never visited (or if it has been a while since you last visited), please take time to check out the exhibitions at the museum. Admission is free, and parking is free (and is located within steps of the museum's door). You won't be disappointed in this hidden gem.

*March 2018*

# HIDDEN KNOXVILLE

## The Savage House and Garden

As East Tennesseans, we are blessed to live in one of the most beautiful places in the world. I recently attended a national meeting of the Garden Club of America, where, upon learning where I lived, attendees often proclaimed that I was the "luckiest of them all" to be from a place with four seasons and natural beauty during each one of them. It is true – we live in an area rich in biodiversity and with a natural beauty that changes throughout the year.

In Knoxville, we are also fortunate to have beautiful public gardens. The Knoxville Botanical Garden and Arboretum has grown into a destination location (and is host to countless brides wanting just the right photograph). I am fortunate to have an office that overlooks the University of Tennessee Gardens in Knoxville, which (along with gardens in Crossville and Jackson) are the State Botanical Gardens of Tennessee. On any given day, you might find me there with a sack lunch from the POD in the vet school. If I need to formulate my thoughts for a project or just clear my head, there truly is no place better. I have also been fortunate enough to visit the gardens at a number of private homes in our area. There is a certain peace that one can find in a garden, and we are fortunate to have a number of beautiful ones in our area.

As a member of the Knoxville Garden Club and as someone who has taken the required courses to become a Tennessee Master Gardener, I have often prided myself as someone who is "in the know" about gardens. As someone who works for the UT Institute of Agriculture, I ought to know about these things.

However, a couple of weeks ago, one of my colleagues at UTIA told me about a garden that he had visited – one that I had never heard of. And one that is in my backyard.

The Savage House and Garden is one of Knoxville's best-kept secrets and is a real treasure to our area. Located at 3237 Garden Drive in Fountain City, the house and its garden are on the National Register of Historic Places. To fully appreciate this hidden gem, you need to know its history.

The Savage House and Garden are named for Arthur Savage, an immigrant from Leamington Spa, England, who moved to America in

1886 when he was fourteen years old to work for his older brother, William, who had a machine shop in Knoxville. Seven years later, Arthur started Ty-Sa-Man, a company that manufactured flour mill machinery and, later, marble cutting machines. It was located in the area that is now World's Fair Park.

In July 1917, Arthur and his wife, Hortense, moved to Fountain City into a house whose backyard had no trees – just a sinkhole and a pigpen. Arthur loved nature and longed for the English gardens of his youth. He immediately started gardening, beginning just outside his back door. Within a year, however, he had an elaborate design of flower beds in the backyard, and he planted a few trees, which grew rapidly.

Also, within a year, Savage had the first of two water towers built, as well as a series of ponds. After a trip back to England in 1925, Savage got ideas for an even larger pond, a pump house, and an elaborate pagoda. He put those ideas to use when he returned to his Fountain City home.

Arthur Savage poured his heart and soul – and considerable financial resources – into his garden. The garden is said to have been at its peak between 1926 and 1930.

Then, things took a turn for the worse. The Great Depression, which started in 1929, caused Savage's business to decline. The resulting decline in income forced Savage to have to reduce (and ultimately eliminate) the time his longtime gardener, Charlie Davis, spent on the job. Then, in 1934, a tornado struck Fountain City, uprooting nineteen trees in the garden. The destruction of the trees tore up the rock foundations in the gardens and caused costly leaks in the ponds. Finally, Savage's death in 1946 caused the gardens to become even more neglected, as there was no one left with the same love of gardening and vision for the gardens that Savage had.

During the next fifty years, the gardens were neglected, but they never were altered. Wildflowers spread, as did English ivy and honeysuckle. The trees that remained grew tall and their canopies spread, causing the kinds of plants that would flourish in the gardens to change from sun-loving specimens to shade dwellers. As happens with nature, they continually evolved.

In 1986, Bill Dohm and Patty Cooper bought the bungalow/craftsman-style house and 1.7-acre garden from Arthur Savage's descendants. (They also own and run the Garden Montessori School nearby). Under their watchful eyes, the Savage Garden has been restored to its former glory. Dohm and Cooper now employ two full-time gardeners, who carefully tend to the plants, paths, and structures in the garden.

Savage Garden boasts a 1926 greenhouse, beautiful entryways and original rock walls and garden art. Savage Garden also features a stone water tower, stone bridges and benches, and Japanese garden art (which was very popular in the early 20th century). The signature structure, though, is a large pagoda, which sits in the garden. If you visit, look closely at the top of the pagoda. The mortar between the large stones contains six little pebbles which were placed by gardener Charlie Davis' daughter to commemorate her sixth birthday.

The Savage Garden is one of our local treasures that is "hidden in plain sight." If you have never visited (or if it has been a while since you last visited), please take time to check out the Savage Garden. Admission is free, and parking is free (and is located within steps of the garden's entryway). You won't be disappointed in this hidden gem.

*April 2018*

# HIDDEN TREASURES

## Love Shack, Baby!

Way back in 1989, the B-52s sang about heading down the Atlanta Highway to the Love Shack, "a little old place where we can get together." Last year, Hugh suggested that we head to the Love Shack in Knoxville. I was a bit perplexed. I thought I had seen some signs for it, but I was certain that I was mistaken about where he meant. I was hoping that he was not referencing the businesses I had seen on Kingston Pike and Clinton Highway, so I went to the internet.

Warning. Be careful when you Google "Love Shack, Knoxville." You are more likely to see adult entertainment stores ranked higher than the pop-up burger stand in the Old City to which Hugh was referring. Chef Tim Love's renowned Love Shack is one of Knoxville's hidden treasures. While most people have heard of his Lonesome Dove Western Bistro on North Central Street in the Old City (one of our favorites), many do not know about the Love Shack. They don't realize that there is a restaurant tucked away in the courtyard behind the Lonesome Dove. As many times as I had been to Lonesome Dove, I had no idea that there was another restaurant behind it.

The Love Shack serves up Chef Love's famous burgers, nachos, fries and more—all made-to-order and all in a family-friendly environment. The "kitchen" is a pop-up tent, where gourmet burgers and more are prepared, and seating consists of picnic tables scattered around the courtyard. On cold nights, you can enjoy a warm fire by the fire pit. On Friday and Saturday nights, you can also enjoy live music. Shorts, t-shirts and flip flops is the suggested attire. Drinks come in red plastic cups (several of which have made it into the rotation at our house), and food is served in paper wrappers or paper bags. It is a no-frills dining experience that is similar to eating at a food truck. What it does have, though, is great food.

As a general rule, I'm not a burger and fries person, but Hugh convinced me that I would really like the Love Shack. On our first visit, he suggested that I try the "Love Burger," which is a fifty-fifty blend of prime tenderloin and prime brisket molded into a patty and grilled, then topped with lettuce, tomato, pickles, American cheese, and Chef Tim Love's famous "love sauce." Hugh and Trace tried the "Dirty Love Burger," which has been lauded by critics as "one of the best in America." The "Dirty Love Burger" is a variation of the "Love Burger" that also includes bacon and a sunny quail egg. For a non-burger person, my burger did not disappoint. Hugh and Trace obviously liked theirs because, when I asked for a bite, I was met with two resounding "nos."

Hugh and Trace also ordered fries. They did let me try a couple, and they were crispy with just the right amount of cracked salt. The Sides menu also includes fried okra with aioli sauce. Being a country girl, I'm a huge fan, so I wondered if the fried okra at the Love Shack could measure up to my standards. It did. Although I shared it with Hugh and Trace, I'll confess – I didn't want to. As we often do, we enjoyed the Love Shack so much on the first visit that we went back the next night. On our second visit, I tried the "Love Bird," which is Chef Love's variation on the chicken sandwich. The "Love Bird" is an organic grilled chicken breast, topped with lettuce, tomato, pickles, cheese, and love sauce sandwiched in a soft bun. It was, quite possibly, the best chicken sandwich I have ever had. Hugh tried the "Dirty Love Bird," which is the Love Bird with bacon and a sunny quail egg. He is generally a "burger man," but he loved it. We added home-made parmesan potato chips, which were also quite good.

The menu also includes a fried portobello burger (the "Boom Boom"), a crispy chicken sandwich, and hot dogs, including the "Shack Dog" (with chopped onion and pickled relish) and "Hot Dog" (with Lonesome Dove Texas Red chili, onion, and cheese). Sides include nachos, Texas Red chili, and onion rings, just to name a few. The Love Shack has a full beer and cocktail menu and is open Thursday through Saturday from eleven in the morning to midnight and Sundays from eleven in the morning to nine at night. If you are there late-night, you can also get home-made doughnuts out of the back of the Lonesome Dove. I'm not a doughnut person, but these are worth the fat and calories. Recently, I suggested to several of my co-workers that we should go to the Love Shack. After I got a couple of raised eyebrows, I explained that we were going to the Old City for burgers and fries. People who work in Ag like really good food, and they really liked the Love Shack. Bonus: we ate and were back on the Ag campus within an hour. The Love Shack has good food at reasonable prices, and it is worth the trip to the Old City. As the B-52s sang back in the 1980s, "Love shack, baby!"

*June 2018*

# BARRISTER BITES

## Bacon Makes Everything Better

Some of my earliest memories are of food…but not necessarily the food itself. Instead, those memories are of sharing food with family, whether it be at dinner, at a holiday gathering, at a family reunion, or one of the homecoming celebrations at church. I can still remember the way that my Aunt Jessie's fried chicken tasted and the smell of my great grandmother's homemade yeast rolls. I can almost taste my grandmother's dressing if I close my eyes and think about it. I recall the birthday cakes that my mom made for us and for family friends, and the smell of my dad's coffee every morning. There is something about food that brings a plethora of pleasant emotions. I remember my childhood fondly, and food played a large role in that.

In those days, I was the willing consumer of the food; however, it was not until law school that I discovered that a big part of the joy of a meal was in the preparation. As a first-year law student at Mercer, I was homesick, and I realized that I could relieve those feelings of loneliness by cooking. I became famous in law school for my turkey, dressing and mashed potato dinners on Sunday night. I would bake a turkey, make dressing, and prepare my famous "yellow mashed potatoes." (They had at least one stick of butter. To quote my roommate, "Who knew that potatoes turned yellow?") My friends and I would enjoy the meal, talk about class and pretty much everything else, and then clean up together.

It was during those times that I realized the true power of food and the sharing of a meal.

As the years have gone by, I still take great pleasure in preparing a meal. In fact, if I were not a lawyer, I think I would want to be a caterer (or at least a party planner). I love to prepare a fancy meal or dessert and then have friends and family over to eat. It is cathartic, and I hope that my child has the same happy memories that I have related to food and the sharing of a meal.

As many things as I enjoy preparing, I've become known for one particular food item: bacon. I love Benton's hickory smoked bacon, and I love to create dishes using it. I first discovered Benton's bacon when Hugh and I moved back to Knoxville in 2006. He brought home a package and told me that, much like him, it would change my life. He was right.

My first foray into bacon prep was the old-fashioned way: I fried it in a skillet on the stove top. As good as it tasted, I hated the mess that it made. More than that, though, I hated when it popped and burned my hands and arms. I decided that there had to be an easier way.

My next experiment involved hot dogs. I came up with the idea of wrapping Benton's smoked bacon around hot dogs and then grilling them for our annual Memorial Day cookout with the neighbors. If you have never had a Benton's bacon wrapped hot dog, you are missing out. They are especially good with mustard and a little bit of chili.

Since that time, I have used Benton's bacon in Brussels sprouts, to wrap green beans into green bean bundles, and on top of beef filets and turkeys. I have even used the grease to season my Lodge skillet, make marinade for beef tenderloin, and to season homemade croutons. The best preparation, however, is the easiest.

I've become known in our neighborhood for my candied bacon. It is our Saturday morning breakfast go-to, and it is my appetizer of choice for neighborhood parties. Last year, I made four pounds of it for the neighborhood Christmas party. It was gone in fewer than fifteen minutes. It's true—bacon makes everything better.

To make candied bacon, I use Benton's hickory smoked bacon. To prepare it, preheat the oven to 350 degrees. Place a cooling rack in a cookie sheet (with sides so the grease does not spill), and coat the rack with Pam or some other sort of cooking spray. Place bacon strips on the cooling rack and sprinkle light brown sugar over the top of the bacon. Place in oven for about 20 minutes or until crisp. Cool and serve. It is that easy.

I'm not the only lawyer who possesses either a love for cooking or culinary skills. Facebook has turned me into a food voyeur. I've seen a number of you post photos of food that you are preparing and photos of you enjoying a home-cooked meal with family and friends.

Going forward, Barrister Bites will highlight our members who have a passion for food. I'll be calling on you to get your thoughts on sharing a meal, favorite foods, and tips to our members on preparing.

There is power in food, and there is power in sharing food. I look forward to featuring our members with special culinary talents, and I look forward to sampling some of those famous creations.

Happy Eating!

*August 2018*

# AROUND THE BAR

## To Palau and Back: KBA Welcomes Hon. Ashby Pate to Supreme Court Dinner

KBA Supreme Court Dinner speaker, the Hon. R. Ashby Pate, may have one of the most interesting resumes of any lawyer practicing in the nation. While most of us who have entered the practice of law have gone from undergraduate studies to law school to a traditional legal job, Pate's journey has been a bit more "non-traditional."

As an undergraduate at the Colorado University-Boulder, Pate found himself in a class taught by anthropology professor Dennis Van Gerven, who often quoted the late writer Kurt Vonnegut on the idea of "skylarking," which Vonnegut defined as an "intolerable lack of seriousness."

"Van Gerven advised us to be willing not to adhere to any specific career path when we graduated," recalls Pate. "He said, 'Skylark for a while.'" And that is exactly what Pate did.

Pate, who studied English, was also an accomplished musician. Following graduation, he toured regionally in the Southeastern United States in two different bands (including one named Wiseblood after a favorite novella by Flannery O'Connor), releasing two albums of original music. Ashby is also the author of a children's book, titled *Sweet Dreams Palau*, published by the Etpison Museum.

As fate would have it though, Pate, a true Renaissance man, found himself in law school at Samford University's Cumberland School of Law. There, he served as Editor-in-Chief of the Law Review. He went on to earn an L.L.M. in International Commercial and Business Law from the University of East Anglia in Norwich, England, where he graduated first in his class and was awarded the Sir Roy Goode Prize in international law.

After graduation from law school, Pate secured a job as judicial clerk to United States District Court Judge U.W. Clemon, one of Alabama's Civil Rights pioneers. While clerking, he noticed a posting for an internship in Palau. It was another opportunity to "skylark"—another opportunity to take the road less-traveled.

For those unfamiliar, Palau is an island country located in the western Pacific Ocean now known for its incredible beauty and remarkable scuba diving. During World War II, however, skirmishes, including the major Battle of Peleliu, were fought between American and Japanese troops as a part of the Mariana and Palau Islands campaign. At the end of the war, Palau (along with other islands in the region) was made a part of the United States-governed Trust Territory of the Pacific Islands. The islands gained full sovereignty in 1994 under a Compact of Free Association. The United States continues to provide defense, funding, and access to social services. Because the island is so small and sparsely populated, Palau often relies on lawyers and judges from the U.S. for their expertise and lack of personal connection to participants in court proceedings.

When Pate arrived in Palau for the clerkship, he worked as senior court counsel for the republic and helped draft legislation that eventually established Palau's first jury trial system, after the Paulauan people voted to do so. His responsibilities ranged from drafting jury trial rules and procedures to discussing the best placement of a jury box in a courtroom. He also authored Palau's first jury trial rules and juror handbook.

When his internship ended, Pate returned to private practice at Lightfoot, Franklin & White in Alabama. However, when Palau's American member of the Supreme Court stepped down in 2012, Ashby Pate became a leading candidate for the position. Although he was only thirty-four years old, the President of Palau, Johnson Toribiong, called to offer him the job in early 2013.

Once on the bench, Pate quickly became known for his keen intellect and probing questions. During his tenure on the Supreme Court of Palau, he presided over several major cases, including the Aimeliik State chief's title dispute, as well as a lawsuit against sitting Vice President Antonio Bells. He also gained notoriety for an order granting a writ of habeas corpus in In Re Angelino, which condemned the solitary confinement conditions in Palau's only correctional facility. The issuance garnered attention in the Asia-Pacific community and among noted international human rights advocates as an "impressive national court application of international human rights norms."

After three years on the bench, the beloved jurist resigned his post to return to his roots in Alabama. He rejoined the Lightfoot firm in Birmingham in 2016. Since his return to private practice, Pate has focused his practice on international disputes, appellate work, and commercial and medical device litigation. He has also resumed his role as an advocate in some of the most important, and sometimes controversial, matters that his firm handles. Most recently, he was appointed co-prosecutor in the widely publicized judicial ethics trial of Alabama's "Ten Commandments" judge, Chief Justice Roy Moore. Pate delivered closing arguments in the trial, arguing that a January 6, 2016, Administrative Order issued by the Chief Justice constituted defiance of the U.S. Supreme Court's same-sex marriage decision in Obergefell v. Hodges. In a unanimous verdict, the Alabama Court of the Judiciary suspended the Chief Justice from office for the remainder of his elected term, without pay.

Pate's career has been marked by leadership in the profession and a dedication to giving back. He is one of only fifty lawyers and judges in Alabama currently serving on the American Law Institute, where he contributes to projects including The Restatement (Fourth) Foreign Relations Law of the United States, The Restatement (Third) The U.S. Law of International Commercial Arbitration, and The Restatement (Third) Torts: Liability for Economic Harm, and other projects published by that prestigious body. He was also chosen as a "Top 40 Under 40."

Additionally, he has been invited to speak to organizations across the country, including giving the keynote address, alongside Justice Anthony Kennedy of the United States Supreme Court, at the Ninth Circuit Court of Appeals' Law Clerk Orientation. He was also the featured speaker at the 2016 American College of Trial Lawyers' meeting in Maui, where he spoke on the power of the human connection and the unique power that lawyers and judges have to create meaningful human connections in this world.

Truly, Hon. Ashby Pate is somewhat of a Renaissance man, and his insight into the unique abilities of lawyers and judges to "be the light" in a world of darkness is inspiring. Please join the KBA in welcoming Justice Pate by attending the Supreme Court Dinner on September 5. You will be glad that you did.

*August 2018*

# BARRISTER BITES

## Making Good Food and Better Memories

My favorite Saturday mornings are spent on the sofa in my family room with the dog on my lap, drinking coffee, and scanning Facebook. I always look forward to seeing how my friends spent Friday night, what their children are doing, or who has taken a really cool trip. My favorite posts, though, are usually courtesy of Chad Tindell. For those of you who don't do Facebook or who haven't yet "friended" Chad, you are missing out. His Facebook posts look like something that you would see in the food sections of Southern Living or Garden & Gun. Without fail, his posts include a description and photos of some delicious concoction that he has created that morning.

I asked Chad about his posts and what inspires him to create such delicious-looking meals. "Cooking is therapeutic for me," says Chad. "I like to get up early in the morning on the weekends and make breakfast, some fresh bread or fire up the smoker. Sometimes at night, after a hard day at work, I will make cookies or prep supper for the following day. All those give me quiet time to reflect."

"But, most of all," Chad continues, "I like cooking because it's doing something for others. I rarely cook for me. I have worked for more than twenty-five years with many local charities, civic groups, and my church. Doing for others is what I love. And that carries over to cooking. My wife, Melissa, is the primary beneficiary (and sometimes guinea pig tester). My office and Melissa's office (at Christian Academy of Knoxville) get a regular delivery of cookies, sometimes biscuits and other treats. My neighbors, church small group and sick friends also get a share. Melissa also says I'm not good at doing nothing, so 'piddling' around the kitchen (as I put it) gives me something to do."

I wondered what inspired Chad to take up cooking. "I grew up with a single mother and was an only child. So, when I was very young, I stayed with my Papaw, as he was known to me. Papaw was a farmer, and I would get dropped off at his house early in the morning. And we would fix breakfast. Sometimes that was 'light bread' with peanut butter and Karo syrup. I think that was how I learned to make something out of whatever I have in the kitchen. But, sometimes, breakfast was sausage, gravy, and biscuits. I learned to make gravy when I was barely big enough to see over the stove. My grandfather left me when I was twelve, far too young with so much more to learn from him. The gravy I make might be good, but it's the memories of my grandfather that make it special."

Chad also relates, "And, I have to give credit to my mother. Mom often worked late, so, I started helping 'cook' before she got home when I was fairly young. My mother loves to cook, also mostly for others. I definitely get that from her. We are both fiercely independent but have managed to 'team cook' for some holidays and friends."

Says Chad, "I am not a 'chef.' I do not make much fancy food. But I hope I make good food that people enjoy."

I asked Chad about some of his best food memories.

"I have so many great food memories. I think that's because food is a lot about people and places. Where food comes from and why. I like to read about food. For southerners, get a copy of *Victuals* by Ronni Lundi or *Soul Food* by Adrian Miller. I was fortunate to meet Ms. Lundi at a Southern food conference and be at her table at Blackberry Farm for dinner. Adrian is from Colorado. I made a point to meet him when he was in town. He ended up going to church with me and to Jackie's Dream for a long Sunday afternoon supper."

"I like local restaurants and 'dives.' I have many favorites. Knoxville is my hometown, and I love it! I also ride motorcycles and, from the twelve states I've visited, have a lot of great food memories. Again, it's more than eating. It's the people and history, along with the food."

"Finally, as for cooking, I will always remember some of the first meals I cooked for Melissa. The first supper was appetizers—dates stuffed with blue cheese and wrapped with bacon, entrée—grilled steelhead trout, with roasted Brussels sprouts, and pound cake and strawberries for dessert."

Chad also relates, "I remember the failures too, things that just didn't turn out just right. A recent pizza off the egg grill comes to mind. You have to laugh and try again. I'm fortunate to have an adventurous wife who overlooks those failures (and others) and has learned that travel means me dragging her to out-of-the way places to find great food, at places with history or a 'story'."

I asked Chad about his favorite food story. He shared this with me: "Prince's Hot Chicken in Nashville (who was making hot chicken long before hot chicken was cool) was a frequent stop when I had to be in court in Nashville. You have to wait, as the chicken is cooked to order. You order through a square hole looking into the kitchen. Most of the tables are large picnic style tables…inside. It is a definite 'dive.' After court one day, I went to Prince's for lunch before heading back to Knoxville. I had my usual suit, tie, starched shirt, French cuffs. The man in line in front of me was a custodian from a local school, in blue coveralls. We could not have looked more different. But, as is often with food, we obviously had something in common. At that time, Prince's had a little black and white TV behind the counter, with a rabbit ears antenna. The custodian and I sat behind the counter for a half hour, laughing and playing The Price is Right on TV. The chicken was fabulous as always, but that's not the memory."

*September 2018*

# BARRISTER BITES

## Smokin' Good Barbecue

I am married to a barbecue aficionado. On our first date, Hugh told me how he spent a great deal of his college years manning a barbecue team called "Huge Hogs BBQ of West Knox." The team was named for him (he acquired the nickname "Huge" as a result of the "freshman fifteen plus"), and he said that brisket was their specialty. On our third date, he took me to his favorite Nashville restaurant – the now defunct "Pig and Pie" on Charlotte Avenue. Many years later, we always seek out great barbecue restaurants when traveling.

But I have heard that some of the best barbecue in Knoxville is not found in a restaurant. Instead, some of the best local barbecue is prepared by our own KBA President Keith Burroughs. Intrigued, I had to ask Keith about how he acquired those skills.

While cooking is now one of Keith's hobbies, he says that was not always the case. "When I was a kid, the kitchen was my mother's domain. She never encouraged any of us to trespass into her sacred area. Quite frankly, my mother was a fabulous cook, so there was never any real reason to try to learn while living at home," said Keith.

That changed, however, when he went to college. "Initially, I started with a gas grill in college. About twenty years ago, I was introduced to my first Weber kettle grill. I immediately fell in love with how predictably and consistently the Weber cooks and heats. Along with a Weber, I found that barbecue is best with a charcoal chimney, Kingsford regular charcoal, and an instant meat thermometer, all available at Lowe's," per Keith.

In more recent years, he has discovered additional tools. "Later, I discovered Pampered Chef cookware, utensils, and all manners of neat cooking trinkets. One of my favorites is the Pampered Chef Salad Dressing Infuser, and, for the most part, we make all of our salad dressings from scratch at our house," said Keith.

He uses those salad dressings for family dinners. "For the last dozen years or more, I cook most of our Saturday night dinners. One of our favorites is grilled chicken breast Greek salad. I like to use the Gerber brand of chicken in the Food City case. It is Amish raised chicken with no hormones or steroids. Brine in a quart of water mixed with one-quarter cup of Kosher salt for at least two hours prior to cooking. Drain and rinse the chicken breast, place in a Pyrex dish and drizzle with light olive oil and sprinkle a light coat of dried oregano and basil. Grill over direct embers to 140-degree internal temperature. Remove and place in Pyrex dish and cover with foil to let rest at least ten minutes prior to slicing. Slice in thin slices going across the chicken breast the most narrow way. Serve over a bed of mixed salad greens, sliced cucumber, red onion, boiled egg, chopped tomatoes, banana peppers, kalamata olives (pitted), rice noodles, feta cheese and drizzle with white balsamic vinaigrette. It is the perfect family meal," Keith said.

I wondered if this was Keith's favorite meal to prepare. "While it is quick and easy, it is not my favorite. In the meat department, I especially like preparing dry rub baby back ribs, pork butts, cedar plank shrimp and salmon and brined chicken breast. I do most of the food preparation on the grill or smoker while my wife, Fran, prepares the sides and dessert. However, I also have several favorite recipes for indoor preparation, like my mother's cucumber, onion, banana pepper and tomato salad (for which there is no recipe), fresh salsa, and my sister's famous recipe for Thanksgiving dressing. I enjoy preparing baby back ribs and pork butts because these are two items that are easy to mess up, but with proper preparation, come out perfect every time. The trick for both is low and slow. You cannot get in a hurry with the preparation of either one. For a quick satisfying treat, the cedar plank citrus shrimp recipe is always a crowd pleaser. And learning to brine chicken makes it turn out juicy and tender every time," shared Keith.

It is no accident that his barbecued food is so good. "One of my best memories about cooking was the day my Series 1400 SmokinTex showed up as a gift from my wife as my combination Father's Day, birthday, and anniversary gift. This all-stainless-steel electric thermostat-controlled smoker is the bomb. Baby back ribs cooked for three and a half hours at 225 degrees guarantees the perfect rib every time, and it only requires two to three ounces of hickory chunks to smoke six whole slabs of ribs. I have cooked up to sixty-five pounds of Boston butts in one run, smoked scrod to make smoked fish dip, perfect beer can chicken, and smoked sausage. With the first run of ribs, my family was hooked. To own your own SmokinTex, just google SmokinTex 1400," Keith relayed.

It is obvious that Keith loves cooking and is quite good at it. "Cooking is one of my hobbies. I am not a naturally creative person, but with food, I can take ordinary ingredients and turn them into something delicious. I am also a pleaser by personality type, and one of the easiest ways to satisfy others is with something yummy to eat. It gives me gratification when someone says 'Wow, that is really good.' I also find cooking relaxing. It is a good excuse to drink a cold beer while watching the grill, and it is something that not everyone can do well."

*October 2018*

# BARRISTER BITES

## Pies, Biscuits and Learning by Doing

Hugh often asks how I learned to cook because, to quote him, "Your mother's idea of homemade is something delivered to the house by the Schwann's man." Truth be told, I learned to cook because I can follow directions in a recipe book. And homemade is often cheaper than pre-made.

I had always thought that my friends who cook learned their skills from their mothers and grandmothers… culinary traditions passed from generation to generation. I have learned, though, that a lot of my friends are a lot like me. Case in point: Dawn Coppock, who is famous for her blackberry pie! She shared:

"Southern cooks usually tell stories about learning the secrets of biscuits, pies, and dumplings by shadowing their mothers or grandmothers. But it wasn't like that for me.

As a kid in the 1970s, I lived in a loud and chaotic house in Holston Hills. I was the second of five children. We had dinner together every night and went camping for vacations. My dad was a professor at Carson-Newman, and my mom taught kindergarten at Chilhowee School, where my grandmother, who lived about a mile away, taught sixth grade. All of them had master's degrees. Ms. Magazine arrived at our house every month, but plenty of people attributed any misbehavior and mismatched clothes to our mom having a job. It was a different time. I am proud of my mom and grandmother and grateful for their examples. But they were not cooks.

Mamaw preferred to eat out—after all, she had worked all day. When she cooked, it was pretty perfunctory. She was enamored with the great modern conveniences like Cool Whip, cream of mushroom soup, and margarine.

Mom loved to have her family around the table; but during my early childhood, the food on that table was icky. Back then, the health food guru, Adelle Davis, attributed all health problems and most social problems, including crime and divorce, to poor diet. Mom had well-worn copies of her books, which sadly included recipes. "Junk food" even in moderation, was a moral failing. Mom would make carob bricks for our birthday cakes and put brewer's yeast in pancakes. She thought raw, unsalted sunflower seeds made a good afterschool snack, and she snuck healthy ingredients like bran, wheat germ, odd oils, and seeds into what-ever she baked. We kids had this "she did it again" look that we would exchange at the first fork full. She would pronounce, "'Food is medicine'—Hippocrates." At our house, it certainly tasted like medicine.

Unlike my mom, I do not 'eat to live.' I was born with a sensitive palate and a decided inclination toward the 'good life' in the classical sense: flowers, landscapes, music, art, poetry, and FOOD. When I was about ten years old, I went from setting the table and making the salad to going straight to the kitchen after school to make dinner by myself. I got home first, and I just couldn't take another plateful of weird.

The budget was tight, and Mom was the shopper. I had to work with the groceries at hand and within Mom's home economics template. Every dinner required a properly set table, green salad or coleslaw, whole grain, protein, and unsweetened iced tea. It was still a menu heavy on beans, brown rice, and ground beef, but pretty soon things tasted a whole lot better.

My first meals were things like spaghetti, tacos, baked chicken, and tuna casserole. I would ask the odd question of mom or dad, but no one taught me to cook. I used directions on the back of packages and cans, and we had that red and white, checked, three-ring cookbook most homes had back then. I turned out to be an intuitive cook. If I ate something at a church supper, I could usually figure out how to make it at home. By the time I was in high school, I made Chinese and Italian meals for company and laid them out like photo spreads in the cookbooks. I still love to set a table.

At sixteen, I had a job at Hardee's on Asheville Highway and learned to make biscuits from Wanda. In college, I bought a copy of the classic, Joy of Cooking. Since then, I've picked different favorites of friends and family and mastered them one at a time with research, practice and, if I'm lucky, a bit of mentoring from a good cook.

I'm fascinated by food history, particular Appalachia. I have my great Aunt Rose's apple stack cake recipe and make it every December 23rd to bring to Christmas dinner as a nod to our family heritage. I create cocktail recipes now too, which is a refreshing departure from my Baptist upbringing.

My pie crust recipe came out of research and experimentation. I love to pick and eat wild blackberries and wanted a pie crust to do them justice. I'm sure I've made over one-hundred blackberry pies. Sour cherry and chicken potpie are two of my other favorites. My husband likes apple, which I can do pretty well, and Boston crème pie. Despite being a prize-winning pie baker, my husband and I don't eat a lot of sugar or white flour at home. I make pies and biscuits for entertaining mostly. Like my mom, I love a house full of friends and relatives. I grow a garden, and I still cook dinner several nights a week, but it is pretty healthy stuff. If I feel I should eat flax oil or chia seeds, I'll slam that separately like medicine. I will not sprinkle it on a perfectly good Tuscan salad or Mango smoothie.

My parents still live in our childhood home. Years ago, I bought the family farm in Strawberry Plains. We all still meet at a Mexican restaurant most Sunday nights and never miss a holiday together. These gathering are much like the dinners of our childhood, but bigger with our spouses and mostly now adult kids. Talk is still boisterous with multiple conversations at once, family news, and inside jokes. My mom loves having us all together. And the food is so much better.

*November 2018*

# MANAGEMENT COUNSEL

## 'Tis The Season: Spread Good Cheer with Holiday Gifts but Beware of the Grinch

'Tis the season. It's that time of year again – the season of giving – when employee appreciation can go a long way in terms of employee happiness and engagement. This is no secret to employers. A recent online poll of U.S. employers found that a majority—more than ninety percent—planned to offer some sort of gift or reward to employees during the holidays.

But, employers, before you really get into the holiday spirit and start passing out awesome holiday gifts or big Christmas bonuses, you need to keep in mind the rules around employee gifts. While you may be playing Santa and celebrating the spirit of the holidays, the IRS may spoil the fun and play the role of the Grinch (but without the heart that gets bigger).

The general tax rule under Internal Revenue Code Section 61 is that all forms of compensation are subject to income tax unless specifically excluded by the Code. This rule, however, is occasionally forgotten when it comes to gift giving to employees at the holidays.

While gifts are generally not considered taxable income, Section 102(c) of the Internal Revenue Code provides that the gift exclusion does not apply when an amount is transferred by or for an employer to an employee. Unfortunately, this includes holiday gifts.

Thus, when an employer gives a gift, it is taxable under Section 102(c) unless another exclusion applies.

The primary exception to the rule that holiday gifts and parties should be included in income is found in Code Section 132(a)(4), which excludes certain de minimis fringe benefits from taxable income. Section 132(e)(1) defines a de minimis fringe benefit as property or service, the value of which is so small as to make accounting for it unreasonably or administratively impractical. So, what does that mean for an employer?

It means that an employer may gift an employee with one of these sought-after gift items without reporting them as taxable income to the employee:

- Controlled, occasional employee use of the office photocopier
- Occasional snacks, coffee, doughnuts, etc.

- Occasional tickets for entertainment events
- Group-term life insurance for employee spouse or dependent with face value not more than $2,000
- Flowers, fruit, books, etc., provided under special circumstances (such as a subscription to the Jelly of the Month Club, a la Clark Griswold in *Christmas Vacation*)
- Personal use of a cell phone provided by an employer primarily for business purposes

It can also include some holiday gifts with de minimis value. Thus, if an employer distributes turkeys, hams, or other merchandise of nominal value to its employees at the holidays, then the value of these items will not constitute salary or wages and will not have to be reported as taxable income.

The determination as to whether an item is de minimis must also take into account the frequency with which similar fringe benefits are provided to the employee. It also must not be a form of disguised compensation.

Whether an item or service is de minimis depends on all the facts and circumstances. In addition, if a benefit is too large to be considered de minimis, the entire value of the benefit is taxable to the employee-- not just the excess over a designated de minimis amount. The IRS has ruled previously in a particular case that items with a value exceeding $100 could not be considered de minimis, even under unusual circumstances.

Unfortunately for our employees, gifts of cash and gift cards (cash equivalent) never fall under the exclusion, no matter how small the amount. Cash (including cash equivalents) is generally intended as a wage and usually provides no administrative burden for which to account. Thus, a $50 cash bonus, a $15 Starbucks card, and a $30 grocery gift card (even if it may be used for the purchase of a turkey or ham) are all considered taxable income and must be reported as wages or compensation to the employee.

An exception to this rule is provided for occasional meal or transportation money to enable the employee to work overtime. The benefit must be provided so that the employee can work an unusual, extended schedule. The benefit is not excludable for any regular scheduled hours, even if they include overtime. The employee must actually work the overtime. Meal money calculated on the basis of number of hours worked is considered taxable, however.

Yes, the holidays are upon us. As you plan office celebrations, keep these "gift giving" rules in mind so that, after your employees are visited by Santa, they are not followed by a visit from The Grinch.

*About this column:* "The cobbler's children have no shoes." This old expression refers to the fact that a busy cobbler will be so busy making shoes for his customers that he has no time to make some for his own children. This syndrome can also apply to lawyers who are so busy providing good service to their clients that they neglect management issues in their own offices. The goal of this column is to provide timely information on management issues.

*December 2018*

# BARRISTER BITES

## World-Famous Christmas Treats

I've often said that law school sucked the creativity right out of me. Prior to law school, I was a master at decorating cakes. I had a collection of Wilton pans and cake decorating materials and could be found making cakes most weekends for my friends' birthdays. I could also make a really good-looking cookie. Something happened, though, during those three years. Sure, I can still make food that tastes really good (I'm pretty good with turkey, beef tenderloin, and cake). Unfortunately, though, nothing is aesthetically appealing.

When Trace was very young, I was in charge of the Easter Egg Hunt at church. For that egg hunt, I found a photo and attempted to make cupcakes that looked like little chicks. Sadly, they looked more like yellow blobs with a triangle of orange for a beak and two black dots for eyes. Parents and children alike were questioning exactly what they were supposed to be. If we had Pinterest back then, the cupcakes would have been a "Pinterest fail." They truly were "ugly ducklings."

The following year, Trace was invited to a Christmas cookie exchange, which meant that the preschool moms would be making delicious treats for our children to exchange. Excited, I went to Williams-Sonoma and purchased cookie cutters and ingredients to make the perfect Christmas cookies. Unfortunately, my cookies did not remotely resemble anything Christmas-y. Instead, they looked like doughy blobs that were a bit overcooked. I ended up purchasing the Pillsbury pre-made dough with little Christmas trees in the center for the exchange. I told myself, "Kids like this stuff. They don't know the difference." Kids may not – but moms do. I had dialed it in, and everyone knew it. Suffice it to say, we have not been invited to a cookie exchange since.

I've always been envious of people who are talented enough to make beautiful Christmas treats – the kind worthy of giving as gifts. While I can do many things, Christmas treat baking is a talent that I do not possess. Stephanie Daniel, though, is a pro. I recall a party at her house several years ago. In addition to many different hors d'oeuvres, she had a plate with the most beautiful cookies I had ever seen. I asked where she had purchased them and was surprised to learn the truth. She made them!

I asked Stephanie how she got into making Christmas treats. She says, "As long as I can remember, I have enjoyed cooking and baking. At Christmas, my mother has always made dozens of batches of baklava and rum balls for giving as gifts. Her homemade treats always brought such joy to the recipients – many even putting in their requests a year in advance to ensure an allotment. I enjoy making something special as a homemade gift for friends, neighbors, teachers and even Santa."

I specifically inquired about the cookies. "When one of my sons was turning two, my mom picked up a couple dozen royal icing cookies from a baker in Middle Tennessee where they live. I asked her how much I owed her and was shocked at how expensive they are. I thought, 'I can figure out how to do this.' It wasn't that simple, but after a while (and lots of practice), I figured it out. I now understand why professional bakers can command what they do for these cookies. I have never sold any cookies, but occasionally I will take on an order for a special friend as a gift."

I asked how long it took to perfect the art. "Over the past several years, I have practiced and practiced making sugar cookies with royal icing. It took me a long time and a lot of failures to get my recipe just right, and humidity and other conditions can really affect it. The royal icing cookies are like miniature works of art. Making them is something that I enjoy."

Recently, at Stephanie's house, I saw baker's boxes filled with her beautiful cookies and tied with lovely ribbons. I asked how many she had made. Per Stephanie, "This year, I have already made forty dozen cookies."

I sure hope one of those boxes finds its way to my house.

*January 2019*

# BARRISTER BITES

## Hiking Tips and Campfire Favorites

Thankfully, no one in my household has ended up with salmonella or e-coli. Let me explain: Hugh and Trace have been involved with Scouting since Trace was a second grader. Their adventures have taken them far and wide, including numerous camping trips over the years. I became a little worried, however, when, after one such adventure, my nine-year -old son remarked, "Well, dad fixed the burgers, and you would have barfed. Mine was red and cold on the inside."

As someone obsessed with food safety, I have been concerned.

At the beginning of sixth grade, Rob Frost's son, Charlie, joined the troop. I've known Rob for a number of years, and he seems to be a bit more cautious than Hugh and Trace. After the first campout that year, Trace came home raving about the food that Rob made. Instead of Hugh's e-coli burgers, Trace had really great food that was fully cooked.

After thanking Rob for making sure that my son doesn't die from food-borne illness on these trips, I asked how he became such a good camp-out cook. Rob says that he boils their adventures (and the food) down to two types: car camping and backpacking.

"Car camping is great. It's also awful. Why is it great? For the same reason it is awful. You can pack your car so full that one more toothpick won't fit. Want to take a cast iron skillet? Play it safe: take two cast iron skillets. You can pack all the food, cooking equipment and many of the comforts of home you want. Your only limit is the size of your vehicle. You're pitching your tent mere steps from where you park, so if you drive a Ford Expedition or another living room on wheels, you are all set. Bring the twenty-person Coleman tent that has a foyer and a chandelier. Two burner camp stove, Dutch oven, coffee pot, cutting boards, Ginsu knives, sharpener for Ginsu knives, generator, you name it- it all can go with you. If you have a good cooler, food really isn't an issue. With car camping, I can make Bananas Foster, grill out steaks and make apple cobbler, and it all tastes like I made it at home," says Rob.

I always feel great when Troop 757 goes on a car campout. Recently, though, a group of them did a three-day backpacking trip down the South Rim of the Grand Canyon. I was concerned about Hugh's ability to pack food and water. He packed a decent amount of water and some protein bars … and pretty much nothing else. The night before they were heading in, Rob was talking about the weight and variety of his food – none of which had been considered by Hugh. Suffice it to say, I was concerned.

Thankfully, all survived… but Rob and Charlie fared much better in the food department than Hugh and Trace. I asked Rob for some backpacking tips.

"What makes the backpacking food great is the setting you are in and the people you are with. The setting can be spectacular- you're with friends and your son and his friends on a mesa down in the Grand Canyon, under a canopy of trees in Cumberland Gap or alongside a stream with a fire burning as snow falls," says Rob.

He continues, "Backpacking is really about the lightness and smallness of everything- your gear, your clothes, and your food. Everything you need for days is slung across your back, so it has to be lightweight. You can try to have one home-like meal on your first day if you can keep it cold enough so it doesn't spoil before you cook it. You can also take tortillas or sandwich thins and cured meat or small containers of peanut butter. After that for us, it's fruit, nuts, trail mix, freeze dried meals and other assorted prepackaged items."

Per Rob, "Freeze dried food is really light to carry, but it has limitations. It takes water, and water is heavy. On our trip to the Grand Canyon, everyone took water down into the canyon with them. However, because of the weight involved, no one took enough for the entire trip. We later hiked an eight-mile loop to a small stream to filter and haul back more water to our campsite and all that we needed for the crawl back up to top of the rim."

He continues, "The taste of the freeze-dried food is enhanced by the hard work put in hiking to the spot where you eat it. The harder the hike, the better the food tastes. If you do a test run of the freeze-dried food in your own kitchen, you may be disappointed. Eating outside in a beautiful setting after a long hike will enhance the taste."

"There are four things I look for in freeze dried meals," says Rob. "First, does it sound good? Mountain House has great granola with milk and blueberries, beef stroganoff and spaghetti. Quaker Oats instant oatmeal is also good."

"Second, will it agree with you? I don't get too adventurous if I'm going to be out in nature for some time- no spicy Thai anything for me."

"Third, what's the salt content? Most freeze-dried food is very high in salt and comes with a long shelf life (I've seen up to thirty years). And, considering most of the time two meals come in one pouch, you might eat the whole pouch. Eating salty meals will wear on you."

"Finally, prep time. Freeze dried food doesn't cook- it marinates in hot water you've boiled. Some take up to twenty minutes to marinate. Freeze dried food can be purchased in pouches where you pour the water in and eat out of the same pouch. Also, remember that for breakfast, lunch, or dinner that Pop-Tarts have no prep time."

I'm thankful for Rob's tips... and also knowing that Trace is safe from food-borne illness when he is around. I'm also thankful that Hugh has been relegated to making coffee.

*February 2019*

# BARRISTER BITES

## Just Desserts and Sweet Temptations

As a general rule, I try to eat healthy and have even been known to give up sugar for months on end. But when February rolls around, nothing says "love" quite like a homemade dessert. I recall making a chocolate trifle a couple of years ago for Valentine's Day. It included chocolate brownies with chocolate chips, chocolate pudding, whipped cream and English toffee bits layered in a trifle bowl. Hugh called it "heaven in a bowl," but I called it "chocolate sin" because it was sinfully good. I had made it for Valentine's dinner, and unfortunately (or fortunately), we had not eaten all of it. Hugh put the leftovers in a Tupperware container and placed them in the refrigerator. Try as I might, I could not sleep… the leftovers were calling my name.

"One bite," I told myself, as I crept down the stairs. Sometime later, Hugh found me, sitting on the floor in front of the refrigerator with an empty Tupperware container and a spoon. I may or may not have even licked the container clean. It's an easy dessert to make, and it is one that our family cannot resist.

We also love turtles in our house (the chocolate, caramel pecan kind). I don't think I have the patience (or time) to make the ones like you find in the candy stores; however, my mom taught me an easy way to make them. You line a cookie sheet with Rollo candies and bake them until they are slightly soft. Then place them on top of the small square pretzels and press a pecan into the top. If you want to make them look like reindeers for Christmas, use regular pretzels. Instead of pecans, press green M&Ms for eyes and a red one for a nose. Voila, Rudolph!

They truly are my favorite candies. When my mom asked what I wanted for Christmas this year, I told her that I wanted a big container of turtles. She ended up making me a very large container of them as one of my Christmas gifts. I ate so many that I made Hugh take the remainder to his office so that I would not be tempted!

Kelly Frere has a similar love of making desserts, and she has become quite famous for them. "My absolute favorite dessert to make is pralines," says Kelly. "My earliest memory is my grandmother in New Orleans teaching me how to get the temperature just right before I started to drop them straight onto her metal tabletop in her kitchen. It takes practice. And a strong arm."

In the Frere house, they are a February treat. "Because they are not easy to make, I usually make them around Mardi Gras. I order the individual wax paper praline bags from New Orleans. It keeps them from sticking, which means they are always perfectly good."

Kelly continues, "I have a pretty good use of the Louisiana food "language" because both my and Matt's families come from there, but the reason these pralines are special is because, after all these years, I am now the person in the family who owns the metal-topped praline table. If you butter the table correctly, temper the candy correctly, and pour them correctly the pralines will lift right off the table and melt in your mouth. None of those stale, hard pralines in our family! They were even part of the Louisiana goodies we offered at our wedding reception in 1980."

Another favorite of Kelly's is Kahlua Chocolate Chip Pecan Pie. "While Matt was in law school at LSU (1983), we took a really cheap trip to Cancun. It was $300 per person, all-inclusive fly out of New Orleans for a four-day/three-night package. We came back with a huge bottle of Kahlua, with the pie recipe attached to it."

Kelly says that it is a "special occasion" dessert. "I make it when-ever I want the person I'm serving to say, 'Man, that's awesome!' It never fails."

Kelly admits that she has modified it a bit. "The first time I made it Matt said, 'You need some pecans in this.' I had used the recipe, but the next time doubled up on the pecans. They're always chopped so that you get pecans in every bite. In the early years, the pecans always came from cousins who grew them on the Mississippi gulf coast."

Ashley Strittmatter is also famous for her desserts. "I have four children, so 'quick and easy' is key when it comes to cooking. One of my favorites is chocolate-dipped Peeps. Now that Peeps are available almost all year, I can make them pretty much any time. To make them, I simply get the meltable chocolate that is sold in the fruit section at the grocery store, heat it in the microwave, and then dip the Peeps. You can place them on waxed paper until the chocolate sets, and then they are ready to eat. My mom started making these years ago, and they have become a 'go-to' when the kids have parties or when they have friends over. Who doesn't love chocolate and marshmallows?!?"

Ashley continues, "Another favorite at our house is home-made kettle corn. Again, my mom taught me to make this, and it is great when the kids have friends over... or when we just want a quick sweet treat. To make it, heat vegetable oil in a large pot over medium heat. Once hot, stir in sugar and popcorn. Cover, and shake the pot constantly to keep the sugar from burning. Once the popping has slowed to once every two to three seconds, remove the pot from the heat and continue to shake for a few minutes until the popping has stopped. Pour into a large bowl, and allow to cool, stirring occasionally to break up large clumps. I usually end up making several batches because the kids cannot get enough of it." May your February be filled with sweet temptations!

*March 2019*

# BARRISTER BITES (OR BREWS)
## The Best Part of Waking Up Is ….

When my parents' first pot of coffee was gone, my dad would make a second and then fill a large green Stanley thermos to take with him to work at UPS. And when he arrived home at night, he would make yet another pot of coffee, which was his beverage of choice with dinner. He truly believed "the best part of waking up is Folgers in your cup."

In law school, a number of my classmates would drink coffee like water in order to pull all-nighters. I enjoyed the caffeine buzz from iced tea (and Diet Coke) but never really got into the coffee craze. It smelled nice but never tasted quite as good as it smelled. It really didn't have much appeal to me. And then I met Hugh.

Hugh is a coffee fanatic. When we first met, he traveled for Disney and practically lived at Starbucks. Every weekend, he would ask me to meet him at Starbucks near where I lived. We would drink coffee and read the Tennessean and discuss the news of the week and plans for the weekend. But those Saturday mornings were usually a highlight. Often, he would surprise me at work during the week with a cup of coffee. And I pretended to like it because I liked him. And then, one fateful day, I decided I did like it. A lot.

Trace is proof that coffee does not hurt a developing baby. Before I knew that I was pregnant, I drank an entire pot of Cuban chicory coffee every morning before work. This happened for at least a month. He's pretty hyper, but I'm not going to blame the coffee for that. Now, I make sure I am up at least an hour and a half before I have to leave for work. I spend my first hour every morning on the sofa with my dog, the local news, and my coffee. It really starts my morning off right.

My current favorite is Black Rifle Coffee Company's Silencer Smooth. It is aptly named, as it is the smoothest coffee that I have ever tried. (I like their CAF and AK-47, too, but Silencer Smooth cannot be beat.) My morning is not complete unless I have two twelve-ounce cups of it, with a little Coffee Mate Sugar Free Hazelnut creamer added in for good measure. If I happened to have made it, I will also top it off with home-made whipped cream. It is my guilty pleasure and truly is the one thing I cannot live without.

My favorite way to prepare it is in the Bunn professional coffee maker that we received as a wedding gift. The Bunn is nearly two decades old but still works like it did the day we got it out of the box. My secret to good coffee with the Bunn is to use extremely cold water. Hugh says that is counter-intuitive because the Bunn just heats the water anyway; however, I think it works quite well. Truly, though, the Bunn is fool proof because even Hugh can make good coffee with it. He doesn't measure the coffee grounds, which is completely against my Type-A personality. With the Bunn, though, that doesn't seem to matter. Hugh also has a Keurig at his office and says that the K-cups by Black Rifle are good for use with it. I'll take his word for it because I cannot get into the Keurig craze – the servings just are not large enough to justify using one.

I've also tried to make the Silencer Smooth in the French press I bought Hugh for Valentine's Day several years ago at the Hermitage Hotel. For what it's worth, the Hermitage Hotel has the best coffee in the entire world. When we are in Nashville, we always have breakfast there just to get the coffee. I asked one time what coffee they used--- certain that it was some sort of rare blend. Not so... it's Royal Cup – same thing that is used in travel centers and law offices throughout the US. That being said, I cannot replicate it at home, even with the best coffee. For the good of my marriage and my relationship with my co-workers, the Bunn had better continue to work for the foreseeable future because it seems to be my best option for really good coffee. I'm not the only lawyer who loves coffee.

Amanda Busby also laments that she cannot live without coffee. "I would definitely say coffee is the top of my list of things I cannot live without. It is just about the perfect beverage. It wakes you up and it is warm. I probably like it so much because it reminds me of my mother and grandmother who spent a lot of time together talking and drinking coffee. My grandmother told me that I could not drink it unless I drank it black and that is still how I like it the best. I remember signing an agreement with one of my mother's friends when I was about twelve agreeing not to drink alcohol, smoke, or drink coffee before I was twenty-one in exchange for her friend's agreement to pay me $100. This was probably one of my first experiences with contracts. In any event, I did not get the $100."

We all have one thing that we cannot live without – that thing that makes life a little more enjoyable, no matter what it may be. Mine happens to be coffee... and I hear Starbucks calling my name.

*May 2019*

# SPEAKER PROFILE

## Servant Leadership Is Not a Title: Renowned Speaker Vicki Clark to Address KBA Supreme Court Dinner

Warren Bennis once said, "Leaders are made, not born. Each of us contains the capacity for leadership." Not all leadership is created equal, however. While the traditional notion of leadership is directional (meaning, "I tell you what to do, and you do it"), Robert Greenleaf coined the term "servant leadership" in 1970 to describe an aspirational leadership style that focuses primarily on the growth and well-being of people and the communities to which they belong. He stated, "The first and most important choice a leader makes is the choice to serve, without which one's capacity to lead is severely limited. A servant leader is a servant first."

Renowned motivational speaker Vicki Clark agrees. "Too many people believe servant leadership is a giant group hug. That is simply not true," she says. "A true servant leader is invested in the people that he or she serves. It is difficult – it's not your traditional directional leadership. A good servant leader listens, is persuasive and builds community."

Vicki is a sought-after speaker who has devoted the last thirty years of her life to building capacity in organizations and inspiring community and business leaders. A noted speaker, facilitator, consultant, and trainer, she has extensive experience in the nonprofit, government and private sectors. Her work includes numerous specialty areas, including inclusion and diversity, board development, strategic planning, effective communications, and leadership development within organizations.

Recently, I sat down with Clark to discuss her upcoming speech to the KBA membership and invited guests at the KBA Supreme Court Dinner on September 4. "I am so very excited to come back to Knoxville," she says. "When I was there last year to speak at the Diversity program, I was taken with how thoughtful and eager everyone was to elevate the Knoxville Bar and Knoxville community to an even higher place. I'm really excited to share some insights into servant leadership with the group."

We opened our conversation with my asking her thoughts on the different types of leadership. Vicki related a story about her mother, a public school secretary. "When you think of the public school secretary, you think of a true servant. They tend to be the problem-solvers, the people everyone goes to for help. That was my mother. She was definitely a leader, but she was not a servant leader. If you know anything about school politics, you know that the school secretary is the one person who really runs the school. My mom was the leader, but she was a leader who told everyone what to do and when to do it. She was a directional leader— and definitely not a servant leader."

Clark acknowledges that servant leadership is more difficult in certain professions – especially professions that are highly competitive and where order and structure are paramount. "Servant leadership is not just for non-profits and religious organizations," she says. "We are all called to be servant leaders. Servant leaders are servants first. Servant leaders are those leaders who work hard to create a just and caring world."

She believes that attorneys are ideal candidates for servant leadership. "I've met a lot of attorneys. They are the perfect servant leaders because they are trained to fight for justice and to create a just and caring world."

"By and large, most people go to law school because they value justice and fairness; those are the people who are natural candidates for servant leadership. But sometimes, they are the people for whom it is the hardest."

I asked Clark what traits that she believed were necessary for servant leadership. She related, "A servant leader must be empathetic – willing to put themselves in someone else's shoes. You cannot lead from your own reality." She continued, "A servant leader must also listen to understand – not just respond. You need to listen to what is being said as well as what is not being said."

Clark and I then discussed the hallmark of servant leadership: humility. She reiterated that a great servant leader is the leader who serves others over his or her own self-centered thinking. She shared her belief that those served should, while being served, become healthier, wiser, freer, more autonomous, and more likely to become servants themselves. She shared that servant leadership can and should be accomplished: one person at a time; one decision at a time; and one encounter at a time.

To illustrate this, she recounted a story about a homeless man in New York who lived in one of the homeless encampments. "One day, he was talking to the others in his group, and one of the men shared that it was his birthday and that he had never had a birthday party. The man who was listening went to one of the nearby bakeries. He told the shop owner that he didn't have any money but that he would like one of the cupcakes that she was going to throw out for one of the men in the homeless camp. He shared that it was the man's birthday and that he had never had a party. The store owner asked how many men were there. He told her that there were twelve. She started packing up twelve cupcakes. 'But we only need one—it's only one person's birthday,' the homeless man told her. She said, 'No. It's a party so everyone needs one.' From that day forward, the shop owner packaged the goods that she was going to have to throw away in order to comply with health regulations for the men in the homeless camp. The man who first asked for the cupcake was a true servant leader. He thought of someone else before he thought of himself. But the shop owner also became a servant leader as a result of the example he set."

Clark concluded with the sentiment that true servant leaders see people for what they can be, and they see the value in everyone. "I never had to unscrew anyone's lightbulb to make mine shine."

*August 2019*

# BARRISTER BITES

## "Summertime, and The Livin' Is Easy"

Most people know that I love to cook and entertain. When a friend asked last week what my easy "go-to meal" for the summer was, though, I had to bite my tongue to keep from saying, "Chick-fil-a drive-thru." Sadly, more often than not, during this busy summer, that would be a true statement. When Ella Fitzgerald sang "Summertime, and the livin' is easy," she surely was not eyeball deep in summer swim season and work travel.

My real "go-to meal" was actually borne out of one of Hugh's auction ideas when he was at Childhelp. He did lots of event-based fundraising and was always trying to come up with new and different auction items. I was rightfully skeptical one year when he told me that he and his buddies were creating an auction item for dinner for twenty that would be hosted and prepared by them. "It will be a summer supper," he said. "We will do all the work," he said. "You won't have to do a thing." I think we all know how that turned out.

My favorite summer supper was borne out of that event, which ended up with Angelia cooking and serving. My "go-to meal" consists of a strawberry salad, grilled chicken with white barbecue sauce, grilled shrimp, tomato pie, grilled corn, and TennTucky cobbler. It is an easy meal, and most of the ingredients can be purchased in "ready to use" form.

The salad consists of mixed greens (pre-bagged), sliced strawberries (I'm lazy, so I buy those already washed and capped), red onion (sliced), bleu cheese (already crumbled), toasted almonds, and Brianna's poppyseed dressing. It is a colorful salad, and it looks like you slaved away slicing and dicing. What your family and friends don't know won't hurt them.

For the chicken, I used the thin-sliced boneless, skinless chicken breasts. They cook quickly on the grill and do not dry out. I make a white barbecue sauce (Hugh's recipe) with mayonnaise, apple cider vinegar, lemon juice, coarsely-ground black pepper, cayenne pepper, horseradish, and Splenda. I can't say that we have a specific recipe... just an ingredient list. I will taste-test it until the combination is right. Then, I fill up a squirt bottle with some of it and put the rest in a large Ziploc bag. I'll add the chicken to the bag and let it marinate until I'm ready to cook. The mayonnaise-y mixture really helps keep the chicken moist during the grilling process.

For the corn, I'll usually get fresh corn (husks still on), pull the husks up, and then tie them with twine like a ponytail. After removing the silks, I like to let the ears stand in a bucket of sea salt and ice-cold water for about 10 minutes to keep them from burning on the grill. While the corn is "chilling," I'll usually mix a stick of butter, a couple of tubes of pureed cilantro, garlic powder, and fresh lime juice. I then brush it on the corn and grill it until it is finished.

Bonus: I discovered that this mixture is really good on shrimp. I will often purchase the large, pre-cooked peel and eat shrimp, toss it in this mixture, and then toss them on the grill. They heat up in about 4 minutes and taste great. (You can also put them on a cooling rack in a cookie sheet and bake them in the oven at 450.) I have seen Trace eat two pounds of them at one sitting this way.

My favorite part of the summer supper is the tomato pie. I'm from Jefferson County, but I had never heard of tomato pie until I met Hugh. I like to tell people that I married him for his tomato pie recipe. It really is that good. To make Hugh's tomato pie, all you need is a deep-dish pie crust, tomatoes, mayonnaise, onion, and shredded cheese. I bake the pie crust in the oven until it slightly brown, fill it half-way with sliced tomatoes (he will peel them... I do not... I'm lazy like that), and then add salt and pepper to taste. I then mix mayonnaise, a pureed white onion (to taste) and shredded cheese until it is a spreadable consistency. Top the tomatoes completely with the mayonnaise-cheese mixture and bake at 350 until it is brown on top. It is one of my very favorite things to eat.

The easiest part of my go-to meal is dessert. This is a family favorite, and, although it is technically a cobbler, Trace calls it "pie" and often asks for it for breakfast. To make the TennTucky cobbler, mix one cup of sugar, one cup of self-rising flour, one cup of milk, and one stick of melted butter. Add it to a greased casserole dish (I use a clear one so I can see the bottom as it cooks). Sprinkle in frozen blackberries (or mixed berries that do not contain strawberries). Sprinkle the top with ¼ cup of sugar and bake at 350 until it is brown and bubbly (usually about an hour). It is great by itself or topped with vanilla ice cream.

I've always heard that summer is supposed to be more relaxed, but that is not the case at our house. We seem to be busier than ever, and I am always looking for ways to do things faster and more efficiently without totally skimping on quality (although Chick-fil-a is pretty darned good). This "go-to meal" has allowed me to keep my sanity on even the most stressful of days. I must also note that all of the above (minus the salad) are just as good (or better) on day two or three.

I'm hoping that summertime livin' is easy for all of you. If it is not, though, maybe these easy recipes will make dinner easier and a little more enjoyable.

*August 2019*

# BARRISTER BITES

## Easy Fall Favorites (Not to Include Hungry Man TV Dinners)

Lately, I've seen the world through the windows of cars and planes. It seems that I have been traveling non-stop for work, which was confirmed a few weeks ago when I was greeted by name at the Delta counter at TYS. Later that same week, I received an email from Delta upgrading me to Gold Medallion status based on the number of flights in a few weeks' time. I've become an expert at packing, luggage selection, and airport navigation. Suffice it to say, life has been busy.

With all that has been going on, I'll admit that I have neglected things at home. Groceries are generally scarce (it does not help that my thirteen-year-old is now eating us out of house and home), and the Bite Squad drivers greet our dog by name. It has been all that I can do to keep up with Trace, Hugh, and late summer/early fall schedules. It's been a "just get by" kind of existence, and creativity-- especially when planning meals-- has gone by the wayside.

A few weeks ago, though, I had two "back-to-back" weeks where I volunteered to provide dinner for the GKAISA Coaches Council and the GKAISA Board. Because I had not had time to experiment with anything new, I decided that I would try for something really good—but really easy. Hugh assisted with menu planning, and we came up with a spread that consisted of some or our favorites-- salad, beef tenderloin, twice-baked potatoes, roasted sweet bell peppers and pie. It's easy... it's good... and I'm willing to share.

The salad is my very favorite salad, and it was borne out of a happy accident (i.e.., throwing things together to see what worked) a few years ago. It consists of six ingredients, all of which are pre-done. I start with the spring mix lettuces as a base in a large bowl (triple-washed and ready to use). I then chunk one or two apples (usually pink lady or gala) and add them to the lettuce. (To prevent them from turning brown if you are not eating immediately, toss them with a little bit of the salad dressing.) Add raw pecan halves, a container of bleu cheese crumbles, and craisins. When you are ready to eat, toss the salad with Stonewall Kitchen's Maple Balsamic dressing (purchased at Fresh Market). The salad is easy, it is pretty, and it tastes great. (Note: It is also good as a meal if you add a grilled chicken breast.)

I like beef tenderloin as a main course, as it is a hard thing to really mess up. I've tried a number of beef tenderloin recipes, but my very favorite comes from my friend Ross Dempster. I start with a 6 or 7-pound tenderloin, which I let rest at room temperature for about an hour. The marinade is key, and it comes out perfect every time. To make it, combine 2 Tbs Kosher salt, 3 Tbs coarsely ground black pepper, 2 Tbs brown sugar, 3 Tbs bacon grease (I use grease from Benton's hickory smoked bacon… I keep a container in the refrigerator at all times), and ½ cup olive oil. Mix well and coat the tenderloin with the marinade. Bake in a roasting pan at 400 degrees until it reaches the desired temperature. (To ensure that it is perfect every time, I use a meat thermometer that can withstand the heat of the oven). While my husband and son prefer that I remove it from the oven when the internal temperature reaches 135 degrees, I usually cook it to an internal temperature of 150 degrees. In my oven, this is a medium – and it suits me just fine. After removing it from the oven, I usually will cover loosely with foil and let it sit for about 15 minutes. Serve with horseradish and Sister Schubert's rolls.

The sweet bell peppers are one of my favorite dishes, and I stole it from my sister-in-law, who got it from Weight Watchers (I'm not joking). Place a bag of small mixed bell peppers in a baking dish. Drizzle with olive oil and top with crumbled feta cheese. Finish with a drizzle of balsamic vinegar, and bake at 350 degrees until the peppers start to brown. They are amazing…. And apparently good for you, too. The twice baked potatoes are the easiest part of the meal. I pick them up from the meat section at Butler and Bailey – they are just as good or better than the ones I make from scratch. To prepare, remove the Saran wrap and bake at 350 until they start to brown on top. I usually serve them with sour cream and crumbled bacon, but they are good by themselves, as well.

For dessert (on days when company is coming), I'll pick up either an apple or a caramel turtle pie from Buttermilk Sky. Again, I figure that I shouldn't waste my time making a pie when theirs are usually better. Both pies are great complements to the flavors of the other foods.

This meal has worked so well that it has become our "every Sunday" dinner (which means that leftovers provide dinner for Monday, Tuesday and sometimes Wednesday). Also, if I am heading out of town, I'll prepare it before I go so that Hugh and Trace have decent food in the house.

During my "travel phase" a couple of months ago, I did not leave food for Hugh and Trace. After all, Hugh is a grown man, and the two of them could fend for themselves. I was a little horrified when I saw a photo of Trace eating a frozen Hungry Man TV dinner. I later learned that Trace was not a fan and had left it for the dog to find. Suffice it to say, little dogs with sensitive tummies and Hungry Man TV dinners are not a good combination. The beef tenderloin meal is always a hit, and there are never leftovers for the dog to find.

*October 2019*

# BARRISTER BITES

## Flavors of Fall and Football

I love fall. After what seemed to be an endless summer, fall has finally arrived. And I could not be more pleased. I love everything about fall: the crispness of the air, the smell of a fire burning in the fireplace, the changing leaves, and the clothes. But most of all, I love football. Especially Vols football. Win or lose, I am there… and I always stay until the band plays the Tennessee Waltz.

Hugh has always said that the whole of Knoxville rises and falls with UT football. His theory is that people are in a better mood when the Vols win. Restaurants are full. People are shopping in our local stores. Cash is flowing. The local economy is booming. Life is good. When the Vols lose, though, the mood of all of Knoxville changes. Until recently, mine did, too. I cried when they beat Florida a couple of years ago. And I've cried when they have lost.

This year, though, I decided that, whether the Vols win or whether they lose, I was going to be happy. My plan was to embrace the season and all of the good things that it has to offer, but especially the tailgate. Whether the team wins or loses, the tailgate offers an opportunity for a really fun party. I saw this firsthand a few years ago at The Grove at Ole Miss. Whether the Rebels are winning or losing, the Ole Miss faithful know how to throw a proper party. I said at the time that Ole Miss always wins the tailgate. And I decided that this year, the tailgate could be my "win."

While I'm really good with the décor, I've never been great with tailgate food. I'm a bit OCD with having food that matches the color scheme, so it's been a challenge. Cheese puffs are easy. Other orange foods are not. I also have a hard time making "small bites" that people can eat quickly. Much like the Vols, though, I have not been deterred.

Bacon-wrapped tater tots with a chipotle dipping sauce have been the clear winner this football season. To make them, get two large bags of tater tots and two packages of bacon. Slice the bacon in half and then wrap the tots with the bacon and place on a baking sheet, crease side down. Bake at 450 until the bacon is done (about 25 minutes). For the sauce, mix ½ cup mayonnaise, ½ cup sour cream, 2 Tbs brown sugar, 2 tsp red wine vinegar, 2 tsp dried oregano, 2 chipotle peppers in adobo sauce, and 2 Tbs of the adobo sauce. Pulse in a food processor until smooth. Skewer the tots with toothpicks and serve with the sauce. I promise that they will not last long. They are yummy goodness on a toothpick.

I've also become a fan of Bloody Mary chili. My sister found this recipe in the NASCAR cookbook a few years ago and has used it to win several chili cook-offs in Northern Virginia. She told me that it was fantastic … and fantastically easy, and it really is. To make the chili, brown 3 lbs. of ground beef in a skillet over medium heat. When cooked completely, drain and set aside. Chop one large onion and one large green pepper. Cook in 2 Tbs olive oil until soft (about 5 minutes). Combine ground beef, onion, and green pepper in a slow cooker. Add 2 Tbs chili powder, 1 Tbs cumin, 2 Tbs red pepper (I like it hot), one 46-ounce bottle of Bloody Mary mix (I like Tom's), one 15 oz can of red beans, one 15 oz can of kidney beans, and one 15 oz can of black beans. Bring to a boil, then reduce heat to a simmer for 2-3 hours. Garnish with sour cream, shredded cheddar cheese for a little orange and white. You can also add chopped scallions, and/or my favorite… Frito's.

My favorite Big Orange tailgate libation happened by accident. I'm not a fan of orange juice or orange sodas, so I had to get creative. I do love peaches, and I had a couple of bags of frozen peaches in the freezer. I combined the two bags of frozen peaches with a bottle of Moscato wine in the Vita Mix and then prepared on the smoothie setting until it had a "smoothie" consistency. It's really easy… and really good.

I will usually get a pre-made cheese ball (Food City's pineapple cheese ball is great), form it into the shape of a football, and then use chives to make "football laces." It is really great with Sociables crackers. For something sweet, one-bite brownies from the deli section at the grocery store cannot be beat. Of course, I always welcome my friends to bring their own additions. (Trace always hopes someone will bring chicken wings.) If you ever come to our tailgate party, he likes traditional wings with the fire rub from Big Kahuna or wet wings from Calhoun's.

To me, fall is the best time of year. It's filled with all of the things I love: cool air, warm clothes, changing leaves and Volunteer football. No matter what happens on the field, if we have been able to spend time each week with friends and share a meal, then I count it as a W. Happy fall, y'all. And Go Vols.

*November 2019*

# BARRISTER BITES

## Barrister Brews

To quote my husband, "Even a blind squirrel finds a nut sometimes." While I usually write about great food and the lawyers who love to make it, I have always wanted to write about a lawyer who brews beer. Unfortunately, as a non-beer drinker, I didn't know one. Then, I had the good fortune to sit next to Judge Michael Simpson at eighth grade parent-teacher night. While we waited for the rest of the parents to get to the classroom, we started talking about "Barrister Bites," and I mentioned that I wanted to find someone who brewed their own beer. Judge Simpson related that he was a home brewer and would be willing to share his secrets.

"I began brewing my own beer just a few years ago and in truth, it was largely an excuse to go and hang out with one of my old friends," says Judge Simpson. "My friend Steve Ogle, who is the Clerk and Master in Blount County, has been brewing his own beer for decades now, and everything that I know about the process I have learned from him. He and I have been friends since the seventh grade, meeting in Mr. Hooper's Science class at what was then Bearden Junior High School. It is somewhat appropriate that we met in science class as the brewing process itself is part cooking and part science experiment."

I asked about how one gets started brewing. He relays, "There are a number of different approaches to this process, and the one we use would probably be considered the easiest and simplest for someone just getting started in their own home kitchen."

"The process begins much like any other recipe with the gathering of all the necessary ingredients. This part has been greatly simplified by the fact that there are readily available kits that can be purchased which contain everything needed to make a batch. These kits are available locally and online and represent a wide variety of different kinds of brews depending upon your particular taste. The equipment required is relatively simple and inexpensive and is also easily obtained and can be cleaned and reused for many years."

"The kit includes a selection of grains which are placed in a cheesecloth bag and steeped in about a gallon of boiling water. Much of the flavor of the final product is determined by the characteristics of the grains provided. Prior to placing the grains in the water, it is a good idea to place the cans of malt extract in the boiling water in order to help liquify the malt as it is very thick, much like molasses, and can be removed from the can much more easily if it is warmed first. After the grains have been given an opportunity to sit in the boiling water for about thirty minutes or so, they are removed, and the malt is added, and the slow boil continues. This is when a wonderful aroma begins to fill the kitchen, much like the smell of fresh bread being baked."

"My friend Steve is an expert, and like most good cooks, he can look, taste and smell and know what to do and when; however, the beginner may want to have a thermometer on hand to monitor temperatures as this can have a significant impact on the flavor and alcohol content of the finished product. During this cooking time both aroma and bittering hops are added to the mix and this, too, provides much of the flavoring of the final brew."

"After cooking is complete, the mixture must be cooled to around room temperature before the yeast can be added. High temperatures will kill the yeast and ruin the batch. We simply pour our gallon or so of mixture into a large glass jar and fill it up with tap water to start cooling down the wort. It is also important to leave some room at the top of the jar to allow for the expansion, bubbling and foaming of the brew during its initial fermentation period. A special air lock is placed in the top of the jar to allow for the escape of carbon dioxide, a by-product of fermentation. Despite the lock in the top and extra room in the jar, it can still make a mess by bubbling over, so a catch tray underneath is a good idea."

I asked if the beer was ready to drink. Judge Simpson said, "No. The mixture needs time and should sit for at least a month. The yeast will dine on the sugars and the brew will begin to clear. After the thirty days, bottling can occur. A small amount of priming sugar is dissolved in about two cups of boiling water and added to the mix. This will wake the now sleeping yeast back up, it will feed on the sugar and the carbon dioxide produced during this second fermentation period will add alcohol content and carbonization. The now bottled beer needs to be cellared for another month before enjoying, but it can be fun to age some of the brews as the time in the bottle will change the flavor over time. If the beer doesn't taste good at first, wait and try another, as it may just need some time to develop."

I asked for final tips for the novice. "Advice to the novice brewer would be that cleanliness is critical. All of the equipment, hoses, bottles and caps must be spotlessly clean and free of bacteria, or the batch will be ruined. This is accomplished either by boiling or washing in a bleach-water solution. The other advice would be to have fun! Find a friend that you can share the experience with and experiment with your recipe. Adding fruit, honey and clearing additives can all drastically change the final beer and make the brew truly unique and original. My favorite part, however, is being able to spend time with my old friend, sharing a few laughs and remembering old times."

*December 2019*

# BARRISTER BITES

## Death, Taxes, And Christmas Breakfast

They say that the only two things in life that are certain are death and taxes. I disagree. I would add Christmas morning in the Nystrom house to that list.

Christmas is a magical time, and there is no time more special in our house than Christmas morning. When Trace was a baby, we invited my mom, Hugh's mom, and my Aunt Doris and Uncle Rodger (who have been surrogate grandparents to Trace) to spend Christmas morning with us to see what Santa had brought to Trace. I like to feed people, so I also found a fool-proof breakfast set-up and menu that was easy and a crowd-pleaser. Family: check. Set table: check. Food: check. All those things combine to make a special holiday morning.

One Christmas morning when Trace was around three, I recall that he bounded down the stairs into the kitchen and exclaimed, "Santa came. He brought plates!" Indeed, the Christmas breakfast has become almost as important as the gifts from Santa.

The menu is always the same: breakfast casserole, pumpkin muffins, smoked gouda cheese grits, clementines, juice and coffee. I once suggested to Trace that we should "change it up" and do French toast. You would have thought I told him that there is no such thing as Santa Claus. Needless to say, we did not change our menu.

The "Sausage, Egg and Cheese Casserole" is the star of the Christmas breakfast, and it is one of the easiest dishes that I make. (Bonus: you can assemble it the night before and bake it on Christmas morning). To prepare the casserole, line a Pyrex dish with rolled out Crescent dinner roll dough. (I prefer reduced fat dough, as it is less greasy). Brown an entire roll of hot sausage, drain, and spread over the top of the dough. Whisk eight eggs and ¼ cup of milk together and pour over the sausage. Top with shredded Colby Jack and Sharp Cheddar Cheese. Bake at 350 until the dough is brown and the cheese is melted and browning on top. If you happen to have leftovers, it is just as good re-heated the next day.

Another family favorite are Pumpkin and Raisin Muffins. To prepare, beat 6 egg whites (I use the ones from a carton) with 3 cups of sugar. Add 1 cup applesauce, 1/3 cup of water and one 16 oz. can of pumpkin. Mix well. Add 3 ½ cups of all-purpose flour, 2 tsp baking soda, 1 ½ tsp salt, 1 Tbs cinnamon, 1 Tbs all-spice, and 4 cups of raisins. Mix well and add to pan for baking. Bake at 350 until muffins are cooked thoroughly and tops are dry. I bake the muffins in pans that look like rosettes. (They make lots of edges.) However, the muffins are equally good in regular muffin pans or mini loaf pans. They are always baked on Christmas Eve and are a favorite treat for Santa.

We also enjoy Smoked Gouda Cheese Grits on Christmas morning. (My recipe is a Paula Deen recipe. It is not a bit healthy, but it is really good.) To prepare, preheat oven to 350 degrees. Grease a casserole dish with butter and set aside. Bring 6 cups chicken broth, 1 tsp salt, 1 tsp pepper, and 1 tsp garlic powder to a boil. Stir in 2 cups regular grits and whisk until completely combined. Reduce heat to low and simmer until the grits are thick (8-10 minutes). Add 16 oz smoked Gouda cheese (cubed), ½ cup milk, and stir. Gradually stir in 4 large eggs, beaten, and ½ cup unsalted butter, stirring until all are combined. Pour the mixture in the casserole dish. Bake for 35 to 40 minutes or until set. As with the casserole, this dish can be prepared the night before and baked on Christmas morning.

To assuage my guilt over the high-fat and high-sugar breakfast, we always have clementines available. Sometimes, they are eaten… but usually they are not. I also try to have an assortment of juices, chocolate milk and coffee and accoutrements. I'm a coffee fan, and I am obsessed with the sugar-free peppermint mocha by Coffee Mate that only seems to be available during the holiday season. If you go to Kroger to find it, chances are I have already purchased all of it. (I bought all eight of their bottles of it last Sunday).

This meal is always a favorite and has been our tradition since the year Trace was born. When Trace was two, Hugh's mom passed away. This year, we lost both my Aunt Doris and my Uncle Rodger. In a letter that he placed in Uncle Rodger's coffin, Trace stated that Christmas morning with all of the people he loves the most has always been his favorite day of the year. He stated that Christmas mornings will never be the same.

He was right. It won't be the same. Knowing how hard this year has been on him, I asked if he wanted to change it up a little bit (after all, at fourteen, he has been known to sleep until noon). His response caught me a little off guard, but I should not have been surprised. "It will be different, but I like our traditions. Our breakfast meal makes me think of happy times. I don't want to change a thing."

I hope your holidays are filled with fun and family. And if you need something easy for breakfast, I hope you will try some of our family favorites.

*January 2020*

# BARRISTER BITES

## Gifts and Granola Goodness

Hugh and I are not gift-givers—not to each other, anyway. When we were younger, Hugh and I always tried to find unique and innovative gifts for each other. While I never managed to be terribly creative, he always did.

One year for my birthday, Hugh bought me a gift certificate for a stay in a haunted hotel because he knew that I enjoy a good ghost tour. What he did not realize was that my enjoyment of a ghost tour is learning about the history of whatever city we were in… not in the stories about ghosts themselves. I did use the gift certificate, but I cannot honestly tell you that I slept at all that night. Suffice it to say, I was happy to check out the next morning.

For Christmas that same year, he bought me a hot air balloon trip across Sonoma. He thought that a balloon trip would be a romantic way to see Northern California. While I enjoy watching hot air balloons in flight, I don't actually enjoy the open air flight itself. I. AM. DEATHLY. AFRAID. OF. HEIGHTS. I recall standing in the center of the basket, with a death grip onto the rail, eyes closed and praying that it would end. I may have kissed the ground when we landed. It was not exactly the romantic trip he had envisioned.

The year that we moved into our house, Hugh bought me a Miele vacuum cleaner for Christmas. His mother was actually appalled that he would buy me an appliance for a holiday and suggested that he refrain from giving gifts without a little input in the future.

As the years have evolved, we have gravitated toward joint purchases and "experiences" in lieu of gifts. This year, our wedding anniversary fell on Thanksgiving weekend. We had already planned to spend Thanksgiving in New York, so it was the perfect excuse to celebrate our anniversary. When we started making plans, we realized that my mom could stay with Trace at the hotel, meaning that we could go to dinner alone to celebrate. (This was the first time that happened in ten years. The last anniversary dinner we had without Trace was number five in Paris.)

After a lot of research and obtaining recommendations, Hugh scored a reservation at Eleven Madison Park, which is recognized as one of the best restaurants in the world. It did not disappoint. For over four hours, we enjoyed a nine-course dinner, which was capped off with a tour of the kitchen with the chef. Each dish was unique and perfectly prepared, and the staff was amazing. It was the dining experience of a lifetime. For a foodie like me, it was pure heaven.

As we were leaving, our server presented us with a menu showing our food selections so that we would remember the meal and a gift bag that contained two jars of their house-made granola. He told us that we could enjoy it for breakfast the next day. I had heard about the restaurant; however, I had not heard of the granola (which I now know to be a famous tradition).

The following morning, as we were getting ready for the Macy's Thanksgiving Day parade, Hugh opened the granola and started eating it straight out of the container. He knows I am not a granola eater, but he told me that I needed to try it. I did. Suffice it to say, we brought two empty jars home with us.

After the busy-ness of Christmas ended, Hugh and I made it our mission to find the Eleven Madison Park granola recipe. With a quick Google search, we found it. Since that time, our kitchen has become "granola central," with six to eight batches prepared each week. It has become "our thing." We have been making jars of it to give as gifts (thank you, A.C. Moore, for the great selection of clearance jars), and a fairly sizable amount gets consumed at our house. Since I cannot give each of you a jar, I thought I might share the recipe.

This one is quick… and it is easy to make. To prepare, preheat oven to 300°F. Line a baking sheet with parchment paper. In a medium bowl, mix together 2 ¾ cups of old-fashioned rolled oats, 1 cup shelled pistachios (I use the pre-shelled salted and roasted one in the bulk area at Fresh Market because I am lazy like that), 1/3 cup raw pumpkin seeds, and 1 cup unsweetened coconut chips (not shredded coconut).

In a small saucepan (or in a microwave-safe container), combine ¾ cup light brown sugar, 1/3 cup extra virgin olive oil, and 1/3 cup maple syrup. Heat to medium and whisk occasionally until sugar is dissolved. Pour over oat mixture and fold until all of the dry ingredients are covered with the sugar-syrup mixture. Spread oats along the prepared baking sheet. Bake until lightly golden, about 30-35 minutes. Remove from oven, cool, and place in a large bowl. Stir in one cup of dried cherries. Scoop into containers to eat or give away. Note: the dried cherries at Fresh Market tend to be sticky. I will put those on the parchment and "bake" them for about 7 minutes while the oven preheats. This tends to dry them out so that they don't stick to the granola.

It is easy – and oh-so-good! We enjoy it spooned into Greek yogurt or straight out of the container. While it does have some sugar, it is a good (and healthy) alternative to chips or other snacks. And even our middle schooler loves it.

*February 2020*

# BARRISTER BITES

## "The Fancy Meal"

It is amazing what happens when (1) you are on a Delta flight at dinnertime with nothing but a Diet Coke, a package of Biscoff cookies and a one-hundred-calorie pack of Cheez-Its, and (2) and the latest edition of *Southern Living* magazine was in the mailbox as you headed for the airport. This was the beginning of what we now call "the fancy meal" at our house.

Back in November, we traveled to New York for Thanksgiving. Our flight was at six thirty on a Tuesday night, which meant that I made a mad dash from work, to home, and then to the airport. We had a direct flight, which meant that we would arrive at the hotel at around nine thirty. Knowing that there was a great restaurant close by that served dinner until midnight, we made the decision that we would not eat dinner until we arrived in New York. I did not plan on working through lunch however, which meant that I may or may not have licked the crumbs from the inside of the Cheez-It bag.

They say that you should never grocery shop while hungry. I will add that you probably should not read a magazine full of recipes while hungry either. During the flight, I read various recipes to Hugh, usually telling him, "We should make that when we get home."

I say that a lot but normally end up preparing the same meals week after week. I've got a few "go-to's" that are easy and usually pretty good. I'm a creature of habit and usually don't venture too far out of my norm. I was intrigued, though, by a recipe for a whole roasted chicken. I had made a lot of turkeys but had never made a chicken unless you count the Fresh Market's rotisserie chicken from the deli section. (We have done that so many times that, when I ask what he wants for dinner, I usually get a quick "not rotisserie chicken" from Trace).

One night when Trace was out (so as to avoid the inevitable 'that looks like rotisserie chicken, so I don't want it' conversation), I decided to try the Southern Living roasted chicken. It took a little longer than the advertised "only 30 minutes to prepare," but it smelled divine while it was cooking. When it was finished, Hugh was so impressed with it that he made a photo and pronounced it "guest-worthy."

"The fancy meal" really is good, and I thought I would share.

To make the chicken, preheat oven to 400°. Core and halve 6 sweet apples (I like Honey Crisp), and place them in the bottom of a roasting pan. Trim and peel 10 shallots and place them in pan with the apples. Drizzle 2 Tbs olive oil over the apples and shallots and sprinkle with ½ tsp each of kosher salt and black pepper. Push apples and shallots to the edge of the roasting pan.

Place a whole chicken (giblets removed, 5-6 lbs.) in the roasting pan. Sprinkle ½ tsp each of kosher salt and black pepper into the cavity of the chicken. Place 2 shallots and 3 large sprigs each of thyme, rosemary and sage into the cavity. Tuck wings under and brush chicken with 2 Tbs olive oil. Sprinkle with 1 ½ tsp each of salt and pepper. Tie legs together with kitchen twine.

Roast chicken in preheated oven until a thermometer inserted in thickest portion of meat registers at least 160°F (about 90 minutes). Remove from oven and let rest for 15 minutes. Transfer chicken to serving platter. Pour drippings over the chicken and sprinkle with 1 tsp each of chopped rosemary, thyme, and sage.

A lot of times, the chicken with apples and shallots is the only thing that we have. Other times, though, I will make a green dish, either green beans or a salad of some sort. My favorite, though, is Brussels sprout slaw with pecans and pomegranate seeds. To prepare, whisk together ½ cup olive oil, ¼ cup champagne vinegar, 2 tsp Dijon mustard, 2 tsp kosher salt, and ½ tsp black pepper. Place 1 ½ lbs. of shaved Brussels sprouts in a large bowl. Add ½ cup of the dressing and toss to combine. Let stand at room temperature until softened (30 minutes to one hour).

Add 1 cup toasted chopped pecans, 1 thinly sliced Anjou pear, and ¼ cup pomegranate arils to Brussels sprouts and toss to combine. Drizzle with remaining dressing just before serving. (For what it's worth and to make this easy, I buy pre-shaved Brussels sprouts, chopped and roasted pecans (and do not use salt in the recipe if they are pre-salted), and the already prepared pomegranate arils. It makes this a quick and easy dish.

Bonus: if you are health-conscious, this meal really fits the bill. It has quickly become a family favorite… and it makes me look like a better cook than I really am! *Bon appetit!*

*March 2020*

# BARRISTER BITES

## The Best Recipes from the Backs of Boxes, Bottles, Cans and Jars

If you have ever read this column, you know that I love to cook. You can often find me at Butler and Bailey on the weekends and at the Fresh Market every night on the way home from work. I love made-from-scratch creations, and I rarely buy processed foods. I'm not a fan of salt, and I very much prefer to use fresh ingredients when I cook.

A couple of weeks ago, I sent Hugh to the grocery store to pick up a couple of things. Hugh is usually pretty slow, but this trip was especially long even for Hugh. After he returned home, Hugh retreated to the garage. I found him there with the trunk open to his 1975 Chevy Caprice convertible. "I'm working on my car," he told me. I'm no dummy – and I know that the engine to a Chevy Caprice is not in the trunk. When I looked inside, I saw bags full of canned goods, non-perishable milk, multiple bags of coffee, bottled water, and various other non-perishable items. "You may have to suck it up and eat Vienna sausages or canned tuna at some point," he told me. Hugh was preparing for potential coronavirus quarantine.

I'm a bit of a picky eater, and I was worried how I could make these cans and boxes palatable. Then, I remembered my mom's favorite cookbook from the 1980s: *Best Recipes from the Backs of Boxes, Bottles, Cans, and Jars.*

My mother was the OG working mom. She worked in a hospital laboratory, kept our house running, drove us to cheerleading and whatever else we were doing, sewed cheerleading uniforms (and Barbie clothes and whatever else we could dream up) and always managed to have a hot meal on the table every night when my dad got home from UPS. We ate lots of Banquet fried chicken and Salisbury steak. We ate salmon patties made from canned tuna, and leftover mashed potatoes were fried into potato cakes. She loved the Schwan's truck that delivered frozen foods, and she loved recipes from the backs of cans and boxes. She always said that companies were not going to put crappy recipes on the boxes and cans and risk losing customers.

My mom's recipes were not generally gourmet dishes, so if you like to make really complex dishes that make people say, "Oh, wow!", then her dishes are not for you. My mom liked things that were easy to make and tasted good. She was a master with the use of cream cheese and cream of anything soup, and she could turn a roll of Ritz crackers into about one-hundred different meals. She did "quick and easy" really well... because that is all that she had time to do.

And most of her dishes will be great in the event we are quarantined.

My favorite of her dishes either came from a package of Crescent dinner rolls or a can of chicken – I'm not sure which, but both should claim it. I think the technical name for the dish is "Savory Crescent Chicken Squares," but we just call them "Chicken Pockets." They are easy and require very little work. To make, heat oven to 350. In a medium bowl, blend 1 package cream cheese (softened) and 2 Tbs melted butter. Add two 5 oz. cans of chicken (boneless, skinless chicken breast), ¼ tsp salt, 1 Tbs pepper, 2 Tbs milk and 1 Tbs chopped onion (dried ones are fine). Separate 1 tube of Crescent rolls into 4 squares and seal the perforations. Spoon ½ cup of the chicken/cheese mixture onto the center and pull the 4 corners together to the top center of the chicken/cheese mixture. Place on ungreased cookie sheet. Brush tops with 1 Tbs butter. Sprinkle with ¾ cup Ritz crackers, crumbled. Bake at 350 for 20-25 minutes or until golden brown.

I am also a fan of her "Easy Lasagna," which really isn't lasagna at all...but it is easy and really good. To prepare, brown one package of ground beef with a chopped onion. Add oregano and salt to taste. Boil 1 package of egg noodles, drain and pour into a baking dish. Soften 1 package of cream cheese and mix with 1 small can of Carnation milk until blended well. Pour over the noodles. Top with ground beef mixture. Add 1 medium jar of spaghetti sauce. Top with 1 package shredded mozzarella cheese. Bake at 350 until bubbly, and cheese is melted.

As a general rule, I don't eat desserts. I love them... but I don't eat them. If I am quarantined at some point, then we will have to have some sort of sweet at our house. My favorite of my mom's desserts from my childhood was called "Chocolate Heath Bar Trifle." I just call it "Chocolate Sin."

Begin by preparing a family-sized box (18-20 ounces) of brownies according to package directions and allow them to cool. Note: I like Ghirardelli chocolate chunk brownies. Prepare 1 (5.9 oz) package of instant chocolate pudding according to directions on box. Crumble half the brownies into the bottom of a trifle bowl. Top with crushed Heath bar

(I use the packages of already-crushed in the baking aisle). Top with one-half of the pudding mixture, being sure to spread to the edges of the bowl. Top with half a container of Cool Whip (spreading to the edges of the bowl). Repeat the layer process with the remaining ingredients. Top with additional chopped Heath bar. Refrigerate overnight.

I am not one to mix my foods. Hugh has often said that the kid plates that are divided were made for me. However, this dessert gets better as it gets mixed together. I have been known to dish it out into smaller containers just so that it will be well-mixed.

They say that you always return to your roots. My mom was a master at making creations from boxes and cans. If we are quarantined (or if we just want to practice social distancing), then I think she taught me well.

*April 2020*

# BARRISTER BITES

## Quarantine Cooking, Part 2

If you read this column last month, you will recall that I was curious as to how I would manage with all of the canned soups, Vienna sausages, Beanie Weenies, and non-perishable milk that Hugh had purchased in the event we were quarantined because of COVID-19. I thought I was prepared because I grew up eating food from the cookbook, *Best Recipes from the Backs of Boxes, Bottles, Cans, and Jars.*

I had no idea that I was about to be tested in truly unimaginable fashion. I had no idea that I would be making my "quarantine recipes" multiple times. I had no idea that I would not be setting foot in a grocery store (or any other store, for that matter) for a very long time. I had no idea that I was going to be at "613 Quarantine" with Hugh and Trace for the foreseeable future. For someone who is usually prepared for most anything, I was not prepared for this. I have not left my house since March 13.

For someone accustomed to grocery shopping every day or two and who eats out at least five times a week, this has been interesting. We made the decision early on that our family would do "extreme social distancing." Trace has mild asthma, and we simply did not want to take a chance on him getting sick. We also knew that we needed to be able to help my mom if she needed it. We have not ventured outside our house, have not had take-out, and have not had pre-made food delivered in over a month. Our only contact with the outside world happens via Zoom.

While Hugh did a great job preparing us for a potential quarantine, it has been an adjustment. During the first week, we decided that we would snack early in the day and then eat one good meal in the late afternoon. Had we not done this, I'm certain that none of us would be able to fit in our clothes since most of the meals that we consume would not qualify as "light" or "low-calorie."

A favorite meal happened quite by accident. We ran out of buns and light bread during the second week but still had a package of hot dogs. I found a couple of boxes of Jiffy corn muffin mix in the pantry and used it to make mini corndogs in a mini-muffin pan. That recipe is definitely a "keeper" (although I feel like I am eating like a five-year-old when we make them).

Another favorite has been cream cheese Easter cookies which a friend posted on Facebook. The recipe calls for sugar, butter, cream cheese, an egg, flour, vanilla extract and sprinkles (which, surprisingly, we had plenty of). To make the cookies, cream 2 sticks of butter and a block of cream cheese with an electric mixer. Add 1 cup sugar, 1 egg and 1 Tbs vanilla extract and beat for one minute. In a separate bowl, whisk together 2 ¾ cups all-purpose flour and 2 tsp of baking powder. Mix contents of both bowls together until a soft dough forms. Cover the dough and chill in the refrigerator for an hour. After the dough has chilled, use a spoon or cookie scoop to make small dough balls. Roll them until they are smooth and round. Put ½ cup sprinkles in a bowl and roll the dough balls until they are covered. Place the dough balls on cookie sheets lined with parchment paper. Gently press the top of the cookies down to flatten a bit. Bake at 350 for 10 minutes until set. Remove and place on cooling racks. They are an amazing treat.

I have run out of ingredients and have had to order some staples. I have tried to order local or semi-local and have had good luck with Benton's Country Hams (bacon and country ham … www.bentonscountryhams2.com), Sweetwater Valley Farm Cheese (our favorites are smoked habanero, smoked gouda, and buttermilk… www.sweetwatervalley.com), and The Old Mill in Pigeon Forge (if you like fried okra, their fried okra batter is AMAZING… www.old-mill.com).

The biggest surprise, though, has been Gullah Gourmet out of South Carolina. I was introduced to Gullah Gourmet at Carolina Gourmet at The Hammock Shops in Pawley's Island. Every year when we make our trek to the beach, I visit Carolina Gourmet. I love all of the kitchen gadgets and cookbooks, but I especially love the food samples that they have (hence the reason I have eleven packages of key lime dip mix in my pantry right now).

When I was cleaning the pantry, I found a Gullah Gourmet mix for shrimp and grits and thought I would check out the internet to see what else they might have. I have ordered Beadah' Lickin' Brownies, Flippidy Flap Jacks, Geechie Peachie Cobbla, Jus' Good Ol' Grits, Mouth Stuffin' Chocolate Chip Muffins, Nana's Been a Nut Bread, Ya Mama's Biscuits, and Yard Bird Batta. All of the mixes can be prepared with water, milk or an egg and require little to no work. Hugh has said that the grits are the best that he has ever had and that our oven-fried chicken made with the Yard Bird Batta rivaled Gus's (I did add a little cayenne pepper). Trace is a fan of the Beadah' Lickin' Brownies and can eat a pan at a single sitting. Bonus: the mixes come in cute little cloth bags with the recipes printed on them and will be great gifts when we can actually get out again. To order, go to www.gullahgourmet.com. You will not be disappointed.

It has been a learning experience. I've learned that I can "make do" with a lot less than I'm used to. I've learned that I am married to a prepper and that I can eat things I normally would not. I've also learned that we would be in a "world of hurt" without my mom's canned foods (like green beans, okra, tomatoes, and corn) and that I really need to learn to can and preserve foods myself. Most importantly, I've learned that time spent with my family is precious (even in these trying times). Stay safe and healthy, friends. I look forward to breaking bread with you soon.

*May 2020*

# BARRISTER BITES

## Making Lots of Dough in Quarantine

They say that "Necessity is the mother of invention." Those words certainly ring true during this COVID-19 lockdown. At our house, I have been making lots of dough. I've been our home's breadwinner during all of this – just not of the green variety.

About a week into the lockdown, I realized that, although Hugh was the ultimate prepper, with the exception of a couple of tubes of Pillsbury crescent rolls and a couple of packages of King's Hawaiian rolls, we did not have any bread in our house. I can make biscuits and cornbread all day. For some meals, though, there is no substitute for honest-to-goodness bread.

When I realized that we were in "knead" of bread, I started scouring the internet for yeast. Apparently, other people had the same idea because I was unable to locate any. I knew there must be another answer, so I looked on the web for recipes for bread that did not require yeast. Thankfully, I found one.

The recipe was for a sourdough bread starter that you made from all-purpose flour and bottled water. It required you to "feed it" more flour and water for several days until it started bubbling. I studied chemistry is college, so I'm pretty decent when it comes to measuring things and combining ingredients. After the requisite number of days, I had a jar of bubbling ooze. Since I didn't have any photos of how this ooze should look, I didn't know if it had done its job. On faith, I followed the recipe.

The recipe called for the dough to be mixed, placed in a warm area to rise, and then baked in a Dutch oven. I have lots of kitchen gadgets, but unfortunately, a Dutch oven was not one of them. Since I had made yeast bread in the past, I had plenty of bread pans, and I figured one of them would work. It's bread, right?

After allowing ample time for the bread to rise, I checked it. It really didn't look like it had risen, but having never made sourdough, I thought that may be normal. I dumped it in the pan and put it in the oven…and then waited. After what seemed like an eternity, it was finally finished.

Once it cooled, I dumped the "loaf" out on the counter and attempted to slice it. My fancy bread knife would not even dent it… no matter how hard I sawed. I was finally able to cut it using a very large butcher knife. Although it was tough, it smelled like bread, so we attempted to eat it. The taste was fine; however, it was so hard on the outside and so dense on the inside, I thought my teeth would break.

I chalked this bad experience up to the lack of a Dutch oven, so I ordered one from Williams-Sonoma. By the time the starter was ready again, I was able to use the Dutch oven to make a beautiful sourdough loaf. Although beautiful, the result was the same. It was horrible.

Not to be deterred, I found a recipe for "yeast water," which is made by mixing bottled water, sugar and raisins and allowing them to ferment. I thought this could be used for bread. After about a week, I checked it. The water/sugar/fruit mixture was covered with a layer of green mold. Needless to say, I had another "fail."

Fortunately for me, my mom found a package of active dry yeast. She made a yeast bread starter and shared it with me. From that, I have made multiple loaves of bread and batches of rolls, and we have been enjoying delicious homemade bread ever since.

Yeast bread has not been my only doughy creation, though.

About a week into the quarantine, in addition to having no bread, we realized that we had no potatoes. Hugh suggested that we order some instant potatoes until we could get the real thing. I went onto Amazon and found instant potatoes in what I believed to be a small milk carton-like container. I knew that they would not "go bad," so I ordered four of them. A few days later, a very large box arrived on my doorstep. I was curious as to why my cartons of potato flakes were in such a large box. When I opened it, I knew.

Instead of cute little cartons of instant potatoes, the box contained four cartons of industrial-size potato flakes. Each carton had sixty-five servings of mashed potatoes! For weeks, we ate mashed potatoes at nearly every meal. We used the leftovers to make fried potato cakes (with egg, onion, and flour... and fried with Benton's bacon grease!). And we still had three and a half large cartons.

I shared the mashed potato dilemma with my sister-in-law, who suggested that I use them to make gnocchi. I googled until I found a recipe for instant potato gnocchi. The recipe called for mashed potato flakes, boiling water, an egg, flour and some spices. I figured that I was not out of a lot if it was horrible—after all, I had plenty of instant mashed potatoes. I tried it.

To make the gnocchi, you just mix all of the ingredients and then knead the dough on a floured surface. I divided it into portions and rolled the portions into "snakes." I then sliced them into ¾ inch pieces and used a fork to make a design. It was just like playing with Play-Doh. I then boiled water and dropped them in in batches. When they floated (it only takes about one minute), I removed them with a slotted spoon and placed them on a rack to dry. To serve, I covered them in pasta sauce and cheese. They were amazing! Bonus: I have enough potato flakes to make them for a year!

If nothing else, this quarantine has given me the opportunity to try new things … and to realize that it is okay to fail sometimes. I've learned to make-do with what I have, and that I have all I "knead" even during these uncertain times.

*June 2020*

# ATTORNEY PROFILE

## Van D. Turner, Jr: A Leader Who Removes Obstacles and Finds Innovative Solutions

It has often been said that the best leaders are the best problem solvers. They have the patience to step back and see the problem at-hand through broadened observation—a type of "circular vision." They see around, beneath and beyond the problem itself. The most effective leaders approach problems through a lens of opportunity and find common ground to reach a solution. They remove obstacles and find innovative solutions.

The Honorable Van Turner, Jr., Memphis attorney, Shelby County Commissioner and founder and president of Memphis Greenspace, Inc. is such a leader.

Elected to the Shelby County Commission for District 12 in 2014, Turner quickly gained a reputation as a commissioner who could resolve seemingly intractable disputes by finding and advocating middle-ground positions. He is known as a compromiser who consistently interposes between squabbling factions and finds compromise solutions that resolve the quarrel.

In December 2016, an intervention by Turner made it possible for the Commission to approve an MWBE program requiring the county to give African American and Caucasian women special consideration to remedy what the Equal Opportunity Compliance director had determined to be discrimination in contracts and purchasing. The measure almost hit a snag when a fellow Commissioner objected that, by not specifying "all women," the measure was actually regressive. Debate ensued. If the ordinance were amended, it would require an additional reading—meaning that the issue would have been held off until the following year.

Turner materialized with a resolution that bridged the gap between the two contending factions, leaving the existing classifications of the ordinance intact, but adding a provision that gave the EOC director free reign to apply the terms of the ordinance to other groups as she deemed appropriate. That allowed for final vote, approving the ordinance by a decisive 11-2 vote. The Commission went on to approve a companion measure applying similar remedial provisions to locally owned businesses, strengthening their potential future share of county purchases and contracts. If there is a problem, Van Turner finds a solution.

For many years, leaders in Memphis wanted to get rid of the Confederate monuments that adorned two of their public parks. In a city where two-thirds of the citizens are African-American, the presence of monuments to J. Harvey Mathes, a Confederate war correspondent and army captain, Jefferson Davis, who led the secession of the Southern states from the United States under the auspices of state's rights to maintain slavery, and Nathan Bedford Forrest, a Confederate general infamous for slaughtering black soldiers and for later co-founding the Ku Klux Klan, was both offensive and nonsensical. While the Memphis City Council had voted in 2015 to remove the statutes from Fourth Bluff Park and Health Sciences Park respectively (and the County Commission passed a resolution supporting the City Council's initiative), they were blocked from doing so by state law. In 2017, Mayor Jim Strickland had requested permission to remove them again. The Tennessee Historical Commission rejected the request.

Mayor Strickland recognized a loophole for removal of the statutes: selling the parks to a private entity would allow the City to skirt the Tennessee Heritage Protection Act, passed in 2013 and amended in 2016, which prohibits the removal, relocation or renaming of a memorial that is on public property. The City could pass an ordinance to transfer the property to a private entity, which could then effectuate the removal of the statues. However, to make the transfer, the City needed an entity to which to transfer the property.

Van Turner had heard about this through the grapevine and knew he had the solution: form a nonprofit to purchase the parks, remove the statues and then maintain the parks for the public to enjoy.

While the creation of the nonprofit would be easy, Turner knew that the controversy surrounding it could be great. As a husband and father, he had cause for concern. As a leader in the community, though, he knew that he needed to make hard decisions that could solve the issue.

Turner reached out to several influential people whose names were given to him by people concerned about the city. He says, "I talked with them and asked if they were interested. Understanding that there would be some publicity—some positive, some negative. Would they be in a position to undergo all of that with their employers, their families? Once we established that everyone knew the risks, we formed Memphis Greenspace, Inc."

Memphis Greenspace, Inc. was created to promote parkland in Memphis so that people from all backgrounds can enjoy livable neighborhoods and share space where people of diverse backgrounds and different ages can come together for recreation, enrichment, and community activities. Importantly, the organization quickly raised a quarter of a million dollars from private donors and to start the process to purchase the parks and get the statues removed.

On December 15, 2017, Memphis's City Council voted to sell Health Science Park and Fourth Bluff Park to a private nonprofit on the condition that they would run them and keep them public. On Wednesday, December 20, Mayor Strickland signed the contract with Memphis Greenspace, and the Council ratified it. Later that evening, at 9:01 pm in a nod to "Take 'Em Down 901," Memphis Greenspace lawfully removed the Forrest statue. The others soon followed.

Legal issues surrounding the transfer of the statues and the remains of Forrest and his wife were resolved earlier this year, and the bodies of Forrest and his wife will be reinterred elsewhere.

When asked about the significance, Van Turner said, "I think it removed, symbolically, a barrier that held our city back." The removal had a more personal meaning to him, though. "My father spent the majority of his youth in LeMoyne-Owen Gardens. The family later moved to Binghampton and at one point, he lived very close to the park. He recalled as a young man not being able to walk through the park without being accompanied by a white and not being able to sit in the park. That left a really bad impression on him and countless other black youth in the community." The statue was removed on his father's 74th birthday.

*September 2020*

# BARRISTER BITES

## Ball Jars and Big Flavor

My husband has often called me a housecat: I don't go outside if the temperature is above eighty or below sixty or if it is raining. I have always been this way. As a child, it was out of necessity. I would break out in welts in the sun during certain times of the year, and I was allergic to all sorts of plants and weeds. Unfortunately, there was no such thing as Allegra or Sudafed, and I was often left to suffer in stuffy, swollen, red silence. Having a dad that grew up on a farm, I found little sympathy at home. His response was always, "Suck it up."

For that reason, I hated Saturdays during spring and summer. My grandmother had a farm, and my aunt and uncle had very large vegetable gardens. And my sister and I were free labor. I recall in the fourth grade telling my dad that there were child labor laws, which meant I could not work. He told me I was not a lawyer. While Amy and I wanted nothing more than to watch cartoons, starting with *Jot* or *Casper* at six in the morning and ending with *American Bandstand* and *Soul Train* at one thirty in the afternoon, my dad wanted nothing more than to see us working. And he always won.

He often said, "If you don't pick it, you don't eat it." I became a master at picking all sorts of vegetables: green beans, cucumbers, okra, tomatoes, corn, beets, potatoes, and anything else that would grow in East Tennessee soil. I've often said that you don't know hot until you pick vegetables and then sit all day on a porch, breaking beans and shucking corn in 100% humidity with nothing but a box fan.

When I got old enough to actually have a job (which, ironically, was as a lifeguard at a swimming pool), my picking, breaking and shucking days ended. At that time, I swore that I would not do it again.

Old age has softened me, and I have done flower gardening for quite some time; however, I have not ventured into my "farm roots" of the past. Until COVID.

In March when everything shut down, Hugh and I went to Dandridge to check on my mom and to be sure that she had enough food. Since her diet often consists of potato chips and Reese's cups, Hugh was worried. And then he saw her basement.

In that basement, my mom had a stash of canned vegetables: green beans, corn, okra, squash, tomatoes, and a plethora of jams and jellies. Hugh remarked that she could eat until 2030 and still have food left over. While we had gone with the intention of sharing our supplies with my mom, she ended up giving us more than we gave her.

After making a few fantastic meals (and getting remarks about how good the food was), I asked my mom the question she thought she would never hear: "Will you teach me to can food?"

Although I wanted to learn, I was a bit cautious at first. My mom uses the pressure canning method, which has always scared me. I recall as a child something going wrong one time and the jiggler (the pressure weight) shooting off the cooker and into the ceiling. The dent is still there. I've also seen the videos of exploding Instant Pots, so I know that bad things can happen.

My mom assured me that I could use the pressure canner and that I would not blow up the house if I followed her directions. For weeks this summer, we sterilized jars and lids, prepared vegetables, and then placed the jars of those vegetables in four to five inches of water and heated the cooker to at least 240 degrees. Mom explained that this was necessary because most vegetables are low in acid and have a pH greater than 4.6. Because of the danger of botulism, we had to use the pressure canner to destroy any bacteria. As someone who overcooks most foods out of precaution because of the chance of food poisoning, I was happy to do anything that would alleviate the fear of botulism.

My mom has several pressure canners, and the newest of them has a very heavy lid, fitted with a vent, a weighted pressure gauge, a safety fuse, and an extra cover-lock as an added precaution. We used Ball jars (which became increasingly hard to find… since apparently a lot of people decided to can food this year) and two-piece self-sealing lids, which consist of a flat disc with a rubber-type sealing compound around one side near the outer edge and a separate screw-type metal band. I learned that (1) wide mouth jars are easier to use than the small mouth jars, and (2) the flat metal lid is not reusable. I also learned that it helps to have a jar lifter, a funnel, and a jar wand (a magnetized wand for removing treated jar lids from hot water). I don't recall my mom having such conveniences when I was a child, but it certainly made the process much easier.

When we finished each run and removed the jars, we waited to hear the lids "pop" as the jars cooled. It became a game to count the number of pops, which was evidence that our efforts were successful.

I now have a pantry full of green beans, okra, squash, and corn. I also have tomatoes, potatoes, and salsa. We should eat well for a while. More than that, though, my mom was able to pass her knowledge of food preservation to me. I'm certain she thought that I would never have an interest in learning, as I have tended to purchase food on as "as-needed" basis (i.e.., the day I am going to prepare it). With all that is happening in the world, it was great to spend so much time learning from my mom. It was also great to end harvest season having not blown up my kitchen.

*October 2020*

# BARRISTER BITES

## Bird Is the Word

I hate birds. Don't get me wrong: I think they can be pretty, and I am amazed by their ability to fly with those fragile wings. However, I am extremely scared of anything that can fly toward my head. I have always had this fear, but it intensified many years ago after a series of unfortunate encounters with a mockingbird.

After law school, I purchased a little red Chevrolet Cavalier Z-24. It was small, fast, and economical. It was perfect for a young, struggling lawyer. I loved that car… And apparently a mockingbird that had taken up residence near my home did, too. For weeks, every time I tried to get into my car, that stupid bird would dive at my head. I tried everything to keep him away: screaming, file folders, an umbrella, a tennis racquet. I even called TWRA to see if they could dispatch him. After the officer finished laughing at my request, he told me that mockingbirds, as the state bird, are a protected species and that I was on my own.

My disdain for birds has continued; however, as long as they are not dive-bombing me, I don't want to see them dead. My husband, on the other hand, has a different philosophy. Hugh is an avid wing shooter and loves nothing more than to spend his free time bird hunting. When Trace was young and we were still in what I term the "toddler bubble," Hugh decided to go hunting with some friends. At the end of the trip, he came home with a bag of bloody birds, which he deposited in our garage freezer. As much as I love cooking, I am disgusted by the sight of raw meat if it has liquid with it. This packet of birds was especially loathsome. I let Hugh know that he was responsible for cooking them, as I had no intention whatsoever of dealing with them.

Unfortunately, a couple of weeks later, our power went off and stayed off for a couple of days. When I went to the garage refrigerator, it looked like something from a horror movie. The bag had not been sealed well, and blood from the birds was running out of the freezer, down the door and into the floor of our garage. After that incident, Hugh's wing shooting days came to an end (at least for a number of years).

As Trace got older, Hugh was hoping that he had found a hunting buddy. Those hopes were realized when Trace, at ten, shot a robin in our backyard with his Red Ryder BB gun. After that incident, I advised Trace that the rule of our house was, "You kill it—you eat it." Again, as much as I dislike birds, I don't want to see them dead.

This year, Hugh decided that Trace was old enough to go dove hunting. He has participated in several Boy Scout shooting courses and has even participated in sporting clays tournaments with Hugh. Hugh has often remarked that Trace is a really good shot, and he was excited to see what Trace could do in a dove field. As they left for their trip, I again advised of the house rule (you kill it, you eat it) … and also advised that I did not want to see bloody birds in my freezer. Per Hugh, Trace shot the first three birds of the day (within the first ten minutes). He also saw Hugh shoot one mid-flight and then catch it in his hand before it hit the ground. Needless to say, Trace was hooked. At the end of the day, they arrived home with a bag full of birds that had been cleaned extremely well (i.e.., not bloody).

As much as I love to cook, I have never tried to prepare wild game. Trace was extremely excited to be able to eat the doves that he shot and decided that he would actually find a recipe and cook them. I was fine with that. Hugh and Trace scoured the internet for recipes and settled on smoked jalapeno dove poppers.

To make them, Trace used dove breasts, fresh jalapenos, a jar of chopped jalapenos, season salt, cream cheese, and bacon. He began by removing the breasts from the bone and dividing each breast into two lobes. He then sprinkled the meat with salt and pepper. Next, he sliced the jalapenos lengthwise and removed the seeds. He then mixed softened cream cheese with chopped jalapenos (from a jar) and season salt. Trace cut the bacon slices in half so that they were the appropriate length to wrap around the poppers.

To prepare the poppers for grilling, Trace spooned some of the cream cheese mixture into each jalapeno, laid a piece of dove meat on top, and then wrapped each one with a bacon slice, securing it with a toothpick. He and Hugh decided that they would be good smoked. (Hugh purchased a Traeger smoker at the start of the COVID shutdown and uses every available opportunity to smoke things.)

They set the smoker temperature to 180° and smoked them for about an hour. Then, they increased the temperature to 375° and grilled them for about ten minutes, turning once, to ensure that the bacon was crisp.

I have never been a huge fan of wild game, but I really enjoyed the dove poppers. They had a complex flavor, and you could taste each of the ingredients with each bite. The dove and the bacon were a nice combination. The jalapenos gave the poppers some heat, and the cream cheese "cooled" them down a bit.

Although I am not a huge fan of bird hunting, I am glad that Hugh has found a hunting buddy in Trace. And the house rule has now changed: "You kill it-- we eat it."

*November 2020*

# BARRISTER BITES

## Cooking with Yves Pons

Aside from my family, my dog and my job, there are two things in this world about which I am passionate: Tennessee basketball and food. I haven't missed many basketball games over the past decade and have even been to a number of away games. On multiple occasions, I have attended alone. I've attended dressed for a cocktail reception several times, and I even went to one game in a ball gown. Suffice it to say, Volunteer basketball is one of my favorite things.

As much as I love Tennessee basketball, I also love food. To me, food is like art. I love preparing new foods to see how flavors meld. It's fun to find menu items that complement each other to make a satisfying meal. Last spring, Hugh and I had planned to travel through Belgium and France while Trace attended a two-week exchange program in Paris. While there, we had scheduled a chocolate-making class in Belgium and a cooking class in Normandy. COVID-19 had other plans, and our trip was cancelled.

I found solace during quarantine in cooking. I learned to make delicious meals with limited ingredients, and we made lots of my childhood favorites from the backs of boxes, bottles, and cans. I've tried my hand at some "fancy" things which have turned out well and others which have not. Although recipes from magazines and watching cooking shows were great, they were a poor substitute for the experiential learning of a class.

It's an amazing thing when your passions collide, and it is even more amazing when your spouse makes the opportunity happen. For my birthday, Hugh signed me up for "Cooking with Yves Pons," a class Yves was hosting to benefit Make-a-Wish East Tennessee. I had seen Yves live-stream a demonstration of how to make perfect French crepes, so I knew this would be an unforgettable experience. The class was going to be hosted via Zoom, and we were given the instructions as to when to expect details.

When I got the ingredient list about a week before the class, I was beyond excited. For the dish, we were told to get a 5-pound bag of potatoes (I used petite reds, which I peeled, cut into 1/3 inch rounds and boiled pre-class), 4 onions (chopped), 2 cloves of garlic, 1 package of smoked beef or turkey bacon (I used Benton's hickory smoked bacon), a pint of heavy whipping cream, Herbs de Provence, and 2 large wheels of brie. Hugh and I guessed that we were making some sort of potato soup but were excited to see what we would learn in the class.

On the evening of the class, Yves told us that we would be making tartiflette, a traditional dish from the Savoy region in the French Alps. He said that the dish is French comfort food and is often served in the colder months because of its heaviness. He said that it is often used to serve large groups because a little is all that you need. As we started the class, he talked to us about his background, about foods he loved (and loved to prepare), and what American foods he likes and dislikes (he loves lobster mac-and-cheese from Ruth's Chris and does not understand the appeal of oatmeal). We also met his wife, Laetitia, who is also French and who is lovely. You could tell that she was just as excited to share a part of France with us as he was.

To make the tartiflette, we sautéed the onions and garlic in olive oil until the onions were golden. We then cut the bacon into small pieces and added it to the onions and garlic and sautéed until the bacon was fully cooked. (Note: because I used Benton's hickory smoked bacon – which tends to be fattier—I actually drained the mixture at the end of this step. Yves used turkey bacon, and he did not drain his). After the bacon was cooked, we added the pint of heavy whipping cream, continuing to stir until it thickened. Toward the end of the process, we added 3 Tbs of Herbs de Provence. Once everything was mixed, we set it aside.

Next, we layered half of the potatoes in a baking dish, covering the bottom. We topped the potatoes with one-half of the onion/garlic/bacon mixture. Then, we repeated the process. Afterwards, we cut the wheels of brie so that they were like hamburger buns and then placed them cut side down on top of the potato mixture in the casserole dish. To complete, we baked at 450 for about 15 minutes (until the brie was melted and started to brown). Yves said that the French generally use reblochon cheese instead of brie; however, it is difficult to find in the U.S. Brie is a nice substitute.

When the dish was finished, it looked and smelled amazing. Hugh and I served it with a salad of mixed greens, chopped apples, and pecans, finished with Stonewall Kitchen's Maple Balsamic dressing (from Fresh Market). The lightness of the salad was a perfect complement to the heaviness of the tartiflette, and the apples were especially good with the melted brie. We were actually able to get twenty-four servings out of the tartiflette over three days. It was every bit as good warmed up as it was the night we prepared it.

If you see that Yves is cooking for Make-a-Wish again, please do yourself a favor and sign up for his class. If you try this recipe and enjoy it, donate to Make-a-Wish East Tennessee in Yves' honor. He is a great teacher, but he is also warm and engaging. He answered a ton of questions about a myriad of topics from the participants, and he does a great Rick Barnes impression. When he found out that it was my birthday, he sang "Happy Birthday" to me in French.

This might go down as the greatest birthday gift in the history of birthday gifts for me.

*December 2020*

# BARRISTER BITES

## Losing the Covid-19

I've got the COVID-19. No, I don't have the virus itself. I have the significant weight gain that has come from working from home for the past ten months.

If you have read my column for any length of time, you know that I enjoy cooking. The work- from-home situation has caused my cooking to go into over-drive. It has become a source of entertainment since we are not venturing out of the house. I've made favorites from my childhood from the backs of boxes and cans. I've canned lots of food. I've scoured cookbooks for new and interesting recipes. It has been fun.

Unfortunately, I also like to eat. In addition to sampling my creations, I also tend to stress-eat. This, combined with the fact that I'm not really getting out, has been bad news.

I gained the COVID-19.

With work-from-home, my wardrobe has consisted of Lululemon pants, t-shirts, and fleece jackets. Since all of these things stretch, the weight crept up without me realizing it. It became obvious, though, when I had to wear a suit for a meeting. Despite having a closet full of work clothes, I had nothing to wear because NOTHING FIT.

The week before Thanksgiving, I decided that things had to change. While my mother said I was crazy for starting a diet during the holidays, I was desperate. I needed to work my way back to healthy and fit.

I have completely transformed my diet. I've cut out most sources of sugar and flour, and I rarely eat processed foods. I eat complex carbohydrates—but only early in the day. I get plenty of lean proteins and healthy fats, and I eat lots of vegetables. I'm eating four to five times a day and am never hungry. I actually feel better than I have in years. It has been an adjustment, though, particularly in the way that I cook. I enjoy really good food, and I've had to come up with ways to make my food so good that I don't feel deprived.

My favorite "go-to" has been Roasted Curry Salmon with Tomatoes. It is a simple, yet flavorful, dish that can be prepared in around twenty minutes. As a bonus, it requires only two dishes to make (a casserole dish and a microwave-safe bowl), so clean-up is a breeze.

To prepare the dish, heat oven to 400°.

Then, cook 2 cups long-grain white rice in the microwave. (I use Fresh Market rice. To cook, combine 2 cups of rice with 3 cups of water in a microwave safe bowl. Cover with plastic wrap and microwave on high for 15 minutes).

Meanwhile, toss 1 pint grape tomatoes, 1 tablespoon olive oil, kosher salt and cracked black pepper in a baking dish. Nestle 4 salmon fillets among the tomatoes. (Note: I prefer steelhead trout, which looks like salmon but is genetically a trout and has a milder flavor). Cover the fillets with curry powder. Roast until the fish is opaque throughout and the tomatoes are soft, 15-18 minutes.

Remove the rice from the microwave. Spray lightly with olive oil. (I like La Tourangelle Extra Virgin Olive Oil Spray.) Sprinkle curry powder on top and mix well with a fork.

Serve the salmon and tomatoes over the rice. Sprinkle with ¼ cup torn basil. It is pretty, and it tastes really good.

To make the dish more diet friendly, I am now eating cauliflower rice instead of real rice. This has been an adjustment since I really do not like cauliflower. I purchase the microwavable bags of cauliflower and cook according to directions. I then add the contents of the bag to a skillet, and then add enough curry powder until it turns yellow. I have found that if you cook it over medium heat until it starts to brown, it develops the consistency of rice and loses any cauliflower flavor it may have had. For someone who does not like cauliflower, it is really quite good.

We have also enjoyed filet mignon tails with skillet tomatoes and spicy green beans. I purchase filet tails (the trimmed off ends that are left after the butcher cuts steaks) at Fresh Market. They are much cheaper and just as good. I usually bake them in the oven on a cast iron skillet to desired doneness, seasoning with a little garlic and cracked pepper. To prepare the tomatoes, add a tablespoon of olive oil to a skillet over medium-high heat. Add 2 pints grape tomatoes and ¼ tsp salt and black pepper to taste. Cook, tossing occasionally, until they begin to soften. Add in ¼ cup fresh oregano and then set aside. Meanwhile, cook a package of microwavable fresh green beans according to package directions. Heat 2 cloves of thinly sliced garlic in the skillet where you prepared tomatoes. Add 1 Tbs olive oil, stirring frequently until fragrant. Add the green beans and ½ tsp each of salt and pepper. Toss to combine. Sprinkle with red pepper and serve with the steak and tomatoes. Not only does this combination taste great together, but it also looks pretty on a plate.

I have found that I sometimes struggle with ways to prepare vegetables that the whole family will eat, especially since I am not using butter and very little salt. My "go-to" vegetable recipe is roasted sweet peppers with feta and balsamic vinegar. I add a bag of small, sweet peppers to a casserole dish. I then drizzle a balsamic vinegar glaze over them. (I like the thicker balsamic vinegars that they sell at Tree and Vine downtown.) Sprinkle ½ cup crumbled feta cheese over the peppers and bake at 400° until they start to brown. This dish has wonderful flavor, and it pairs well with most meats. I prefer them with either a petite filet mignon or baked chicken with smoked paprika, but they really pair well with most anything.

Hugh, Trace, and I are currently the only ones consuming these healthy dishes; however, per Hugh, they are "good enough for company." Happy Eating in the New Year!

*January 2021*

# BARRISTER BITES

## Hoarders, Gluttons and Banana Pudding

I don't know if I think my husband is sentimental—or if I think he is just a hoarder. Hugh says that there is a fine line between the two, and I'm not exactly sure where I think he lands. Hugh keeps everything. Restaurant menus, ticket stubs, a box of candy that a Disney guest gave him in 1992, his tonsils. When I say "everything," I mean everything. Because of the sheer volume of things he keeps, Hugh also tends to misplace things.

Usually, when Hugh misplaces things, I end up cleaning the house to try to find whatever it is that he has lost. Christmas at our house was no different this year. During the Christmas break, Hugh had some time on his hands and began a mad search for the memorabilia (i.e., programs, menus, newspapers, airplane boarding passes, etc.) from our 2016 trip to Pearl Harbor. As he was frantically searching through drawers in the cabinet in our living room, I was having heart palpitations because I cannot stand disorganization and clutter. Although I told him that his paperwork was not there, he kept digging … until I shooed him away so that I could organize the drawers and prove once and for all that his memorabilia was not there.

Fortunately for me, his hoarding and losing things caused me to make one of the great discoveries of 2020. While going through the paperwork,

I found IT... the thing I thought was gone forever.... I found my grandmother's Famous Banana Pudding recipe.

For you to understand the significance of this discovery, I need to share some background information. I have always loved banana pudding. My mom made the Jell-O Instant Pudding version for us often, and it was good. However, it could not compare to the banana pudding my Mamaw French made for holidays.

Banana pudding was a staple on my grandmother's table at Thanksgiving and Christmas, and she always served it in a blue covered bowl. She has been gone for fifteen years and was unable to cook for many before then, but my memories of her banana pudding in that pretty blue bowl have not faded.

The love for banana pudding may be genetic because Trace loves it as much as I do. When Trace was about six, we went to a buffet that had banana pudding in martini glasses. After Trace had devoured six of them, we made him stop. Had we not done that, I am scared to think how many he would have eaten.

A couple of years later, Hugh and I planned a tailgate party before a UT football game. We are huge fans of Sweet P's BBQ and decided that it would be the perfect tailgate food. I meticulously planned everything out. I prepared a lot of food; however, Sweet P's was the centerpiece to our culinary celebration. In addition to various meats, greens, and mac-and-cheese, I ordered extra of my two favorites: potato salad and banana pudding.

Prior to the game, the adults, including my cousin Todd, were enjoying the food while Trace played football and generally ran around with his friends like eight-year-old boys do. Todd was on his second trip through the buffet and saw that the banana pudding was low. He didn't want to eat the last of the pudding. I told him not to worry.... We had plenty. After all, I had ordered two each of the banana pudding and potato salad. Todd grabbed a spoon and started eating straight out of the container.

As Todd was finishing the banana pudding, Trace returned, ready to eat. He didn't want barbecue; he didn't want mac-and-cheese; he didn't want any of the tailgate food. He just wanted banana pudding. Todd teased him that he was eating the last of it.

I directed Trace to the cooler to get the other container of banana pudding. When Trace opened the first container, it was potato salad—not banana pudding. He repeated the process with the second container. Same result. Potato salad. To this day, I don't think I have ever seen Trace look so dejected. Many years later, Trace still talks about the day Uncle Todd ate all of the banana pudding.

While Sweet P's banana pudding is great, it doesn't compare to my grandmother's. A few years ago, my aunt found my grandmother's recipe and gave it to me. I made it several times, and it was always as good as I remembered. And then the recipe disappeared from my folder of recipes. I had searched for it for years, and I had become convinced it was gone forever. Thanks to Hugh's hoarding, though, I found it tucked away in a drawer with some newspaper articles that we had saved. That day, I felt like all was right in the universe.

This recipe is too good not to share. To make Mamaw French's Famous Banana pudding, separate 4 large eggs. Add egg yolks to a mixing bowl and whisk in 4 cups evaporated milk. Transfer to a saucepan. Add 1 ¾ cups sugar and 5 tsp cornstarch. Cook over medium heat until thick, whisking constantly to avoid lumps. Add ½ stick of butter and 1 Tbs vanilla. When butter melts, remove from heat. Layer pudding mixture with sliced bananas and Nilla Wafers. I use lots of them because I love both bananas and Nilla Wafers. Let cool in refrigerator (if you can wait that long), and then eat and enjoy. This recipe is supposed to serve four. In our family, though, it becomes *The Hunger Games* when Mamaw French's Banana Pudding is on the table.

*March 2021*

# BARRISTER BITES

## Preppers, Cows and Springtime Suppers

If anyone asks how I am these days, I normally answer with "It's been quite a year." I don't think any of us fully envisioned what the last nine months of 2020 and the first few months of 2021 would look like. No one really knew what steps we would take to adapt.

As I think I have written before, I am married to a "prepper." Before the pandemic began in earnest (and certainly before shutdowns in the US), Hugh followed news in Europe about the need to prepare for quarantine and lockdown. Our garage soon became known as the "grocery store," as Hugh made sure that we had enough non-perishable food to last at least eight weeks. To say we were prepared for what was to come is an understatement.

Last spring, reports were rampant about the coming "meat shortage." I recall reports on the local news (and personal accounts from friends and family) that there was no meat in our grocery store coolers. As a "prepper," Hugh quickly found a solution. We would buy a cow. Literally. We bought a cow.

If you wonder how much meat a single cow will provide, it is a lot. I'm not a beef eater; however, I quickly adapted. Last summer, we enjoyed lots of grilled and smoked beef, and I found 1,000 ways to prepare ground beef this winter. With spring, though, I'm ready to grill again. And, like the Chick-fil-a cows, I am ready to "Eat More Chicken."

My favorite warm weather "go-to meal" was borne out of one of Hugh's silent auction ideas. He has done lots of event-based fundraising and is always trying to come up with new and different auction items. I was rightfully skeptical one year when he told me that he and his buddies were creating an auction item for dinner for twenty that would be hosted and prepared by them. "We will do all the work," he said. "You won't have to do a thing." I think we all know how that turned out. Angelia was cook and server.

My "go-to meal" is good for both larger gatherings and small groups. It consists of a strawberry salad, grilled chicken with white barbecue sauce, grilled shrimp, tomato pie, grilled corn, and TennTucky cobbler. It is an easy meal, and most of the ingredients can be purchased in "ready to use" form.

The salad consists of mixed greens (pre-bagged), sliced strawberries (I buy those already washed and capped), red onion (sliced), crumbled bleu cheese, toasted almonds, and Brianna's poppyseed dressing. It is a colorful salad, and it looks like you slaved away slicing and dicing. What your family and friends don't know won't hurt them.

For the chicken, use the thin-sliced boneless, skinless chicken breasts. They cook quickly on the grill and do not dry out. I make a white barbecue sauce (Hugh's recipe) with mayonnaise, apple cider vinegar, lemon juice, coarsely-ground black pepper, cayenne pepper, horseradish, and Splenda. We don't have a specific recipe… just an ingredient list. I will taste-test it until the combination is right. Then, put a little in a squirt bottle and the rest in a large Ziploc bag. Add the chicken to the bag and let it marinate until ready to cook. The mayonnaise-y mixture really helps keep the chicken moist during the grilling process.

My favorite part of the meal is the tomato pie. I'm from Jefferson County, but I had never heard of tomato pie until I met Hugh. I like to tell people that I married him for his tomato pie recipe. It really is that good. To make Hugh's tomato pie, all you need is a deep-dish pie crust, tomatoes, mayonnaise, onion, and shredded cheese. Bake the pie crust in the oven until it slightly brown, fill it half-way with sliced tomatoes, and then add salt and pepper to taste. Then, mix mayonnaise, a pureed white onion (to taste) and shredded cheese until it is a spreadable consistency. Top the tomatoes completely with the mayonnaise-cheese mixture and bake at 350 until it is brown on top. It is one of my very favorite things to eat.

The easiest part of this meal is dessert. It is a family favorite, and, although it is technically a cobbler, Trace calls it "pie." To make the TennTucky cobbler, mix one cup of sugar, one cup of self-rising flour, one cup of milk, and one stick of melted butter. Add it to a greased casserole dish (I use a clear one so I can see the bottom as it cooks). Sprinkle in frozen blackberries (or mixed  berries that do not contain strawberries). Sprinkle the top with ¼ cup of sugar and bake at 350 until it is brown and bubbly (usually about an hour). It is great by itself or topped with vanilla ice cream.

As the weather warms, I am always looking for ways to do things faster and more efficiently without totally skimping on quality. This "go-to meal" reminds us of years past spent with friends and gives us something to look forward to as we contemplate gathering once again.

*April 2021*

# BARRISTER BITES

## "Where's The (Ground) Beef?" Hint: Not at Wendy's

I am married to a "prepper." My first glimpse into Hugh's obsession with prepping was the duffle bag in his car when we first met. I think he saw the fear on my face and quickly explained that he was not a serial killer… he was a serial worrier. In sales for Disney, he spent most of his life in his car, and he needed to be prepared in case of accident, bad weather, and other unfortunate events.

His "bug-out bag" (as he described it) contained items like water, non-perishable food, first aid items, extra clothing, flashlights and other "disaster planning" items. In the days before MapQuest and cell phones with internet, he also had books of maps and atlases for everywhere in the U.S. He also carried a Swiss Army knife or Leatherman tool wherever he went. Like all good Boy Scouts, Hugh was completely prepared for most any situation he could encounter. When we were hearing reports out of Europe about the coming pandemic and shutdowns last February, I really didn't worry. My own personal prepper did enough of that for both of us. He stocked up on non-perishable food items, water, toiletries, and cleaning supplies that we might need. When things shut down in March, we did not leave our house; nor did we have anything delivered. We didn't need to… Hugh had everything we could ever need.

When we started hearing about the coming "meat shortage," Hugh took his prepping to a new level. In a house of carnivores, Hugh couldn't fathom the thought of being without meat. He was determined that we would buy a cow. And we did.

We bought a cow. Literally. We bought a cow.

If you wonder how much meat a single cow will provide, it is a lot. When the very large truck arrived from Simpson's Meats (great local producer, by the way), I was a little concerned about what it contained. I was excited as they brought out beef brisket, various cuts of steak, roasts, ribs, and other meats. But then I saw the ground beef. When Mr. Simpson began unloading the ground beef, it was like a clown car. It just kept coming. And coming. And coming. I actually started wondering if we were going to have to buy another freezer to hold it all.

I am not a burger eater; however, the single-cow burgers from Simpson's (and from our cow) are phenomenal. The burgers are lean, and the flavor is probably the best I have ever had. But you can only eat so many burgers.

Hugh says that I have become much like Bubba from *Forrest Gump*, who had about a hundred different ways to prepare shrimp. I think I have at least that many recipes that use ground beef.

My go-to is an easy meat sauce, which I use for spaghetti, baked ziti, lasagna, and other Italian dishes. Pre-COVID, I would spend hours making a meat sauce, using home-canned tomatoes and other fresh ingredients. Once I started cooking so much with the "stay-at-home" and "shelter-in-place" directives, I became all about convenience. To make an easy meat sauce, finely chop two onions and two cloves of garlic and heat in a couple Tbs olive oil. Add 2 lbs. ground beef and cook until browned. Add 4 Tbs Italian seasoning, 1 Tbs cayenne pepper, and two jars of Newman's Own Sockarooni sauce. Cover and heat on low for 30 minutes. We most frequently use this sauce with spaghetti; however, I have also used it with baked ziti and lasagna. (If you are making traditional lasagna, I cannot recommend Barilla Oven-ready Lasagna noodles enough. They are hard like normal noodles that you cook, but you place them in your dish and bake…no boiling required).

We have also become fans of Ground Beef Stroganoff. My mom made this for us when I was a child, and I found the recipe when I was rummaging through my cookbooks from law school. It's easy, and it is great when you don't have a lot of time to spend cooking. To prepare, cook a package of egg noodles according to package directions. In a large skillet over medium heat, brown 1 lb. ground beef along with a diced yellow onion and 2 cloves minced garlic until thoroughly cooked.

Then, drain the ground beef to remove excess fat from the pan. Put the pan back on the stove over medium heat (but don't add the ground beef back in yet). Add 3 Tbs butter to the pan and allow it to melt. Then, add 3 Tbs flour to pan, whisk it and let it absorb butter. Add 1 ½ cups beef broth and whisk vigorously to remove any lumps, turning the heat up to high, bringing it to a boil for 2-3 minutes until you see it thicken slightly. Bring the temperature down to medium and whisk in 1 cup sour cream and 1 can cream of mushroom soup. Stir until mixed well. Add ground beef back to mixture until reheated. Serve over egg noodles. It has been a hit with the entire family and takes about 30 minutes from start to finish.

We have also enjoyed Beef Taco Bake. To make it, brown 1 lb. ground beef. Drain off fat. Add 1 can tomato soup, 1 cup salsa, ½ cup milk, 6 flour (or 8 corn) tortillas (cut in 1" pieces), and 1 cup shredded cheddar cheese. Spoon into a baking dish. Bake at 400 for 30 minutes or until hot. Sprinkle with cheese and serve. It is quick and easy, and there is not a lot of clean up. If you grew up in the '80s and ever wondered "Where's the (Ground) Beef?" now you know.

*May 2021*

# BARRISTER BITES

## Everything Is Fine ... When You Have Cheese and Wine

Growing up, I lived on cheese: Kraft American singles, Velveeta, and the shredded mozzarella that came in a bag from the White Store in Dandridge. As I got older, I discovered an entirely different world of cheeses: feta, bleu, stilton. You name it—I tried it. And, except for a couple of varieties, I loved it all. I didn't know what to do with it, but I loved it.

During a trip to a fromagerie in Paris in 2009, I learned how to make a "proper" cheese board. The proprietor said that we needed five cheeses (arranged from mildest to most intense): a soft cheese (like brie, camembert, or reblochon), a hard cheese (like Gruyere), a goat cheese, a bleu cheese, and another cheese of your choosing. He also suggested adding a baguette, some grapes, fig jam, almonds, and a glass of wine. To me, it was perfection. And when we came home from France, it was often dinner.

I love a good cheese board, but the pandemic stifled my ability to get a lot of the cheeses that I normally kept on hand. I went almost an entire year without going to a grocery store. While they did a great job, I found that the Instacart shoppers couldn't always find the cheese varieties that I liked. At the UT Institute of Agriculture, though, we pride ourselves on Real. Life. Solutions. And I found my own.

During the pandemic, I made a concerted effort to shop local. Fortunately, UTIA made it easy to indulge my need for both wine and cheese. I am insanely proud of the work that we do at the Institute of Agriculture, and we produce cheese and partner with producers of wine – the key ingredients to make the perfect cheese board for summer entertaining (or just summer eating).

All Vol Cheese has been in production for over five years. It is made by UT Food Science students in partnership with Sweetwater Valley Farm. Through the partnership, students get real-life experiences in dairy operations and cheese production from start to finish. They see first-hand what it takes—all the way from raising cows, to generating milk, to how milk is turned into cheese, and then packaged and sent to market. Throughout this process they learn about manufacturing, safety, and regulatory issues, all of which better prepare them to become valuable owners and employees in the industry.

They also make some really good cheese. Students produce four varieties of cheese: Checkerboard Mild Cheddar (a mild white cheddar with a silky texture and flavor), Game Day Sharp Cheddar (a crisp, yellow cheddar with a sharp flavor), Smokey's Smoked Gouda (my personal favorite… a rich gouda with a heavy smoky flavor… great for both eating and cooking), and Torchbearer Jalapeno (also a favorite… hot and spicy).

They have also collaborated with the Department of Industrial & Systems Engineering and Sweetwater Valley Farm to create Power T cheese. This product is hand-cut by students and is a combination of orange and white cheddars. It comes either as orange with a white Power T or white with an orange Power T. It is the perfect gift for the Tennessee fan on your shopping list, and it tastes as good as it looks.

These cheeses make the perfect cheese board for entertaining on a hot summer day and are a must for this fall's tailgates. I like to pair them with toasted sourdough bread, Benton's prosciutto, Benton's smoked hickory bacon (coated with brown sugar and baked in the oven), or Simpson's Farm summer sausage.

No cheese board is complete without a good wine, and UTIA has again supplied me with a Real. Life. Solution. Earlier this year, we introduced the Vino Volunteer project and UT Wines.

UTIA has partnered with the Tennessee Farm Winegrowers Alliance to release three limited edition wines: Smokey's Red, Volunteer Orange and White, and UT Tailgate Sangria. Bottled by Mountain Valley Winery, each blend features Tennessee-grown grapes. These wines were produced to raise awareness of the Tennessee wine industry and to support viticulture research at UTIA. A portion of the proceeds from every bottle of UT Wine purchased goes toward the Peter Howard Endowment for Wine and Ag Tourism, directly supporting the viticulture industry in the state of Tennessee through student internships at Tennessee vineyards, wineries and other agritourism locations.

My personal favorite is the Volunteer Orange and White. It is made from Blount County grown Villard Blanc (a French hybrid grape). It is similar to a pinot grigio or a smooth sauvignon blanc and goes well with most anything. The aromas and flavors are suggestive of green apple and fresh melon, with a simple, clean, and refreshing finish. I like to serve it very cold, and it is quite refreshing on a hot afternoon. I like to pair it with Smoky's Smoked Gouda or the Power T cheese.

I am not necessarily a red wine drinker, but Smokey's Red is great with the Game Day Sharp Cheddar. Smokey's Red is made from East Tennessee grown Chambourcin and Middle Tennessee grown Syrah. It is a robust red with aromas of cherry and plum.

If I'm feeling festive (like on a Taco Tuesday), I love to drink the Tailgate Sangria. It is a lively blend of fruits like strawberry and mango. Made from red muscadine grapes sourced from Monroe and McMinn Counties, it has a deep garnet color that is rich in flavor with notes of strawberry and tropical fruit, followed by hints of spicy elderberry. It is slightly sweet, with a smooth finish. I like to freeze berries and grapes and add it to it. It is the perfect refreshment on a hot summer day, and it goes great with spicy foods.

If you are interested in supporting UT Ag students and if you enjoy local products, please give All Vol Cheese and UT Wines a try. All Vol Cheese will be back in stock soon and can be purchased at https://AllVolCheese.Tennessee.edu. UT Wines are available now at www. UTWines.com. You won't be disappointed.

*June 2021*

# BARRISTER BITES

## FOR THE LOVE OF FOOD, I HAVE RAISED A COOK!

For the last twenty years or so, I have not been greeted with even as much as a "How was your day?" at the end of the workday. It has always been, "Hey, Mom/Angelia/Honey. What's for dinner?" That has always been a pretty fair question because, for the past two decades, I have been almost solely responsible for putting food on the table at our house. I do love to cook; however, I will confess that there have been times I have tried to "wait them out" so that they would just eat cereal and call it a night. Sometimes, I'm tired, and cooking is the last thing I want to do. I've always sort of "gone it alone" and figured that it would be that way forever.

Recently, though, things have changed.

For the love of food, I have a cook at my house! My fifteen-year-old son has become our chef/short-order cook in residence. This recent change was brought about by two somewhat expected events. First, Trace spent eight days at Sea Base High Adventure camp with the Boy Scouts on a fishing expedition. He loves to fish, and I knew that he was going to have the trip of a lifetime. As a part of that trip though, the Scouts were expected to cook their catches of the day and then clean up after themselves. To my surprise, Trace actually enjoyed the cooking (and eating) as much as the fishing. For a week, I received photos of restaurant-quality food courtesy of some Boy Scouts. And my son was responsible for a lot of it.

Second, Trace decided he wanted a job this summer. He applied and was hired as a lifeguard at Knoxville Racquet Club. However, because of his age (fifteen), he learned that he would not get many shifts. His boss did tell the younger guards that she needed help in the snack bar. Trace said that no one was volunteering, so he stepped up. To quote him, "It pays more, AND I get tips."

He loves his job. I'm not sure whether it is because he loves to cook or whether he loves the money he can make by cooking, but I will take it either way. And he practices his culinary skills at home. This is a win for everyone.

A couple of weeks ago, Trace called me at work to let me know that he was preparing dinner. Hugh had taken him shopping, and he was going to prepare halibut and a salad. I was skeptical, but he was so proud, and it was a meal I did not have to prepare.

For the halibut, Trace used halibut filets. He combined ¼ cup olive oil, 2 Tbs lemon juice, 3 cloves minced garlic, 1 Tbs black pepper and 1 Tbs lemon pepper seasoning in a zip lock bag. He then added the halibut and refrigerated for 1 hour. He preheated the oven to 400 °, placed the halibut in a cast iron skillet, topped each filet with a slice of lemon and baked until the fish was opaque and the lemon slices were browned. Trace's salad was a mixture of cubed watermelon, cucumbers, fresh mint, and dried basil. It was simple, but it was delicious.

The total preparation time on this meal was about 30 minutes, and the cooking time was quick. It was one of the best meals I have had in a very long time, and Trace even cleaned the kitchen after dinner. Again, this is a win for everyone.

At his job at KRC, Trace's dishes are more of the "kid food" variety. He makes hamburgers, chicken sandwiches, quesadillas, nachos, and salads. He works every day, and he practices at home to see what he can do to make his food better. Apparently, it is working.

A friend recently reached out to let me know that her daughter said Trace's quesadillas are the best that she had ever had. Of course, I asked for his secret.

For cheese quesadillas, Trace says the key to making a really good one is to cook the quesadilla in the same spot where you just finished a hamburger. He says that the hamburger grease adds extra flavor and that the quesadilla gets extra crispy. He also adds lots of shredded cheese. He says that the best quesadillas are a mixture of cheeses, and he likes the Kraft Four-Cheese Mexican Blend. He says that it melts well and the variety of cheese give it a more complex flavor.

He has also had rave reviews for his burgers, and he says that the secret is in the bun—a trick he says he learned from me. Trace butters the bun and then places it on the griddle until the butter is melted and the bread is slightly browned. He says it adds flavor to the burger and gives a nice crunch when you bite into it. A dear friend once told me that, "Apple trees make apples." I love food. I love to cook. And I love that my son enjoys these things as well. Trace's culinary skills are quite good, and I am delighted. Maybe, just maybe, he takes after me a little bit.

*August 2021*

# BARRISTER BITES

## Toasted Almonds, Fire and Double Ovens

My mom always said, "Be careful what you wish for." In the last Barrister Bites, I lamented the fact that, for 20 years, I was met every night with one question: "What are you making for dinner?" I was so proud that Trace not only accepted a job in the snack bar at the Knoxville Racquet Club (where he expertly made burgers, salads, quesadillas, and other fast-food delicacies) but that he also was often cooking dinner for the family.

Hugh apparently read the column (or someone spilled the beans about it) and wanted in on the action. On the Sunday night before the GKAISA City Championship Swim Meet (which included 2,000 swimmers and of which I was in charge), Hugh decided that HE was going to prepare dinner. He found some sort of baked chicken dish and broccoli salad on the internet and decided that would be the evening's fare. I was busy and hungry, so I was thrilled.

Unbeknownst to me, the broccoli salad required toasted almonds. Hugh put them in a roasting pan on broil and continued to work on the other items. During that time, he received a phone call. If you know Hugh well, you know that he can be hyper-focused but that he can be easily distracted by things like telephone calls. He took the call outside (so as not to bother me). This meant that he forgot about the almonds.

When Hugh realized that he had forgot about the toasting almonds, he ran back into the kitchen. In case you did not know, almonds combust. I was upstairs and did not realize anything was wrong until I heard the fire alarm going "FIRE. FIRE." And Hugh shouting expletives, which I will not publish.

Apparently, when Hugh opened the oven door, flames shot out. I heard the commotion and ran down the stairs when I heard Hugh yell, "Trace, get the fire extinguisher!!" They were able to extinguish the flames, but the controls on the oven were melted, and soot and fire extinguisher foam covered our kitchen.

Hugh was surprised that I was not mad. I had wanted a husband that cooks… and he was trying. And I got something else that I had wanted: new double ovens.

When we moved into our house and remodeled our kitchen in 2005, I wanted double ovens. However, the appliance salesman told me that would be wasteful in a family of 3 and that I would be better served with a wall oven and a convection microwave. He was wrong. I have always regretted not getting double ovens. I love to cook, and I love to entertain. There have been multiple instances in which two ovens would have made things so much easier.

After the Great Fire Fiasco, we headed to Friedman's to look at appliances. There were lots of really nice ones, but I had my eyes on what had eluded me 16 years ago. Although it took almost a month (and lots of eating out), I got my double ovens... Wolf M-Series ovens with red knobs that match my kitchen!

When they arrived, I read over the Owner's Manual with the same attention to detail that I use when reading the Internal Revenue Code. The ovens also came with a cookbook that featured dishes made using all 10 cooking settings. I knew that I needed to try one of them as the first meal.

I chose Pork Tenderloin and Roasted Cauliflower, which was prepared on convection mode. With convection mode, I had the benefit of cooking both dishes at the same time so that the whole meal came out of the oven together. This recipe also benefitted from the oven not needing to be preheated, which meant that we had food that much sooner. To prepare, I placed a 1 lb. pork tenderloin on a large plate and patted it dry with a paper towel. I then combined 2 tsp chopped fresh rosemary, 2 tsp chopped fresh thyme, 1 tsp freshly ground pepper, 1 clove of chopped garlic, and 2 Tbs olive oil in a small bowl and then rubbed it on the tenderloin. The tenderloin was placed on a baking tray and set aside. I then broke 1 lb. cauliflower into florets and halved them. I tossed the cauliflower with 1 Tbs olive oil and ½ tsp kosher salt and placed it on a baking sheet lined with parchment paper.

I set the oven on convection at 400° and placed both dishes in the oven. When the pork reached an internal temperature of 160°, I removed both dishes from the oven, allowed the pork to rest for 5 minutes and then served both dishes together. They were amazing. Since we had the ovens installed, my grocery bill has increased, and my dining-out bill has gone down considerably. I cook something in those ovens almost every night. And the food just tastes better. My mom was right. You do need to be careful what you wish for. I wished for a husband that would cook and ended up with a kitchen fire. But I also wished for double ovens—which I now have. It's safe to say that I no longer wish for a husband who cooks.

*September 2021*

# BARRISTER BITES

## LET'S TALK TURKEY ... AND EAT PIE

For as long as I can remember, I have loved fall. My dad always said that he thought fall was sad because it got darker earlier, the leaves turned and fell off the trees, and it ushered in winter weather (which he always said was torture for a UPS man). I could understand his point of view, but I have never shared it. To me, fall is a magical time, and there is nothing better than the month of November.

Of all of the "eating holidays" (for us, Thanksgiving, Christmas and Easter), Thanksgiving is the best. Thanksgiving is the unique holiday where we can focus on the fact that we are thankful for all kinds of things... including really good food, old traditions, and new ones as Trace gets older.

As the years have gone by, our traditions have changed. Our family has celebrated at home, at other people's homes, and at restaurants. We have even managed to make it to New York for the Macy's Thanksgiving Day parade a couple of times. No matter where we are, though, Thanksgiving has always featured great food. Now, the highlight of the Thanksgiving meal is the dessert—the Deep-Dish Apple Bourbon Streusel Pie from the Williams-Sonoma recipe.

This "pie" is prepared in a rectangular baking dish and combines elements of many classics—pecan pie, Dutch apple pie and pastry-heavy slab pie—to create something completely new. It is great when you are serving a crowd, as it will easily serve 12-14 people.

To make the pie filling, you will need 3 lbs. *each* of Granny Smith apples and Pink Lady apples (peeled, cored, and cut into slices ¼ thick), ¾ cup firmly packed light brown sugar, ½ cup granulated sugar, 1 ½ tsp ground cinnamon, ¼ tsp salt, ¼ tsp freshly grated nutmeg, ¼ cup cornstarch, ½ cup bourbon (I prefer Prichard's chocolate bourbon), 2 Tbs vanilla extract. PLEASE NOTE: It is not a typo in the recipe when it calls for 6 lbs. of apples. *You will actually use that many.* To peel, slice and core, I use the Williams-Sonoma apple peeler/slicer/corer. It makes the preparation of the apples much easier, and the crank on the machine is quite the workout (which will be needed if you eat this pie).

For the streusel, you will need 2/3 cup all-purpose flour, ½ cup granulated sugar, ½ cup firmly packed light brown sugar, 1 Tbs ground cinnamon, ½ tsp salt, 1 cup roughly chopped pecans, and 7 Tbs cold, unsalted butter (diced).

For the pie crust, I just use the Pillsbury pie crust rolled dough that is found in the refrigerator aisle at the grocery store. Pillsbury can make a pie crust much better than me—plus, it saves a TON of time.

To prepare the pie, roll the dough out into your baking dish, covering the bottom and sides so that it extends just beyond the rim of the dish. Refrigerate for 30 minutes.

Position a rack in the lower third of the oven and preheat to 375°.

For the filling: In a large bowl, stir together the apples, brown sugar, granulated sugar, cinnamon, salt, nutmeg, cornstarch, bourbon, and vanilla until well combined.

For the streusel, in a bowl, stir together the flour, granulated sugar, brown sugar, cinnamon, salt and pecans. Add the butter and work it in with your fingers, pinching to form pea-size pieces.

Pour the apple mixture into the pie shell and sprinkle the streusel on top. If you want to be fancy, use Thanksgiving cookie cutters and another piece of pie crust dough to make decorative cutouts. Those can be placed on the sides of the pie and the top, as desired. I'm not fancy, so I don't do this.

Bake until the streusel is golden brown and the apples are tender, about an hour and 45 minutes. If the top of the pie has browned after 1 hour, tent it loosely with aluminum foil and allow it to continue to bake. Transfer the pie to a wire rack and let cool for at least 2 hours before serving. While this pie is wonderful by itself, I actually prefer it heated and then topped with vanilla ice cream.

While this pie takes about an hour to make and then nearly two to cook, it is worth the effort. Even if we don't celebrate Thanksgiving at home, we always celebrate with this pie at some point in November. And for that, we give thanks.

*December 2021*

# BARRISTER BITES

## MAKE YOUR HOLIDAYS FESTIVE WITHOUT THE FUSS

I have always loved Christmas. I love everything about it: the music, the decorations, the Hallmark Channel movies, and the food. I especially love the food. For someone who loves to cook and entertain, Christmas truly is the most wonderful time of the year.

For as long as I can remember, Hugh and I have hosted a Christmas morning breakfast for my family (which has become more of a Christmas morning brunch since we now have a teenager). Most years, we also host Christmas dinner, which includes Hugh's family, some of mine, and friends who are more like family. I've been able to experiment with all sorts of fancy foods (poached pears, tartiflette), and, for a number of years, Christmas dinner was like Thanksgiving dinner on steroids, featuring turkey and its accoutrements as well as beef and ham and dishes that complemented them.

A few years ago after the presents had been opened, and I was left with tired feet, dishwater hands, and a bunch of dirty dishes, I realized that I was going from Santa's elf to the Grinch pretty quickly. Christmas was over, and I didn't get to enjoy any of it. I had been in the kitchen all day, and I had missed the spirit of the holiday.

That night, I vowed that I would not miss the fun again. I needed to come up with a dinner that left me with time to actually enjoy celebrating Christmas with our family. I spent the year pouring over recipes to come up with something festive without the fuss.

Christmas dinner at our house now features a simple salad, beef tenderloin, burgundy mushrooms, twice-baked potatoes, and Sister Schubert's rolls. It is a great dinner that can be prepared for a large group in very little time. These recipes have become my "go-to's" and have not failed me yet. If you want festive without fuss, then this might be the menu for you, too.

For the salad, use triple-washed mixed greens topped with raw pecans, cubed apple, bleu cheese, and dried cranberries. Toss with Stonewall Kitchen's maple balsamic vinaigrette dressing. It is easy and it is amazingly good. For twice-baked potatoes, I use the pre-made version from either

Butler and Bailey (my favorite) or Fresh Market (also really good). I just unpackage them and pop them in the oven until they are warm. I also use Sister Schubert's premade rolls. I have tried (and failed) with homemade bread more times that I can count, and Sister Schubert is a most appreciated substitute.

The beef tenderloin and burgundy mushroom recipes were passed down from dear friends, who are both impressive cooks. Our friend Ross was gracious enough to give me his beef recipe, and it is probably the best I have ever made. (I've tried a number of different methods, but his is the best.) The burgundy mushrooms are courtesy of my friend Melissa. She had made them for a party that Hugh attended several years ago when I was out of town for work, and he called me at midnight to tell me that they were the best thing he had ever eaten. I have used both for a couple of years, and I want to share them with you.

The beef tenderloin starts with a 6-7 lb. beef tenderloin (trimmed and tied). For best results, let the meat sit out an hour before you cook it to get it to room temperature. Preheat oven to 450°. In the meantime, get a bowl and combine 2 Tbs Kosher salt, 2 Tbs black pepper, 2 Tbs sugar, 3 Tbs bacon grease (I keep grease from Benton's smoked bacon in the refrigerator), and ½ cup olive oil. Mix well and set aside.

Heat a griddle on medium high and put 1 Tbs of butter and 1 Tbs olive oil on griddle top. Once melted, place the tenderloin on the griddle and brown on all sides (about 1-2 minutes each side). Take the tenderloin from the griddle and place on a broiling rack that sits in a roasting pan. (Don't put the meat directly on the bottom of the roasting pan.)

Stir the marinade and pour a little of it at a time over the meat. Rub the marinade all over the tenderloin, paying close attention that you get it in all the crevices. Use all of the mixture. It will look like it is drowning, but it is fine.

Place a roasting thermometer in the largest part of the tenderloin. (I use one that attaches to a display on the counter. It works better than the oven probe.) Cook to 140° and remove from oven. Move the meat from a rack to a cutting board and cover with foil for at least 20 minutes to rest. Slice meat as desired and serve with horseradish. This will serve 8-10 people.

The burgundy mushrooms are a favorite and are just as easy. To prepare, wash 4 lbs. button mushrooms and throw into a large pot. Add 2 sticks of butter, 1 ½ Tbs Worcestershire sauce, 2 bottles of burgundy wine (although any rich red wine will do), 1 Tbs fresh ground black pepper, 2 cups boiling water, 4 chicken bouillon cubes, 4 beef bouillon cubes, and stir to combine. Bring to a boil over medium-high heat. Reduce heat to low and simmer, covered, for 6 hours. (I transfer to a very large crock pot and heat on low heat.) Remove the lid and continue cooking, uncovered, for an additional 3-4 hours. Serve straight from the pot or put them in a serving bowl (duh!). Have crusty bread ready to soak up all the deliciousness. In the meantime, get a part-time job to pay for the gas or electric bill for cooking these. They are yummy and serve 8-10 people.

If you want festive without the fuss during this holiday season, I hope this menu and these recipes will help. No matter how you celebrate, though, I hope it is wonderful!

*January 2022*

# ACKNOWLEDGEMENTS

For years, I told Hugh that he needed to collect my columns for Trace after my death so that our son could see that there was so much more to me than the "make your bed, brush your teeth, do your homework" mom he saw every day. I am so thankful that Hugh worked hard to collect my writings while I am still very much alive. I'm also thankful for Marsha Watson, Jody Dyer, and the Honorable Cindy Wyrick for their help in making this book possible. I am truly honored and humbled. I could not stop crying when I saw the proof on Christmas Day, 2021. This book is probably the nicest gift I will ever receive. I've got the best husband in the world, and I thank God for him every day.

As I read these columns again, memories of the past two decades came flooding back: of the things we did, the places we saw, and, most importantly, the friends we've made along the way. Thank you to all of my friends who contributed to my columns over the years. I could not have written them without you. I appreciate your time and I appreciate you allowing me to share your stories as a part of my own.

To all who have read these columns over the years and to those who are now reading this book, thank you for allowing me to share my family and friends' lives and adventures with you. I hope you enjoy reading these columns as much I enjoyed writing them.

Angelia